Nirali's New Series

CONCISE STUDY SERIES

(50 Marks)

ANALOG AND DIGITAL ELECTRONICS

Sem - I

S.E ELECTRICAL ENGINEERING

As per New Revised Syllabus of University of Pune

(Pattern 2012)

S. S. Kulkarni
M. E. (E & TC)
Associate Professor
Sinhgad Academy of Engineering
Kondhawa, Pune.

N 2840

ANALOG AND DIGITAL ELECTRONICS (SE ELECT.)

First Edition : June 2014

© : author

The text of this publication, or any part thereof, should not be reproduced or transmitted in any form or stored in any computer storage system or device for distribution including photocopy, recording, taping or information retrieval system or reproduced on any disc, tape, perforated media or other information storage device etc., without the written permission of Authors with whom the rights are reserved. Breach of this condition is liable for legal action.

Every effort has been made to avoid errors or omissions in this publication. In spite of this, errors may have crept in. Any mistake, error or discrepancy so noted and shall be brought to our notice shall be taken care of in the next edition. It is notified that neither the publisher nor the authors or seller shall be responsible for any damage or loss of action to any one, of any kind, in any manner, therefrom.

Published By :
NIRALI PRAKASHAN
Abhyudaya Pragati, 1312, Shivaji Nagar,
Off J.M. Road, PUNE – 411005
Tel - (020) 25512336/37/39, Fax - (020) 25511379
Email : niralipune@pragationline.com

Printed at
Repro Knowledgecast Limited
India

DISTRIBUTION CENTRES
PUNE

Nirali Prakashan
119, Budhwar Peth, Jogeshwari Mandir Lane
Pune 411002, Maharashtra
Tel : (020) 2445 2044, 66022708, Fax : (020) 2445 1538
Email : bookorder@pragationline.com

Nirali Prakashan
S. No. 28/25, Dhyari,
Near Pari Company, Pune 411041
Tel : (022) 24690204 Fax : (020) 24690316
Email : dhyari@pragationline.com
bookorder@pragationline.com

MUMBAI
Nirali Prakashan
385, S.V.P. Road, Rasdhara Co-op. Hsg. Society Ltd.,
Girgaum, Mumbai 400004, Maharashtra
Tel : (022) 2385 6339 / 2386 9976, Fax : (022) 2386 9976
Email : niralimumbai@pragationline.com

DISTRIBUTION BRANCHES

NAGPUR
Pratibha Book Distributors
Above Maratha Mandir, Shop No. 3, First Floor,
Rani Jhanshi Square, Sitabuldi, Nagpur 440012,
Maharashtra, Tel : (0712) 254 7129

BENGALURU
Pragati Book House
House No. 1, Sanjeevappa Lane, Avenue Road Cross,
Opp. Rice Church, Bengaluru – 560002.
Tel : (080) 64513344, 64513355,
Mob : 9880582331, 9845021552
Email:bharatsavla@yahoo.com

JALGAON
Nirali Prakashan
34, V. V. Golani Market, Navi Peth, Jalgaon 425001,
Maharashtra, Tel : (0257) 222 0395
Mob : 94234 91860

KOLHAPUR
Nirali Prakashan
New Mahadvar Road,
Kedar Plaza, 1st Floor Opp. IDBI Bank
Kolhapur 416 012, Maharashtra. Mob : 9855046155

CHENNAI
Pragati Books
9/1, Montieth Road, Behind Taas Mahal, Egmore,
Chennai 600008 Tamil Nadu, Tel : (044) 6518 3535,
Mob : 94440 01782 / 98450 21552 / 98805 82331, Email : bharatsavla@yahoo.com

RETAIL OUTLETS
PUNE

Pragati Book Centre
157, Budhwar Peth, Opp. Ratan Talkies,
Pune 411002, Maharashtra
Tel : (020) 2445 8887 / 6602 2707, Fax : (020) 2445 8887

Pragati Book Centre
Amber Chamber, 28/A, Budhwar Peth,
Appa Balwant Chowk, Pune : 411002, Maharashtra,
Tel : (020) 20240335 / 66281669
Email : pbcpune@pragationline.com

Pragati Book Centre
676/B, Budhwar Peth, Opp. Jogeshwari Mandir,
Pune 411002, Maharashtra
Tel : (020) 6601 7784 / 6602 0855

PBC Book Sellers & Stationers
152, Budhwar Peth, Pune 411002, Maharashtra
Tel : (020) 2445 2254 / 6609 2463

MUMBAI
Pragati Book Corner
Indira Niwas, 111 - A, Bhavani Shankar Road, Dadar (W), Mumbai 400028, Maharashtra
Tel : (022) 2422 3526 / 6662 5254, Email : pbcmumbai@pragationline.com

www.pragationline.com   info@pragationline.com

Dear Students,

It gives us great pleasure to introduce a New Series "**C**oncise **S**tudy **S**eries" for Second Year Engineering students. These "**CSS**" books are written by Experienced and Eminent Professors of respective subjects.

The specialty of this new Series "**CSS**" is that it:

- Covers full syllabus of University of Pune.
- Contains Matter written in Simple and Lucid language.
- Includes "To the Point" Topics and well arranged articles.
- Includes Most Likely Questions.
- Includes Previous Years University Question Papers.
- Available in all leading stores at Affordable Price.

Happy Studying and Best of Luck!!!

Nirali Prakashan

SYLLABUS

Unit 1 : Numbering Systems

Numbering systems binary, octal, decimal and hexadecimal and their conversion, codes- BCD, Grey and excess3, Binary arithmetic:- addition and subtraction by 1's and 2's compliment. Booleans algebra, De-Morgan's theory etc. K-map: - structure for two, three and four variables, SOP and POS form reduction of Boolean expressions by K-map.

Unit 2 : Concept of Combinational & Sequential Circuits

Flip flops – R-S, Clocked S-R, D latches, Edge triggered D flip-flops, Edge triggered JK flip flops, JK Master - slave flip flop, Register- Buffer registers, shift registers, controlled shift registers, ring counter, Counters – asynchronous counters, synchronous counter, u p - d own counter , twisted ring counters, N – module counters.

Unit 3 : Op-Amp

Block diagrams of 741 and 324, ideal and practical parameters open loop and close loop configuration of Op-Amp. Applications of Op- Amp- Comparator, Schmitt trigger, zero crossing detectors, V-I and I-V converters, voltage regulators using ICs 78xx, 79xx, LM 317 and LM 723.

Unit 4 : Waveform Generation Using OP-AMP

Waveform generation using Op-amp - sine, square, saw tooth and triangular generator, peak detector, Instrumentation amplifier, Half and full wave precision rectifiers IC 555 – construction, working and modes of operation- astable, monostable and multivibrators, Sequence generator, Active filters-Its configuration with frequency response, Analysis of first order low pass and high pass filters.

Unit 5 : BJT Amplifier

Introduction, Class A amplifier, AC-DC load line analysis, Single stage a n d Multistage BJT amplifier, direct coupled, RC coupled and transformer coupled, Darlington pair, Push-Pull amplifier and differential amplifier FET-construction, Parameters, Characteristics.

Unit 6 : Diode Rectifiers

Introduction, Single phase half wave rectifier with R, RL and RC loads. Single phase full wave rectifier – Center tap and bridge rectifier supplying R and RL load and performance parameters. Three phase full wave bridge rectifier with R and RL load. Comparison of single phase half wave and full wave rectifiers, comparison of single phase full wave bridge and three phase full wave bridge rectifiers. Consideration of LC filters.

CONTENTS

Unit 1 : Number Systems and Boolean Algebra   1.1-1.40

1.1	Number systems	1.1
	1.1.1 Binary Number System	1.1
	1.1.2 Decimal Number System	1.1
	1.1.3 Octal Number System	1.2
	1.1.4 Hexadecimal Number System	1.2
1.2	Conversion of any radix numbers to decimal number	1.2
	1.2.1 Conversion of Binary to Decimal	1.3
	1.2.2 Conversion of Octal to Decimal	1.3
	1.2.3 Conversion of Hexadecimal Number to Decimal Number	1.3
1.3	Conversion from decimal to other number system	1.4
	1.3.1 Conversion of Decimal to Binary	1.4
	1.3.2 Conversion of Decimal to Octal	1.5
	1.3.3 Conversion of Hexadecimal to Decimal	1.5
1.4	Remaining radix conversion	1.6
	1.4.1 Conversion of Binary to Octal	1.6
	1.4.2 Converting Octal to Binary	1.6
	1.4.3 Converting of Hexadecimal to Binary	1.7
	1.4.4 Converting of Binary to Hexadecimal	1.7
	1.4.5 Converting Octal to Hexadecimal	1.8
	1.4.6 Converting Hexadecimal to Octal	1.9
1.5	Signed Binary Number Representation	1.9
	1.5.1 Signed Magnitude	1.9
	1.5.2 One's Complement	1.10
	1.5.3 Two's Complement	1.11
1.6	Binary arithmetic	1.11
	1.6.1 Binary Addition	1.11
	1.6.2 Binary Subtraction	1.13
1.7	Codes	1.16
	1.7.1 BCD Code	1.17
	1.7.2 Excess 3 Code	1.18
	1.7.3 Gray Code	1.19

1.8	Code conversion	1.22
	1.8.1 Converting Binary code to Gray code	1.22
	1.8.2 Converting Gray to Binary	1.22
	1.8.3 Binary to BCD Conversion	1.23
	1.8.4 BCD to Binary Conversion	1.23
	1.8.5 BCD to Excess-3 Conversion	1.23
	1.8.6 Excess-3 to BCD Conversion	1.24
1.9	Boolean Algebra	1.24
	1.9.1 Axioms of Boolean Algebra	1.24
	1.9.2 Laws of Boolean Algebra	1.25
	1.9.3 Rules of Boolean Algebra	1.26
	1.9.4 DeMorgan's Theorems	1.26
1.10	Sum of products (SOP) Form	1.28
	1.10.1 Standard Terms and Standard (or Canonical) Forms	1.28
	1.10.2 Sum Term or Maximum Term (M)	1.28
	1.10.3 Product or Minimum Term (m)	1.29
	1.10.4 Standard (or Canonical) Forms	1.29
	1.10.5 Sum of Products (SOP) Form	1.29
1.11	Product of Sum (POS) Form	1.31
	1.11.1 Product-of-Sums (POS) Form	1.31
1.12	Reduction Techniques	1.32
	1.12.1 Boolean Algebra Simplification Technique	1.32
	1.12.2 Reduction of Boolean Equation using K-map	1.33
	1.12.3 Representing SOP Equation on K-map	1.34
	1.12.4 Representing POS Equation on K-map	1.35
1.13	K-map Reduction Techniques	1.35
	1.13.1 Prime Implicant and Essential Prime Implicant	1.38
	1.13.2 Don't Care Condition	1.39
	1.13.3 Limitations of Karnaugh Map	1.40
UNIT II : Sequential Logic		**2.1-2.56**
2.1	Logic Circuits	2.1
	2.1.1 Combinational Circuit	2.1
	2.1.2 Sequential Logic Circuit	2.2

	2.1.3	Comparison of Combinational and Sequential Circuit	2.2
	2.1.4	Sequential Circuit Types	2.3
2.2	Latch vs Flip-Flop		2.3
2.3	Level Triggered and Edge Triggered		2.4
	2.3.1	Level Triggered	2.4
	2.3.2	Edge Triggered	2.5
2.4	Latch		2.6
	2.4.1	SR Latch using NAND Gate	2.6
	2.4.2	SR Latch using NOR Gate	2.9
	2.4.3	D Latch	2.10
2.5	Clocked S-R Flip-Flop		2.11
2.6	Clocked S-R flip flop with Preset and Clear Inputs		2.12
2.7	JK Flip Flop		2.14
	2.7.1	Master Slave JK (MS JK) Flip Flop	2.16
2.8	D Flip Flop		2.17
2.9	T Flip Flop		2.19
2.10	Registers		2.20
	2.10.1	Buffer Register	2.20
2.11	Shift register		2.20
	2.11.1	Serial In Serial Out Shift Register	2.21
	2.11.2	Serial in Parallel Out Shift Register	2.23
	2.11.3	Parallel In Serial Out Shift Register	2.23
	2.11.4	Parallel In Parallel Out Shift Register	2.26
	2.11.5	Bi-directional Shift Register	2.27
	2.11.6	Universal Register	2.29
2.12	Counters		2.29
	2.12.1	Classification of Counter	2.29
2.13	Asynchronous (Ripple) Counters		2.30
	2.13.1	3-Bit Asynchronous Up (Ripple) Counter	2.31
	2.13.2	4-Bit Asynchronous Up Counter	2.33
	2.13.3	3-bit Asynchronous Down Counter	2.35
	2.13.4	4 Bit up / down Ripple Counter	2.36
	2.13.5	MOD-N counter (Modulus of the counter)	2.37

2.14	Synchronous Counter	2.39
	2.14.1 3-bit Synchronous Counter	2.40
	2.14.2 4-bit Synchronous Counter	2.42
	2.14.3 3-bit Up/Down Synchronous Counter	2.44
	2.14.4 Modulo N Synchronous Counter	2.46
	2.14.5 BCD Synchronous Counter	2.49
2.15	Ring Counter	2.51
	2.15.1 Johnson Counter	2.53
2.16	Difference between Synchronous and Asynchronous Counters	2.56
UNIT III : Operational Amplifier		**3.1-3.34**
3.1	Introduction	3.1
3.2	Block Diagram of an Operational Amplifier	3.1
3.3	Equivalent Circuit of an Op-amp	3.2
3.4	Ideal Op-Amp Characteristics	3.2
3.5	Practical Op-Amp Characteristics	3.4
	3.5.1 Comparison of Ideal and Practical Characteristics	3.6
3.6	Op-Amp Configuration	3.6
	3.6.1 Open Loop Configuration of Op-Amp	3.6
	3.6.2 Closed loop operation of op-amp	3.8
3.7	Comparison of Ideal Vs Practical Characteristics of IC 741C	3.8
3.8	Applications of Op-Amp	3.9
	3.8.1 Op-amp Comparators	3.9
	3.8.2 Schmitt Trigger	3.13
	3.8.3 Comparison of Schmitt Trigger and Comparator	3.16
	3.8.4 Zero Crossing Detector	3.16
	3.8.5 Current to Voltage Converter	3.17
	3.8.6 Voltage to Current Converter with Floating Load	3.21
3.9	Voltage Regulators	3.22
	3.9.1 Types of Voltage Regulators	3.23
	3.9.2 Advantages of Voltage Regulators	3.23
	3.9.3 Applications of Voltage Regulators	3.23
3.10	Block Diagram Of 3 Pin IC Regulator	3.24
	3.10.1 IC 78XX : Positive Voltage Regulators	3.24
	3.10.2 IC 79XX Negative Voltage Regulator Series :	3.26

3.11	Performance Parameters Of Voltage Regulators	3.27
3.12	Adjustable Voltage Regulators	3.28
	3.12.1 LM 317 Regulator	3.28
	3.12.2 IC µA 723 Voltage Regulator	3.30

UNIT IV : Waveform Generation Using OP-AMP   4.1-4.34

4.1	Sine Wave Generators	4.1
	4.1.1 Barkhausen Criterion for Oscillations	4.1
4.2	RC phase-shift Oscillator Using IC 741	4.2
	4.2.1 Wein Bridge Oscillator using IC 741	4.3
4.3	A Square Wave Generator (Astable)	4.4
4.4	Triangular Wave Generator using Op-amp	4.5
4.5	Peak Detector	4.6
4.6	Instrumentation Amplifiers	4.7
	4.6.1 Instrumentation Amplifier Using Transducer Bridge	4.9
	4.6.2 Instrumentation Amplifier Using Three Op-amps	4.10
4.7	Precision Rectifiers	4.12
	4.7.1 Precision Half Wave rectifier	4.12
	4.7.2 Full Wave Precision Rectifiers	4.14
4.8	Timer IC 555	4.15
	4.8.1 Pin Description	4.17
4.9	Multivibrators	4.18
	4.9.1 IC 555 as a Monostable Multivibrator	4.18
	4.9.2 IC 555 as an Astable Multivibrator	4.21
	4.9.3 Bistable Multivibrator	4.24
4.10	Active Filters	4.24
	4.10.1 First Order Low pass Butterworth Filter	4.25
	4.10.2 First Order High pass Butterworth Filter	4.28
	4.10.3 Band-pass Filters	4.31

UNIT V : Bipolar Junction Transistor   5.1-5.42

5.1	Introduction	5.1
5.2	Classification of Amplifier	5.1
5.3	Load Line Analysis	5.3
	5.3.1 DC Load Line	5.3
	5.3.2 The Quiescent Point (Q point)	5.4

		5.3.3 AC Load Line	5.5
		5.3.4 Factors Affecting the Stability of Q Point	5.5
5.4	Power Amplifiers		5.5
5.5	Class-A Power Amplifier		5.6
5.6	Class-B Push Pull Amplifier		5.8
5.7	Types of Coupling (Quantitative Analysis)		5.9
		5.7.1 Direct Coupled Amplifier	5.10
		5.7.2 Transformer Coupled Amplifier	5.10
		5.7.3 RC Coupled Amplifier	5.11
		5.7.4 Multistage RC Coupled CE Amplifier	5.13
		5.7.5 Differential Amplifier	5.15
5.8	Field-Effect Transistors		5.18
		5.8.1 Introduction	5.18
		5.8.2 Types of FETs	5.18
5.9	Junction Field-Effect Transistors (JFETs)		5.18
5.10	Construction of JFET		5.19
		5.10.1 Construction of N-channel JFET	5.19
		5.10.2 Construction of P-channel JFET	5.19
		5.10.3 Symbols of JFET	5.20
5.11	Working Principle of N-Channel JFET		5.20
5.12	Characteristics of N-Channel JFET		5.23
		5.12.1 Drain Characteristics	5.23
		5.12.2 Transfer Characteristics	5.25
5.13	Parameters of JFET		5.25
5.14	Relation Among FET Parameters		5.27
5.15	Applications of JFET		5.27
		5.15.1 Electronic Switch	5.27
		5.15.2 Analog Multiplexer	5.29
5.16	Advantages of FET over BJT		5.30
5.17	Disadvantages of JFET		5.30
5.18	Metal Oxide Semiconductor FET		5.30
		5.18.1 Types of MOSFET	5.30

5.19	Depletion Type N-Channel MOSFET	5.31
	5.19.1 Construction	5.31
	5.19.2 Working Principle	5.31
	5.19.3 Static Characteristics	5.33
5.20	Enhancement Type N-Channel MOSFET	5.34
	5.20.1 Construction	5.34
	5.20.2 Working Principle	5.35
	5.20.3 Static Characteristics	5.35
5.21	Symbols of MOSFET	5.37
	5.21.1 Depletion-type MOSFET	5.37
	5.21.2 Enhancement-Type MOSFET	5.37
5.22	Applications of MOSFET	5.38
	5.22.1 Advantages of N-channel MOSFETs over P-channel	5.38
	5.22.2 Handling Precautions for MOSFET	5.38
	5.22.3 Advantages of MOSFET over JFET	5.38
	5.22.4 Comparison of JFET and MOSFET	5.39
5.23	CMOS	5.39
	5.23.1 Working Principle	5.40
	5.23.2 Advantage of CMOS	5.41
5.24	Comparison between JFET and BJT	5.41
	5.24.1 Comparison between JFET and BJT	5.41
	5.24.2 Comparison between N-channel and P-channel JFET	5.42
UNIT VI : Diode Rectifiers		**6.1-6.24**
6.1	Introduction	6.1
	6.1.1 Types of Rectifiers	6.1
6.2	Half-Wave Rectifier (HWR)	6.1
	6.2.1 Analysis of Half-Wave Rectifier	6.2
	6.2.2 Disadvantages of Half-Wave Rectifier	6.6
6.3	Single Phase Half Wave Rectifier With RL Load	6.6
	6.3.1 Single Phase Half Wave Rectifier with RC Load	6.8
	6.3.2 Single Phase Half Wave Rectifier with Freewheeling Diode	6.8
	6.3.3 Diode Circuit with RL Load	6.9
	6.3.4 Diode circuit with RC Load	6.10

6.4	Full-Wave Rectifier With Centre Tapped Transformer (FWR)	6.12
	6.4.1 Analysis of Full-Wae Rectifier Circuit	6.12
	6.4.2 Single Phase Full Wave Rectifier with RL Load	6.16
6.5	Bridge Rectifier	6.17
	6.5.1 Performance Parameters of a Bridge Rectifier	6.18
	6.5.2 Single Phase Bridge Rectifier with RL Load	6.19
6.6	Three Phase Rectifiers	6.20
	6.6.1 Three Phase Bridge Rectifier with R Load	6.20
	6.6.2 Three Phase Bridge Rectifier with RL Load	6.22
6.7	Comparison of Diode Rectifiers	6.23
	6.7.1 Comparison of Single Phase Half Wave and Full Wave	6.23
	6.7.2 Comparison of Single Phase and Three Phase Bridge	6.24

Unit - I

NUMBER SYSTEMS AND BOOLEAN ALGEBRA

1.1 NUMBER SYSTEMS

Q. Explain different types of number systems ?

- Binary Number System
- Decimal Number System
- Octal Number System
- Hexadecimal Number System

1.1.1 Binary Number System

Q. Explain binary number system in detail. [Dec 10, 12, 3 M]

- The binary number system is used in digital electronics. It has the following characteristics.

Two digits : 0, 1

Base : 2

Weights : Powers of Base 2 (2^0, 2^1, 2^2, 2^3...) or (1, 2, 4, 8).

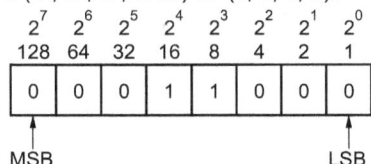

Fig. 1.1 : Binary number system

- In the binary system, 1's and 0's are arranged into columns.
- Each column is weighted. The first column on the right has a binary weight of 2^{10}. This equivalent to decimal 1 and is referred to as the Least Significant Bit (LSB).
- The number in the far left hand column is called Most Significant Bit (MSB).

1.1.2 Decimal Number System

- In decimal number system, we can express any decimal number in units, ten hundreds, thousands and so on.

e.g. 6597.8 this number can be represented as

$6000 + 500 + 90 + 7 + 0.8 = 6597.8 = 6597.8_{10}$

radix and base of decimal number system is 10.

	10^3	10^2	10^1	10^0		10^{-1}
In power	6	5	9	7	•	8
of 10	6×10^3	5×10^2	9×10^1	7×10^0	•	8×10^{-1}

Fig. 1.2

1.1.3 Octal Number System

- The octal number system consists of eight digits of decimal number system : 0, 1, 2, 3, 4, 5, 6 and 7. So its base is 8.

  e.g. The octal number 8531.74 can be represented in power of 8 as shown in Fig. 1.3.

8^3	8^2	8^1	8^0		8^{-1}	8^{-2}
8	5	3	1	•	7	4
8×8^3	5×8^2	3×8^1	1×8^0	•	7×8^{-1}	4×8^{-2}

Fig. 1.3

1.1.4 Hexadecimal Number System

Q. Explain hexadecimal number system in detail	(Dec 12, 3 M)

- The hexadecimal number system abase of 16 having 16 characters.

  0, 1, 2, 3, 4, 5, 6, 7, 8, 9, A, B, C, D, E, F.

- It is easy to convert hexadecimal number to binary and vice versa.

  e.g. 3FD. 48 can be represented in power of 16 as shown in Fig. 1.4 below.

16^2	16^1	16^0		16^{-1}	16^{-2}
3	F	D	•	4	8
3×16^2	$F \times 16^1$	$D \times 16^0$	•	4×16^{-1}	8×16^{-2}

Fig. 1.4

1.2 CONVERSION OF ANY RADIX NUMBERS TO DECIMAL NUMBER

- To convert from any radix r to Decimal. The formula for converting any Radix to Decimal.

$$N = A_{n-1}r^{n-1} + A_{n-2}r^{n-2} + \ldots + A_1 r^1 + A_0 r^0 + A_{-i}r^{-i} + \ldots + C_{-m}r^{-m} \quad \ldots(1)$$

where   N = Number in decimal

A = Digit
r = Radix or base of number system number of digits
m = The fractional part of the number
n = The number of digit in the fractional part of the number

1.2.1 Conversion of Binary to Decimal

Q. Convert following number into decimal. $(101101.10101)_2$ **[Dec. 07, 6 M]**

Example 1.1 : Convert binary number 1011.01 into its decimal equivalent.

Solution : Given binary number is 1011.01

Using formula given in equation 1.

$$(1011.01) = (1 \times 2^3 + 0 \times 2^2 + 1 \times 2^1 + 1 \times 2^0 + 0 \times 2^{-1} + 1 \times 2^{-2})$$

$$= 1 \times 8 + 0 \times 4 + 1 \times 2 + 1 \times 1 + 0 \times \frac{1}{2} + 1 \times \frac{1}{4}$$

$$= 8 + 0 + 2 + 1 + \frac{1}{4}$$

$$= (11.25)_{10}$$

1.2.2 Conversion of Octal to Decimal

Q. Convert the following octal number into its equivalent decimal.
(a) (555) octal   (b) (777) octal   **[May 07, 6 M]**
Q. For a maximum 3-digit octal number obtain a equivalent decimal number.
     [May 11, 1 M]
Q. Convert the following into its equivalent decimal numbers. $(327.4051)_8$ **[Dec. 12, 2 M]**

Example 1.2 :

$(321)_8 = (\ )_{10}$

Solution : Given number is $(321)_8$

Using formula given in equation 1.

$$(321)_8 = 3 \times 8^2 + 2 \times 8^1 + 2 \times 8^0 = 3 \times 64 + 2 \times 8 + 2 \times 1$$

$$= 192 + 16 + 2$$

$$(321)_8 = (210)_{10}$$

1.2.3 Conversion of Hexadecimal Number to Decimal Number

Q. Express following number in decimal. Show your step by step calculation. $(16.5)_{16}$

[May 07, 6 M]

Example 1.3 :

Convert hexadecimal number $(4D7.2)_{16}$ into its equivalent decimal number.

Solution : Given number is $(4D7.2)_{16}$

$$(4D7.2) = 4 \times 16^2 + 13 \times 16^1 + 7 \times 16^0 + 2 \times 16^{-1}$$

$$= 4 \times 144 + 13 \times 16 + 7 \times 1 + \frac{2}{16}$$

$$= 576 + 208 + 7 + 0.125$$

$$(4D7.2)_{16} = (791.125)_{10}$$

1.3 CONVERSION FROM DECIMAL TO OTHER NUMBER SYSTEM

- In this we need to first consider the given number having decimal point we need to separate integer part and fractional parts.
- Then convert each part different method and then combine for last answer.

1.3.1 Conversion of Decimal to Binary

Q.	Express the following numbers in binary	
(i)	$(13.65625)_{Decimal}$ (ii) $(428.10)_{Decimal}$	**[May 11, 2 M]**
Q.	Express the following numbers in binary	
(i)	$(0.6875)_{10}$ (ii) $(11\ 01.11)_{10}$	**[May 11, 2 M]**

Example 1.4 : Convert 125.12 decimal into binary number.

Solution : Integer part

Division	Remainder
125 ÷ 2 = 62	1
62 ÷ 2 = 31	0
31 ÷ 2 = 15	1
15 ÷ 2 = 7	1
7 ÷ 2 = 3	1
3 ÷ 2 = 1	1
1 ÷ 2 = 0	1

(LSD at top, MSD at bottom)

$$(125)_{10} = (1111101)_2$$

Fractional part

0.12	0.24	0.48	0.96
× 2	× 2	× 2	× 2
0.24	0.48	0.96	1.92

$$(0.12)_{10} = (0001)_2$$

∴ $(125.12)_{10} = (1111101.0001)_2$

1.3.2 Conversion of Decimal to Octal

Q. Convert the following number into octal form $(3287.51)_{10}$ **[Dec. 12, 2 M]**

Example 1.5 : Convert $(338.025)_{10}$ into octal.

Solution : Integer part

Division	Remainder
338 ÷ 8 = 42	2
42 ÷ 8 = 5	2
5 ÷ 8 = 0	5

(LSD ↑ MSD)

$$(338)_8 = (522)_{10}$$

Fractional part :

0.025	0.200	0.600	0.800
× 8	× 8	× 8	× 8
0.200	1.600	4.800	6.400
↓	↓	↓	↓
0	1	4	6

$$(0.025)_8 = (0146)_{10}$$

∴ Final answer $(338.0.25)_8 = (522.0146)_{10}$

1.3.3 Conversion of Hexadecimal to Decimal

Q. Convert the following number into decimal number.   **[Dec. 11, May 12, 4 M]**
  (i) $(1FFF)_{16}$ (ii) $(BF8)_{16}$

Q. Convert the following number into decimal number.
  (i) $(5A.FF)_{16}$ (ii) $(3FFF)_{16}$

Example 1.6 : Convert $(438)_{16}$ into decimal.

Solution : Integer part

Division	Remainder
438 ÷ 16 = 26	0
26 ÷ 16 = 1	1
10 ÷ 16 = 0	10 = A

LSD ↑ (bottom to top) MSD

$(438)_{16}$ = (A10)
$(438)_{16}$ = $(A10)_{10}$

1.4 REMAINING RADIX CONVERSION

1.4.1 Conversion of Binary to Octal

> **Q.** Convert the following octal number into octal. **[May 11, 2 M]**
> (i) $(11100110.110)_2$

- Converting binary to octal is also a simple process. Break the binary digits into groups of three starting from the binary point and convert each group into its appropriate octal digit.
- For whole numbers, it may be necessary to add a zero as the MSB in order to complete a grouping of three bits. Note that this does not change the value of the binary number. Similarly, when representing fractions, it may be necessary to add a trailing zero in the LSB in order to form a complete grouping of three.

Example 1.7 : Converting $(010111)_2$ to Octal

    111 = 7 (LSB)
    010 = 2 (MSB)

Thus, $(010111)_2$ = $(27)_8$

Example 1.8 : Converting $(0.110111)_2$ to Octal

    110 = 6 (MSB)
    111 = 5 (LSB)

Thus, $(0.110101)_2$ = $(0.65)_8$

1.4.2 Converting Octal to Binary

> **Q.** Convert the following octal number into binary.
> (a) $(123456)_8$ (b) $(5726.34)_8$
> (c) $(337)_8$ (d) $(0.53652)_8$

- The primary application of octal numbers is representing binary numbers, as it is easier to read large numbers in octal form that in binary form. Because each octal digit can be represented by a three-bit binary number (see Table 1.1, it is very easy to convert from octal to binary.
- Simply replace each octal digit with the appropriate three-bit binary number as indicated in the examples below.

Table 1.1 : Octal and binary numbers

Octal Digit	Binary Digit
0	000
1	001
2	010
3	011
4	100
5	101
6	110
7	111

$13_8 = (001011)_2$

$(37.12)_8 = (011111.001010)_2$

1.4.3 Converting of Hexadecimal to Binary

Q. Convert the following hexadecimal to Binary numbers.
(1) A72E (2) BD6.7 (3) 0.AF54 (4) DF (5) FF [May 13, 10 M]

- Because each hexadecimal digit can be represented by a four-bit binary number it is very easy to convert from hexadecimal to binary. Simply replace each hexadecimal digit with the appropriate four-bit binary number as indicated in the examples below.

Example 1.9 :

$A3_{16} = (10100011)_2$

$(37.12)_{16} = (00110111 . 00010010)_2$

1.4.4 Converting of Binary to Hexadecimal

Q. Convert $(10110)_2$ into hex. number. [May 12, 4 M]

- Converting binary to hexadecimal is another simple process. Break the binary digits into groups of four starting from the binary point and convert each group into its appropriate hexadecimal digit.

- For whole numbers, it may be necessary to add a zero as the MSB in order to complete a grouping of four bits. Note that this addition does not change the value of the binary number.
- Similarly, when representing fractions, it may be necessary to add a trailing zero in the LSB in order to form a complete grouping of four.

Example 1.10 :

(a) Converting $(1010111)_2$ to hexadecimal.

$$0111 = 7 \text{ (LSB)}$$
$$0101 = 5 \text{ (MSB)}$$

Thus, $(1010111)_2 = (57)_{16}$

(b) Converting $(0.00111111)_2$ to hexadecimal.

$$0011 = 3 \text{ (MSB)}$$
$$1111 = F \text{ (LSB)}$$

Thus, $(0.00111111)_2 = (0.3F)_{16}$

1.4.5 Converting Octal to Hexadecimal

Q. Convert the following octal numbers into its equivalent hex.	[May 10, 4 M]
(i) $(555)_{octal}$ (ii) $(777)_{octal}$	
Q. Convert $(36)_8$ into hexadecimal.	[May 12, 2 M]
Q. Convert $(377)_8$ into hexadecimal.	[Dec. 11, 2 M]

- To convert an octal number to hexadecimal follow the steps given below.

Step 1 : First convert octal to its binary.

Step 2 : Then convert binary number into hexadecimal.

Example 1.11 :

Convert $(777)_8$ into hex.

Step 1 : Convert $(777)_8$ into binary.

$$(777)_8 = (111111111)$$

Step 2 : For equivalent hexadecimal group the binary number into group of 4.

$$(777)_8 = (\underline{0001} \ \underline{1111} \ \underline{1111})$$
$$\downarrow \quad \downarrow \quad \downarrow$$
$$1 \quad F \quad F$$

∴ $(777)_8 = (1FF)_{16}$

1.4.6 Converting Hexadecimal to Octal

Q. Convert hexadecimal numbers into octal numbers. [May 13, 10 M]
(1) A72E (2) BD6.7 (3) 0.AF54 (4) DF (5) FF

- To convert hexadecimal numbers into octal follow the below steps.

Step 1 : First write down given hexadecimal numbers into 4 group of binary numbers.

Step 2 : Then remove the group of four binary.

Step 3 : Make group of 3 binary bits starting from the LSB side.

Example 1.12 :

Convert hexadecimal numbers 5DB into octal.

Step 1 : Given number is 5DB.

Binary from of 5DB is = 01011.1011011

Step 2 : Rewrite number with removing group space.

$$= (\underline{010} \ \underline{111} \ \underline{011} \ \underline{011})$$
$$\qquad \downarrow \ \ \ \downarrow \ \ \ \downarrow \ \ \ \downarrow$$
$$\qquad 2 \ \ \ 7 \ \ \ 3 \ \ \ 3$$

$(5DB)_6 = (2733)_8$

1.5 SIGNED BINARY NUMBER REPRESENTATION

Q. What do you mean by signed magnitude representation of a number ? [Dec. 07, 2 M]
Q. What are different ways of representing signed binary numbers ? Explain with examples ? [Dec. 11, 6 M]

- Signed Magnitude
- One's Complement
- Two's Complement

1.5.1 Signed Magnitude

- The simplest way to indicate negation is signed magnitude. In signed magnitude, the left-most bit is not actually part of the number, but is just the equivalent of a + / − sign.
- "0" indicates that the number is positive, "1" indicates negative. In 8 bits, 00001100 would be 12 (break this down into (1*2 ^3) + (1 * 2 ^2)). To indicate - 12, we would simply put a "1" rather than a "0" as the first bit : 10001100.
- The +ve or −ve signs are also represented in the binary form i.e. by using 0 or 1 so a 0 is used to represent the (+ve) sign and 1 is used to represent (−ve) sign.

- The most significant Bit (MSB) of binary number is used to represent the sign and the remaining bits are used for representing the magnitude.

  e.g. 8 bit signed binary number show in Fig. 1.5

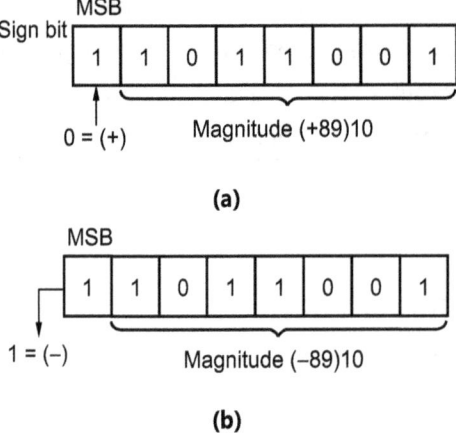

Fig. 1.5 : 8-bit signed binary numbers

This type of numbers is called number or signed magnitude number.

- For an 8 bit sign magnitude number the largest negative number is (–127) to largest positive, number is (127) i.e. from 0 to 255.

Advantages :

- We can easily find out the magnitude by deleting the sign bit.
- The simplicity of sign magnitude.

Disadvantage :

- Signed number require complicated circuits.

1.5.2 One's Complement

- In one's complement, positive numbers are represented as usual in regular binary. However, negative numbers are represented differently. To negate a number, replace all zeros with ones, and ones with zeros-flip the bits. Thus, 12 would be 00001100, and –12 would be 11110011.
- As in signed magnitude, the leftmost bit indicates the sign (1 is negative, 0 is positive). To compute the value of a negative number, flip the bits and translate as before.

1.5.3 Two's Complement

- Begin with the number in one's complement. Add 1 if the number is negative. Twelve would be represented as 00001100, and − 12 as 11110100. to verify this, let's subtract 1 from 11110100, to get 11110011. If we flip the bits, we get 00001100, or 12 in decimal.

Example 1.13 :
Represent the decimal numbers 25 and − 25 in the 8 bit signed magnitude 1's complement and 2's complement forms.

Solution :

Step 1 : (i) Representation of 25 signed magnitude

$$25 = 0 \quad 0011001$$
$$\downarrow \qquad \quad \downarrow$$
$$\text{sign} \quad \text{Magnitude}$$

Step 2 : (ii) Representation of −25 in signed magnitude form.

$$25 = 1 \quad 0011001$$
$$\downarrow \qquad \quad \downarrow$$
$$\text{sign} \quad \text{Magnitude}$$

Step 3 : (iii) Representation of − 25 in 1's complement form

$$25 = 00011001 \quad \text{...sign magnitude}$$
$$\downarrow$$
$$\text{invert all bits}$$
$$-25 = 11100110 \quad \text{...1's complement form}$$

Step 4 : (iv) Representation of − 25 in 2's complement form

$$25 = 00011001 \quad \text{...sign magnitude}$$
$$\text{invert all bits + add 1}$$
$$-25 = 11100111 \quad \text{...2's complement form}$$

1.6 BINARY ARITHMETIC

1.6.1 Binary Addition

Q. Perform addition of $(11001001)_2$ and $(10101111)_2$.

- The binary addition is the most basic operation of binary arithmetic. The two bit binary digit addition is shown in following table.

Table 1.2 : Truth table for half adder

Sr. No.	Operations	Sum	Carry
0	0 + 0	0	0
1	0 + 1	1	0
2	1 + 0	1	0
3	1 + 1	0	1

- The 3 bit (i.e. two significant bit and a previous carry) is called a full addition is shown in following table.

Table 1.3 : Truth table for full adder

Inputs			Outputs	
A	B	C_{in}	Sum	Cout
0	0	0	0	0
0	0	1	1	0
0	1	0	1	0
0	1	1	0	1
1	0	0	1	0
1	0	1	0	1
1	1	0	0	1
1	1	1	1	1

Binary addition method steps :

Step 1 : Add bits column wise from LSB with carry if any

Step 2 : If carry is generated write at the top of next column.

Step 3 : Write the sum at the bottom of the same column.

Example 1.14 : $(8)_{10}$ and $(12)_{10}$

Step 1 : First convert both number into binary.

$$(8)_{10} = (1000)_2$$
$$(12)_{10} = (1100)_2$$

Step 2 : Add bits column wise from the LSB with carry if any.

```
        1         ...carry
     + 1000       ...number 1
       1100      ...number 2
       ─────
       10100
```

$$= (10100)_2$$

1.6.2 Binary Subtraction

- The subtraction for 2 bit procedure is given below in table 1.4.

Table 1.4

Sr. No.	Operations	Sub	Borrow
1	0-0	0	0
2	0-1	1	1
3	1-0	1	0
4	1-1	0	0

Subtraction method steps :
1. Subtract bits column wise starting from LSB with barrow if any.
2. Write borrow at the next column top.
3. Write difference bottom of the same column.

Example 1.15 :

Perform binary subtraction $(11101100)_2 - (00110010)_2$

Solution :

```
           10
       0 0 10 0 10
       1 1 1 0 1 1 0 0    ...number 1
      - 0 0 1 1 0 0 1 0   ...number 2
       1 0 1 1 1 0 1 0    Result
```

1.6.2.1 Binary subtraction using 1's complement method

Q. Perform binary subtraction using 1's complement form.

Steps :
1. First take 1's complement of second number.
2. Add first number and 1's complement of second number.
3. If the carry is generated then result is + ve and true form. Then add carry to the result to get final answer.
4. If the carry is not generated then result is –ve and in 1's complement form.

Example 1.16 :

Perform binary subtraction using 1's complement method.
$$(28)_{10} - (15)_{10}$$

Step 1 : First convert both numbers into binary.

$$(28)_{10} = (011100)_2$$
$$(15)_{10} = (001111)_2$$

Step 2 : Take 1's complement of second number i.e. $(15)_{10}$

$$(001111) = (15)_{10}$$
↓ 1's complement
110000

Step 3 : Add first number and 1's complement of second number.

```
  011100
+ 110000
--------
 1001100
        ↓
      carry
```

Step 4 : Carry is generated so result is positive add carry to the result to get final result.

```
  001100
+      1
--------
  001101   final answer
```

$001101 = (13)_{10}$

1.6.2.2 Binary subtraction using 2's complement method

> **Q.** Perform the following arithmetic's operations using 2's complement form
> (i) 8 + 12 (ii) –8 + 12 (iii) 8 – 12 (iv) –8 – 12   **[May 05, 8 M]**
>
> **Q.** Perform subtraction using 2's complement method.
> (i) 96 – 78 (ii) 57 –77 (iii) 88 – 99

Steps :

1. First take 2's complement of second number.
2. Add first number to the 2's complement of second number.
3. If carry is generated then result number is positive and true form. Remove carry or ignore carry.
4. If carry is not generated then the result number is –ve and in the 2's complement form.

Example 1.17 : Perform following substructure using 2's complement method

(a) $(4)_{10} - (9)_{10}$.   **[Dec. 06, 2 M]**

Step 1 : First write both number in the binary form.

$$(4)_{10} = 0100$$
$$(9)_{10} = 1001$$

Step 2 : Obtain 2's complement of $(9)_{10}$

$$(9)_{10} = 1001$$
$$\downarrow \text{ 2's complement}$$
$$0111$$

Step 3 : Add $(4)_{10}$ to 2's complement of $(9)_{10}$

$$(4)_{10} = 0100$$
$$+$$
$$\underline{\text{2's complement of } (9)_{10} = 0111}$$
$$\quad 0 \quad\quad 1011$$
$$\quad \downarrow \quad\quad \downarrow$$
$$\text{final carry} \quad \text{answer}$$

zero shows the result is negative and in its 2's complement form.

Step 4 : Convert the answer into true form

$$\text{Answer} \quad 1011$$
$$\text{Subtract } - \quad \underline{\quad 1}$$
$$1010$$
$$\downarrow \text{ invert all bits}$$
$$0101 \quad \text{(answer in true form)}$$

Thus the answer is $-(0101)_2$ i.e. $(-5)_{10}$.

(b) $(10011)_2 - (1101)_2$

Step 1 : Take 2's complement of second number.

$$01101$$
$$\downarrow \text{ invert all bits}$$
$$10010$$
$$\underline{+ 1}$$
$$10011$$

Step 2 : Add $(10011)_2$ to 2's complement of $(01101)_2$.

$$10011 \quad\quad \text{...number 1}$$
$$+ \underline{\;10011} \quad\quad \text{...number 2 2's complement}$$
$$1\,00110$$
$$| \text{ result answer}$$
$$\text{carry}$$

Step 3 : Carry is 1 so number is positive discard carry.

$$\text{final answer} = 00110$$

1.7 CODES

Q. What are the different types of codes used in digital systems ? Explain them.

- The codes are used to represent the given digital information in particular format.
- The codes are used to store and transmit the data efficiency. All codes are represented finally as '0' and '1' which computers can understand. There are various types of codes which are enlisted below.

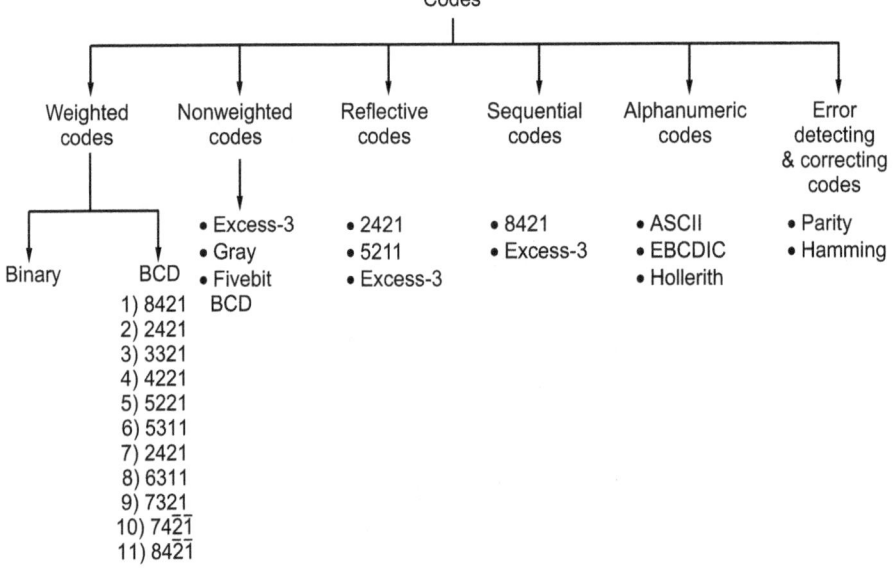

Fig. 1.6

- **Weighted codes :** The weight of digit or bit depends on its position e.g. the weight of 6 in 647 is 600, 4 is 0 and 7 is 1.

- **Non weighted codes :** Non weighted codes are not assigned with any weight to each digit position i.e. each digit position within the number is not assigned fixed value excess-3 and gray codes are the non weighted codes.

- **Reflective codes :** A code is said to be reflective when the code for 9 is the complement for 0, the code for 8 is complement for 1, 7 for 2, 6 for 3 and 5 for 4.

  e.g.   2 + 4 + 2 + 1

  code for 9   1   1   1   1

                   ↓ complement

  code for 0   0   0   0   0

- **Sequential codes :** In this codes each succeeding code is one binary number greater than its preceding code. This type of codes mainly used in mathematical manipulation.

The 8421 and excess – 3 are sequential codes.

- **Alphanumerical Code :** The binary codes of alphabets, number and special symbols are known as alpha numerical codes. e.g. ASCII (American Standard Code for Information Interchange) code.
- **Error detecting and Correcting Codes :** Special types of codes like parity or Hamming codes are used to detect errors when digital data is transmitted over long distance.

Thus, codes are used to represent binary information and reliable communication. In this chapter we will study three important codes Viz. BCD (Binary Coded Decimal), Gray and seven segment code.

1.7.1 BCD Code

Q. Write short note on BCD code. [3 M]

- Each digit of decimal number is represented by four bits. For example digit '5' is represented as '0101'. The BCD code is also called as 8-4-2-1 code where 8,4,2 and 1 represent weights of binary symbol in the respective positions. The examples of BCD codes are given below ;

Decimal	4	2	8	6	3
BCD	0100	0010	1000	0110	0011

- BCD code for 0 to 9 digits are given as;

Decimal digit	BCD code
0	0 0 0 0
1	0 0 0 1
2	0 0 1 0
3	0 0 1 1
4	0 1 0 0
5	0 1 0 1
6	0 1 1 0
7	0 1 1 1
8	1 0 0 0
9	1 0 0 1

- The remaining 4 digit binary representations i.e. 1010, 1011, 1100, 1101, 1110 and 1111 are invalid BCD codes.

BCD Arithmetic : The arithmetic of BCD code is complex. It can be used to perform addition and subtraction.

Rules :
1. If four bits sum is equal to or less than 9, no correction is needed. The sum is in proper BCD form.
2. If the four bit sum is greater than of 9 or if a carry is generated from the four bit sum, the sum is invalid.
3. To correct the invalid sum add 6 $(0110)_2$ to the four bit sum. If carry results from this addition, add it to the next higher order BCD digit.

1.7.2 Excess 3 Code

Q. Explain Excess-3 code in detail	[Dec. 10, 6 M]
Q. Write short note on Excess-3 code with example	[May 11, 4 M]
Q. Explain Excess-3 code	[Dec 11, Dec 12, 3 M]

- Excess – 3 wide is derived from the natural BCD code by adding 3 to each coded number.
- It is non-weighted code.
- Table 1.7 shows excess-3 codes to represent single digit.
- The excess – 3 codes are obtained as follows

$$\text{Decimal number} \longrightarrow 8421 \text{ BCD number} \xrightarrow{\text{add } 0011} \text{Excess-3 code.}$$

Table 1.5

Decimal Number	BCD 8 4 2 1	Excess – 3
0	0 0 0 0	0 0 1 1
1	0 0 0 1	0 1 0 0
2	0 0 1 0	0 1 0 1
3	0 0 1 1	0 1 1 0
4	0 1 0 0	0 1 1 1
5	0 1 0 1	1 0 0 0
6	0 1 1 0	1 0 0 1
7	0 1 1 1	1 0 1 0
8	1 0 0 0	1 0 1 1
9	1 0 0 1	1 1 0 0

- The excess-3 is also called as sequential code, because each succeeding code is one binary number than its preceding code.

- The excess-3 is also known as self complementary because we get the 9's complement of number just complete of number just complement of each bit by means replacing ?

Example 1.18 : What is Excess-3 code of binary number ?

0010 B, 0110 B and 0111 B

(a) 0010 B

add (0011) to the number

```
  0010
+ 0011
  ----
  0101
```

(b) 0010 B

add (0011) to each number

```
  0110
+ 0011
  ----
  1001
```

(c) 0111 B

add (0011) to the given number

```
  0111
+ 0011
  ----
  1010
```

1.7.3 Gray Code

> **Q.** What will be the gray code 4-bit binary number ? [Dec. 11, Dec. 12, 3 M]
>
> **Q.** What is Gray code covert binary number.
>
> 1100B, 0111B and 1101 B into gray number.

- Gray is a non-weighted code.
- The feature of gray code is that the only one bit will change, each time the decimal number is incremented this is shown in table 1.8.

Table 1.6

Decimal Code	Binary code	Gray code
0	0000	0000
1	0001	0001
2	0010	0011
3	0011	0010
4	0100	0110
5	0101	0111
6	0110	0101
7	0111	0100
8	1000	1100
9	1001	1101
10	1010	1111
11	1011	1110
12	1100	1010
13	1101	1011
14	1110	1001
15	1111	1000

- Gray code also exhibits the reflective property.
- The two least significant bits for decimal 4 to 7 are the mirror images of those for decimal 3 to 0.
- The three least significant bits for decimal 8 through 15 are mirror images of those for decimal 7 through 0.

1.7.3.1 Application of Gray Code

- Gray code is mostly used in the shaft position encoders.
- A shaft position encoder produces a code coordinate which represents the angular position of the shaft. The shaft position encoder consist of alight source, an optical disc and alight detector as shown in Fig. 1.7 (a).

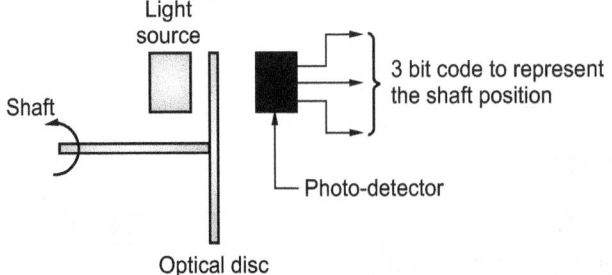

Fig. 1.7 (a) : Shaft position encoder

- Patterns of opaque and transparent segments is etched out on the optical disc. So corresponding to the black position. The photo detector produces a "1" and corresponding to the transparent portion a "0" is produced.
- The patterns on the disc are according to the code required to be produced at the detector output.
- Fig. 1.7 (b) shows the patterns for binary code and Fig. 1.7 (c) shows the pattern for producing gray code.

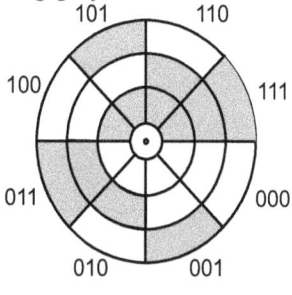

(b) Pattern for binary code

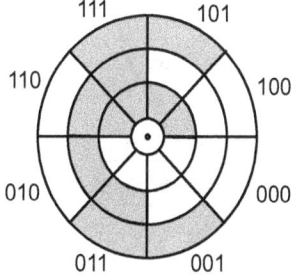

(c) Pattern for gray code

Fig. 1.7

1.7.3.2 Advantages of Gray Code

Q. Give the advantages of Gray Code.

- The advantage of Gray code over straight binary code is that Gray code changes by only 1 bit as it sequences from one number to the next.
- The 3-bit Gray code representations for number 0 through 7 are listed below. Design a decoder to convert a 3-bit binary number into a Gray code number. Your decoder should have three inputs and three outputs and it should convert a binary number, say 011 (decimal 3), to a Gray code number, 010 for all the eight decimal numbers 0 to 7.

Table 1.7

Decimal	Binary b_2, b_1, b_0	Gray g_2, g_1, g_0
0	000	000
1	001	001
2	010	011
3	011	010
4	100	110
5	101	111
6	110	101
7	111	100

1.8 CODE CONVERSION

1.8.1 Converting Binary code to Gray code

Q. Find gray codes for the following binary number.
  (i) 11001100 (ii) 01011110 [Dec. 08, 2M]

Q. Explain rule for any sequence binary to gray code conversion. [May 12, 2 M]

A binary number can be converted in gray by following steps :

Step 1 : First take MSB as it is.

Step 2 : Add this MSB bit to the next position bit, recording the sum and neglecting any carry.

Step 3 : Take successive sums until complete.

Example 1.32 : Convert binary 11001100 [Dec. 08, 1 M]

Given binary number

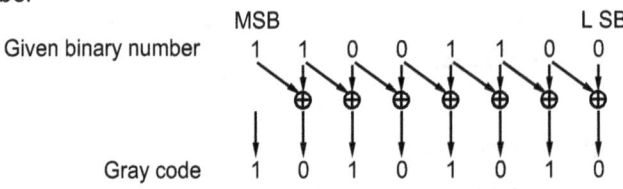

$\therefore \quad (11001100)_2 = (10101010)_{gray}$

In general from the conversion of binary to gray takes place as follows

G_3 (MSB) = B_3 (MSB) $G_2 = B_3 \oplus B_2$

$G_1 = B_2 \oplus B_1$ (LSB) $G_0 = B_1 \oplus B_3$

1.8.2 Converting Gray to Binary

Q. Explain rule for any sequence gray to binary code conversion.

For gray to binary conversion, follows the steps given below.

Step 1 : The MSB of gray and binary are same. So write it directly.

Step 2 : Add binary MSB to the next bit of gray code. Record the result and ignore the carriers.

Step 3 : Continue above process till the LSB is reached.

Example 1.20 : Convert 11101 gray to binary.

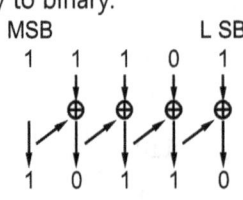

$\therefore \quad (11101)_{gray} = (1011)_2$

In general we can say that the conversion below 4-bit gray number $G_3G_2G_1G_0$ into a 4-bit binary number $B_3B_2B_1B_0$ it takes places as below

$$B_3 \text{ (MSB)} = G_3 \text{ (MSB)} \qquad B_2 = B_3 \oplus G_2$$
$$B_1 = B_2 \oplus G_1 \qquad B_0 = B_1 \oplus G_0$$

1.8.3 Binary to BCD Conversion

For the binary to BCD conversion two steps to be followed are as shown below :

(i) First write binary number into decimal number.

(ii) the from decimal number convert into BCD.

Example 1.21 : Convert $(1101)_2$ into BCD.

Step 1 : Write given number into decimal number

$$(1101)_2 = 1 \times 2^3 + 1 \times 2^2 + 0 \times 2^1 + 1 \times 2^0$$
$$= 8 + 4 + 0 + 1$$
$$= (13)_{10}$$

Step 2 : Convert 13 into BCD.

$$\therefore \qquad (13)_{10} = (0001\ 0011)_{BCD}$$

1.8.4 BCD to Binary Conversion

> **Q.** Represent 37 into BCD.

Step 1 : Convert BCD to decimal number

Step 2 : Convert BCD to decimal number to binary number

Example 1.35 : Convert $(0101\ 0101)_{BCD}$ into binary number

Step 1 : Convert given BCD to decimal number

$$(0101.0101)_{BCD} = (55)_{10}$$

Step 2 : Convert $(55)_{10}$ to binary

$$(55)_{10} = (110011)_2$$
$$\therefore \qquad (0101\ 0101) = (110011)_2$$

1.8.5 BCD to Excess-3 Conversion

For BCD to excess-3 conversion steps are given below.

Step 1 : First convert BCD to decimal.

Step 2 : Add $(3)_{10}$ to this decimal number

Step 3 : Convert into binary to get the excess-3 code

Example 1.22 : Convert $(1001)_{BCD}$ to excess – 3

Step 1 : Convert BCD to decimal

$$(1001)_{BCD} = (9)_{10}$$

Step 2 : Add $(3)_{10}$ to decimal number

$$\therefore \quad 9$$
$$+ \quad 3$$
$$\overline{12} \text{ ...Answer}$$

Step 3 : Convert answer to binary number

$$(12)_{10} = (1100)$$

$$\therefore \quad (1001)_{BCD} = (1100)_{Excess\text{-}3}$$

1.8.6 Excess-3 to BCD Conversion

The same procedure like BCD to excess-3 only change is subtract $(3)_{10}$ from decimal number

Example 1.23 : $(10011010)_{excess\text{-}3}$ convert into BCD.
Solution :

```
       11   111     ...carry
      1001 1010    ...Excess-3
    − 0011 0011    ...(03)₁₀
      ─────────
      0110 0111    ...BCD answer
```

1.9 BOOLEAN ALGEBRA

Q. State and prove any two theorem of Boolean algebra. [May 12, 4 M]

- The rules for manipulation of binary numbers developed by George Boole are known as Boolean algebra.
- A Boolean variable can only take binary values i.e. '1' or '0' just like ordinary algebra.
- Boolean algebra has also its own certain operators like AND (·), OR (+), NOT (−) and XOR (⊕).

1.9.1 Axioms of Boolean Algebra

- Axioms and postulates of Boolean algebra are a set of logical expressions that we accept without proof and upon which we can built useful theorems or laws.

- Axioms are nothing but logical expressions of the basic three gates i.e. AND, OR and NOT.

  Axiom 1 : 0.0 = 0
  Axiom 2 : 0.1 = 0
  Axiom 3 : 1.0 = 0
  Axiom 4 : 1.1 = 1
  Axiom 5 : 0 + 0 = 0

  Axiom 6 : 0 + 1 = 1
  Axiom 7 : 1 + 0 = 1
  Axiom 8 : 1 + 1 = 1
  Axiom 9 : $\bar{1} = 0$
  Axiom 10 : $\bar{0} = 1$

1.9.2 Laws of Boolean Algebra

Sr. No.	Category of Law	Laws
1.	AND Laws	$A \cdot 0 = 0$ $A \cdot 1 = A$ $A \cdot A = A$ $A \cdot \bar{A} = 0$
2.	OR Laws	$A + 0 = A$ $A + 1 = 1$ $A + A = A$ $A + \bar{A} = 1$
3.	NOT or Inversion Laws	$\bar{\bar{A}} = A$
4.	Commutative laws (allows change of position of variables)	$A + B = B + A$ $A \cdot B = B \cdot A$
5.	Associative laws (allows grouping of variables)	$A + (B + C) = (A + B) + C$ $A \cdot (B \cdot C) = (A \cdot B) \cdot C$
6.	Distributive Laws (allows factoring or distribution of terms)	$A \cdot (B + C) = A \cdot B + A \cdot C$ $A + (B \cdot C) = (A + B) \cdot (A + C)$ $A + (\bar{A} \cdot B) = A + B$
7.	Impotence laws (means same value)	$A \cdot A = A$ $A + A = A$
8.	Identity laws	$A \cdot 1 = A$ $A + 1 = 1$
9.	Null laws	$A \cdot 0 = 0$ $A + 0 = A$
10.	Absorption laws	$A + (A \cdot B) = A$ $A (A + B) = A$

1.9.3 Rules of Boolean Algebra

The rules that are followed in Boolean algebra are given below :
- Capital letters are used for representing variables and functions of variables.
- It will be assumed that the positive logic is used unless until the problem statement specifically mentions negative logic.
- The complement of a variable is represented by a "bar" (¯) over the variable letter.
- The logic AND function is shown by a "dot" (·) between the two variables, e.g. A · B. Many times, this dot is not written i.e. AB.
- Boolean addition is logical OR operation. It is different than mathematical addition. For example,

$$1 + 1 = 1 \text{ in Boolean algebra}$$
$$1 + 1 = 0 \text{ with carry 1 in mathematics}$$

1.9.4 DeMorgan's Theorems

> **Q.** What are DeMorgan's theorem ? How will define them in terms of your own words ?
> **[Dec. 05, May 08, Dec. 09, 4 M]**

- Boolean algebra was initially ignored by both mathematicians and technocrats. Bas Augustus DeMorgan was the first to put Boolean algebra to practice. DeMorgan discovered two important theorems which are known as DeMorgan's theorems.

The two theorems are,

1. $\overline{A + B} = \overline{A} \cdot \overline{B}$

2. $\overline{A \cdot B} = \overline{A} + \overline{B}$

1.9.4.1 DeMorgan's first theorem

- The statement of DeMorgan's first theorem goes like this, "Complement of a sum of variables is equal to the product of their individual complements".

$$\overline{A + B} = \overline{A} \cdot \overline{B}$$

Truth Table Proof :

A	B	$\overline{A}$	$\overline{B}$	A + B	L.H.S. = $\overline{A + B}$	R.H.S. = $\overline{A} \cdot \overline{B}$
0	0	1	1	0	1	1
0	1	1	0	1	0	0
1	0	0	1	1	0	0
1	1	0	0	1	0	0

Logic Diagram :

$$A \overset{A}{\underset{B}{\rightarrow}} \!$$

— Y = $\overline{A+B}$ ≡   — Y = $\overline{A} \cdot \overline{B}$

Fig. 1.8 : Logic diagram of DeMorgan's first theorem

Thus, NOR gate is equivalent to a bubbled AND gate.

1.9.4.2 DeMorgan's second theorem

- The statement of DeMorgan's second theorem goes like this, *"Complement of a product of variables is equal to the sum of their individual complements"*.

$$\overline{A \cdot B} = \overline{A} + \overline{B}$$

Truth Table Proof :

A	B	$\overline{A}$	$\overline{B}$	A·B	L.H.S. = $\overline{A \cdot B}$	R.H.S. = $\overline{A} + \overline{B}$
0	0	1	1	0	1	1
0	1	1	0	0	1	1
1	0	0	1	0	1	1
1	1	0	0	1	0	0

Logic Diagram :

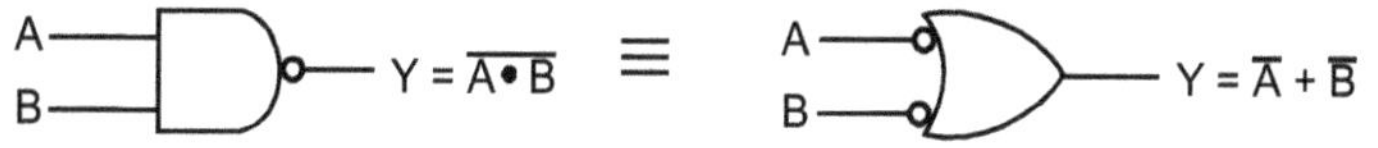

— Y = $\overline{A \cdot B}$ ≡   — Y = $\overline{A} + \overline{B}$

Fig. 1.9 : Logic diagram of DeMorgan's second theorem

- Thus, a NAND gate is equivalent to bubbled OR gate.

Q. Using Boolean Algebra show that

Example 1.24 :

$$Y = (A + B)(A + C)$$

Solution :

$$Y = (A + B)(A + C)$$
$$= AA + AC + BA + BC \quad \text{(Distributive law)}$$
$$= A + AC + AB + BC \quad (\because AA = A)$$
$$= A(1 + C) + AB + BC$$
$$= A + AB + BC \quad (\because 1 + C = 1)$$
$$= A(1 + B) + BC \quad (\because 1 + B = 1)$$
$$= A + BC$$

1.9.4.3 Duality theorem

- The distinction between positive and negative logic gives rise to principle of duality.
- Because an OR gate is the positive logic system becomes AND gate in the negative logic system and vice-versa. Given a Boolean identity, we can produce a dual identity by changing '+' signs to '·' and vice-versa.

	Boolean Expression	Dual
1.	$A \cdot 0 = 0$	$A + 1 = 1$
2.	$A \cdot 1 = A$	$A + 0 = A$
3.	$A \cdot A = A$	$A + A = A$
4.	$A \cdot \overline{A} = 0$	$A + \overline{A} = 1$
5.	$A \cdot B = B \cdot A$	$A + B = B + A$

Example 1.25 : $(B + A)(B + D)(A + C)(C + D) = BC + AD$

Solution :

$$\begin{aligned}
LHS &= (B + A)(B + D)(A + C)(C + D) \\
&= (BB + BD + AB + AD)(AC + CC + AD + CD) \quad \because A \cdot A = A \\
&= (B + BD + AB + AD)(AC + AD + C + CD) \\
&= (B[1 + D + A] + AD)(C[1 + A + D] + AD) \quad \because A + 1 = 1 \\
&= (B + AD)(C + AD) \\
&= BC + BAD + CAD + AD \cdot AD \quad \because A \cdot A = A \\
&= BC + AD(B + C + 1) \\
&= BC + AD \quad \because A + 1 = 1
\end{aligned}$$

LHS = RHS

1.10 SUM OF PRODUCTS (SOP) FORM

Q. What is the sum of product form?

1.10.1 Standard Terms and Standard (or Canonical) Forms

- The object of a Boolean algebra is to describe the behaviour and logic structure.
- The behaviour of the logic circuit can be expressed in standard forms using standard terms.

1.10.2 Sum Term or Maximum Term (M)

- The output of OR gate is called **su**m term.
- In OR gate, the output is logic '1' for maximum number of combinations of inputs.
- So, the output of OR gate is also called Maximum term or Maxterm (M).
- A sum term of any 'n' variable functions containing all the 'n' literals is called a maxterm. The 'n' variables functions have 2^n maxterms.
- These are denoted as $M_0, M_1, M_2, \ldots M_n$.
- Each variables taking value '0' appears in uncomplemented form in maxterm and each variable taking '1' value appears in complemented form.

1.10.3 Product or Minimum Term (m)

- The output of AND gate is called product term.
- In AND gate, the output is logic '1' for minimum number of combinations of inputs. So, the output of AND gate is also called 'Minimum term or minterm (m).
- A product term of any 'n' variable functions containing all literals is called a minterm. The 'n' variable functions have 2^n minterms. These are denoted as $m_0, m_1, m_2, ..., m_n$.
- In minterms, each variables taking value '1' appears in uncomplemented form.

Table 1.8 : Maxterms and minterms of two-variables

Decimal Equivalent	Variables		Minterms		Maxterms	
	A	B	m_i	Notation	M_i	Notation
0	0	0	$\bar{A}\bar{B}$	m_0	$A + B$	M_0
1	0	1	$\bar{A}B$	m_1	$A + \bar{B}$	M_1
2	1	0	$A\bar{B}$	m_2	$\bar{A} + B$	M_2
3	1	1	AB	m_3	$\bar{A} + \bar{B}$	M_3

1.10.4 Standard (or Canonical) Forms

- If a function is expressed in such a way that each variable is present in each term.

1.10.5 Sum of Products (SOP) Form

- The output of AND gate is called product term.
- The output of OR gate is called sum term.
- The output of AND-OR gate circuit is called sum-of-products (SOP) form.
- Consider the equation,

$$Y = \bar{A}B + AB$$

- Each term in the equation is called the fundamental minterm. From table mentioned earlier, the output Y can be written as,

$$Y = m_1 + m_3 = \Sigma\, m_1, m_3$$
$$= \Sigma\, m_i$$

where, $\quad i = 1, 3$
$$= \Sigma\, 1, 3$$

- The SOP form can be converted to standard SOP form by ANDing the terms in the expression with terms formed by ORing.
- The variable and its complement which are not present in that term.
- Following steps are followed to convert a given SOP form to standard SOP form :

    (i) Write down all the terms.

    (ii) If one or more variables are missing in any term, expand that term by multiplying it with the sum of each one of the missing variable and its complement.

    For example, $\quad Y = AB + A\bar{B}C$

- The variable C is missing in first term. So, multiply the first term by $(C + \bar{C})$.

    $$Y = AB(C + \bar{C}) + A\bar{B}C$$

    (iii) Drop out the redundant terms.

Example 1.26 :

Convert $Y = \bar{A}B + A\bar{C} + \bar{B}C$ into standard SOP form.

Solution :
$$Y = \bar{A}B + A\bar{C} + \bar{B}C$$
$$= \bar{A}B(C + \bar{C}) + A\bar{C}(B + \bar{B}) + \bar{B}C(A + \bar{A})$$
$$= \bar{A}BC + \bar{A}B\bar{C} + A\bar{C}B + A\bar{C}\bar{B} + \bar{B}CA + \bar{B}C\bar{A}$$
$$= \bar{A}BC + \bar{A}B\bar{C} + A\bar{C}B + A\bar{C}\bar{B} + \underbrace{AB\bar{C} + \bar{A}\bar{B}C}_{\text{Redundant terms}}$$

$$= \bar{A}BC + \bar{A}B\bar{C} + A\bar{C}B + A\bar{C}\bar{B} + A\bar{B}C$$

Example 1.27 :

Simplify $\quad Y = \Sigma m\,(0, 1, 2, 3, 4, 5, 6, 7)$

Solution :

The given expression has all the minterms of a three variable table.

$$\therefore \quad Y = \bar{A}\bar{B}\bar{C} + \bar{A}\bar{B}C + \bar{A}B\bar{C} + \bar{A}BC + A\bar{B}\bar{C} + A\bar{B}C + AB\bar{C} + ABC$$

$$= \bar{A}\bar{B}(C + \bar{C}) + \bar{A}B(\bar{C} + C) + A\bar{B}(\bar{C} + C) + AB(\bar{C} + C)$$

$$= \overline{AB} + \overline{A}B + \overline{A}\overline{B} + AB$$

$$= \overline{A}(\overline{B} + B) + A(\overline{B} + B)$$

$$= \overline{A} + A$$

$$Y = 1$$

∴ The answer is always 'true' (1) because the given expression contains all possible minterms.

1.11 PRODUCT OF SUMS (POS) FORM

Q. What is the product of sum form?

1.11.1 Product-of-Sums (POS) Form

- The output of OR-AND gate circuit is called Product-Of-Sums (POS) form.

  Consider the equation,

  $$Y = (A + B) \cdot (\overline{A} + B)$$

  $$Y = M_0, M_2 = \pi(0, 2)$$

  where, π stands for the product of maxterms.

- The POS form can be converted to standard POS form by ORing the terms in the expression with terms formed by ANDing the variable and its complement which are not present in that term.

- Following steps are followed to convert a POS form to standard POS form.

(i) Write down all the terms.

(ii) If one or more variables are missing in any sum terms, expand that term by adding the products of each of the missing term and its complement.

(iii) Drop out the redundant terms.

Example 1.28 :

Convert $Y = (A + B) \cdot (A + C) \cdot (B + \overline{C})$ into standard POS form.

Solution :

$$Y = (A + B) \cdot (A + C) \cdot (B + \overline{C})$$

$$= (A + B + C \cdot \overline{C}) \cdot (A + B \cdot \overline{B} + C) \cdot (B + \overline{C} + A \cdot \overline{A})$$

We use $X + YZ = (X + Y) \cdot (X + Z)$ law to expand the equation.

$$= (A + B + C)(A + B + \bar{C})(A + C + B)$$
$$(A + B + C)(B + \bar{C} + A)(B + \bar{C} + \bar{A})$$
$$= (A + B + C)(A + B + \bar{C})(A + \bar{B} + C)$$
$$(\bar{A} + B + \bar{C}) \qquad (\because \text{Redundant terms})$$

Example 1.29 :
Simplify the following three variable expression.
$$Y = \pi M(1, 3, 5, 7)$$

Solution :
The given Boolean expression is in POS form. From the table, we can rewrite the Boolean expression as

$$Y = \underbrace{(A + B + \bar{C})}_{N_1} \underbrace{(A + \bar{B} + \bar{C})}_{N_3} \underbrace{(\bar{A} + B + \bar{C})}_{N_5} \underbrace{(\bar{A} + \bar{B} + \bar{C})}_{N_7}$$

$$= (AA + A\bar{B} + A\bar{C} + BA + B\bar{B} + B\bar{C} + \bar{C}A + \bar{C}B + \bar{C}\bar{C})(\bar{A} + B + \bar{C})(\bar{A} + \bar{B} + \bar{C})$$

$$= (A + A\bar{B} + A\bar{C} + AB + 0 + B\bar{C})(\bar{A} + B + \bar{C})(\bar{A} + \bar{B} + \bar{C})$$

$$= (A + (1 + \bar{C}) + A(\bar{B} + B) + \bar{C}B)(\bar{A}(\bar{B} + B) + \bar{A}\bar{C} + \bar{C})$$

$$= (A + A + \bar{C}B)(\bar{A} + \bar{A}\bar{C} + \bar{C})$$

$$= (A + \bar{C}B)(\bar{A} + \bar{C}\bar{A})$$

$$= A\bar{A} + A\bar{C}\bar{A} + \bar{C}B\bar{A} + \bar{C}B\bar{C}\bar{A}$$

$$= 0 + 0 + \bar{C}B\bar{A} + \bar{C}B\bar{C}\bar{A} = \bar{A}B\bar{C} + \bar{A}B\bar{C}$$

$$Y = \bar{A}B\bar{C}$$

1.12 REDUCTION TECHNIQUES

1.12.1 Boolean Algebra Simplification Technique

Q. List out the reduction techniques.

- A good digital circuit must have minimum number of logic gates.
- Less number of gates means minimum propagation delay, skew, power dissipation.
- The number of logic gates can be reduced only if the number of terms in the Boolean expression can be reduced.

- There are four methods that are used to simplify or reduce the Boolean equations.
1. Algebraic (Boolean Laws, DeMorgan's Theorems).
2. Karnaugh (K) Map.
3. Variable Entered Mapping (VEM).
4. Quine-McClauskey (Q-M) Tabular Method.
- The K-map is the simplest and the most commonly used method.

1.12.2 Reduction of Boolean Equation using K-map

- The K-map method is a systematic approach for simplifying a Boolean expression.
- This method was proposed by Veitch and then modified by Karnaugh, hence it is called Karnaugh map.
- The basis of K-map method is graphical representation of minterms or maxterms in a chart called Karnaugh map (K-map). K-map contains cells.
- Each cell represents one of the 2^n possible product cells that can be formed from n variables.
- Thus, n-variable K-map has 4 cells, 3-variable k-map has 8 cells and 4-variable K-map has 16 cells.
- Product terms are assigned to the cells of a K-map by labelling each row and each column of the map with a variable, with its complements or with a combination of variables and complements. Fig. 1.11 depicts the 2-variable, 3-variable and 4-variable maps.

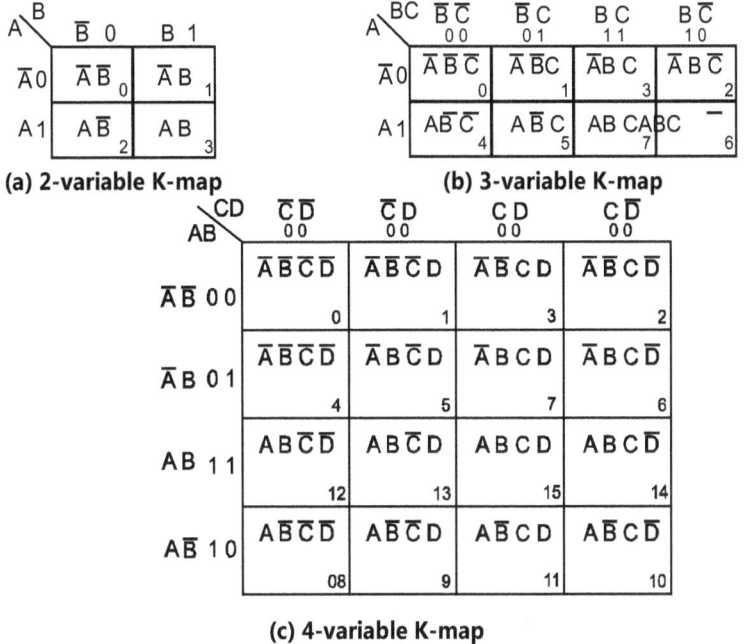

(c) 4-variable K-map

Fig. 1.10

- It is important to note that only one variable changes, when we move from one cell to another along any row or any column.
- Therefore, the third column and the third row in a two-variable K-map have '11' binary representation instead of '10'.
- This peculiar arrangement of K-map has special significance as mentioned below.
- When two inputs change simultaneously then digital circuit output goes in a metastable state.
- Output can swing to either logic '1' or logic '0' state in metastable state.
- This state is to be avoided by prohibiting two inputs from switching simultaneously.
- We know that any logic function can be represented in SOP or POS form. The given Boolean expression can be used to fill entries in the truth table and truth table can be represented on K-map.
- With little practice, it is also possible to fill entries in k-map directly.

1.12.3 Representing SOP Equation on K-map

Example 1.30 :
Plot Boolean expression.

$$Y = \overline{A}B\overline{C}\overline{D} + \overline{A}BC\overline{D} + AB\overline{C}\overline{D}$$

Solution :
- The Boolean expression has four variables, so we use 4-variable k-map.
- Represent each product term by '1' in corresponding cell.
- Note that number of 1's in K-map is equal to the product terms in the given Boolean expression.
- Fill 0's in all other cells.

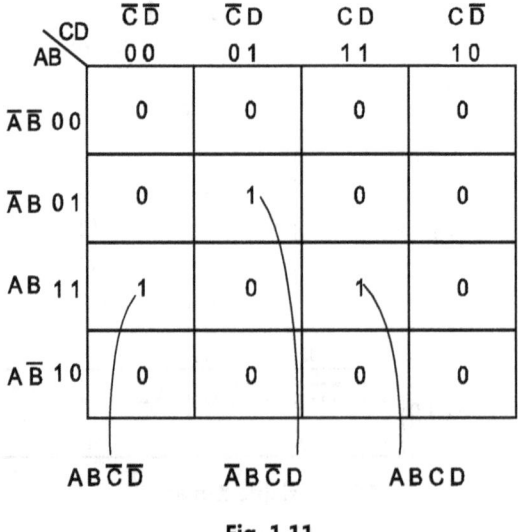

Fig. 1.11

1.12.4 Representing POS Equation on K-map

Example 1.31 :
Plot Boolean expression.

$$Z = (X + \bar{Y})(\bar{X} + \bar{Y})$$

Solution :
- The Boolean expression has two variables, so we use 2-variable K-map.

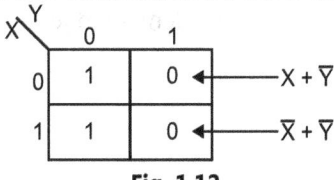

Fig. 1.12

- Represent each sum term by '0' in the corresponding cell.
- Note that number of '0's in K-map is equal to the sum terms in the given Boolean expression.
- Fill '1's in all other cells.

1.13 K-MAP REDUCTION TECHNIQUES

> **Q.** Simplify following logical expression using K-maps.
>
> $y = \bar{A}\bar{B}\bar{C} + \bar{A}\bar{B}C + \bar{A}B\bar{C} + A\bar{B}\bar{C} + AB\bar{C}$
>
> **Q.** Solve the following using minimization technique.   **[Dec. 09, 1 M]**
>
> $z = f(A, B, C, D) = \Sigma (0, 2, 4, 7, 11, 13, 15)$
>
> **Q.** Simplify the following function   **[May 13, 4 M]**
>
> $f_1(A, B, C, D) = \Sigma m (0, 3, 5, 6, 9, 10, 12, 15)$

- In K-map minterms are represented by 1's and maxterms are represented by 0's.
- The objective of K-map reduction or simplification technique is to reduce the number of logic gates.
- Once the logic or Boolean expression is plotted on K-map, we use grouping technique to simplify the given Boolean expression as follows :

(a) Grouping Two Adjacent Ones (or Pair) :

- Consider a Boolean expression $Y = ABC + AB\bar{C}$.

  It can be seen from the given Boolean expression that we will require two three-input AND gates and one two-input OR gate to implement the logic equation.

- Now, if we plot the equation in a 3-variable K-map.

A\BC	$\bar{B}\bar{C}$	$\bar{B}C$	BC	$B\bar{C}$
$\bar{A}$	0	0	0	0
A	0	0	1	1

Fig. 1.13 : Grouping on two adjacent ones

- It can be noticed that when the two adjacent 1's are grouped then only one variable appears in its complemented and uncomplemented form i.e. C and $\bar{C}$.

$$Y = ABC + AB\bar{C}$$
$$= AB(C + \bar{C})$$
$$= AB \qquad (\because C + \bar{C} = 1)$$

- So, these two terms can be combined together to eliminate the variable C.
- Once this third variable is eliminated then it is possible to use two-input AND gate instead of three-input AND.

These adjacent 1's can be also in vertical or any other form as shown in Fig. 1.14.

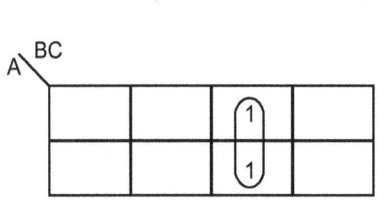
(a) Vertical adjacent cells

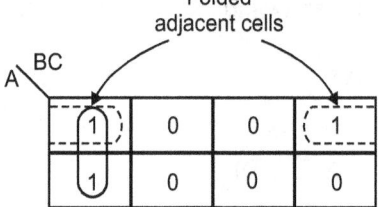
(b) Folded adjacent cells and overlapped pairs

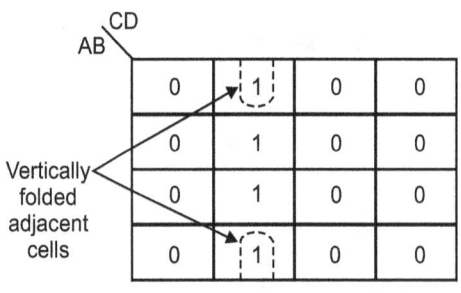
(c) Vertically folded adjacent cells

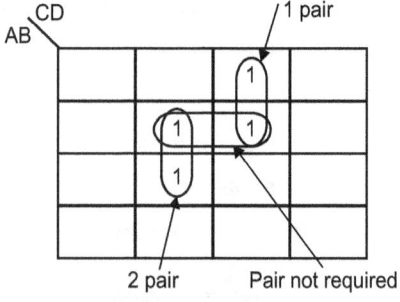
(d) Combining of pair

Fig. 1.14 : Various combinations of 1 pairs

(b) Grouping of Four Adjacent Ones (Quad):

- We can group four adjacent ones to eliminate two variables out of four variables.
- The several ways to form four adjacent ones or quads are shown in Fig. 1.15.

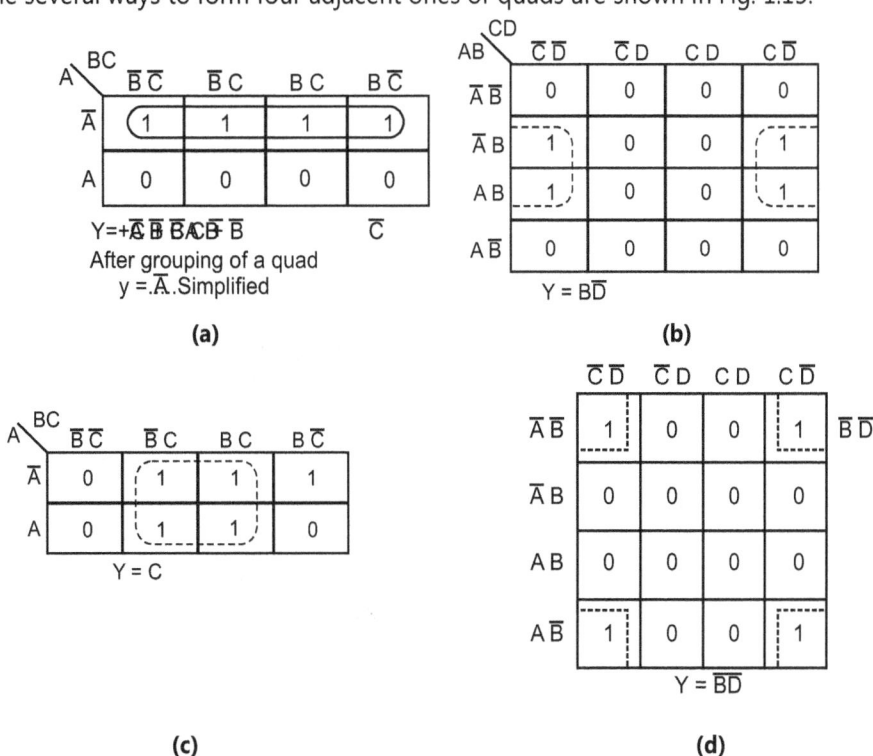

$Y = \bar{A}\bar{B} + \bar{B}\bar{C} + \bar{B}$

After grouping of a quad
$y = \bar{A}$. Simplified

(a)

$Y = \bar{B}\bar{D}$

(b)

$Y = C$

(c)

$Y = \bar{B}\bar{D}$

(d)

Fig. 1.15

(c) Grouping of Eight Adjacent Ones (octet)

- We can group four adjacent ones to eliminate three variables out of four variables.

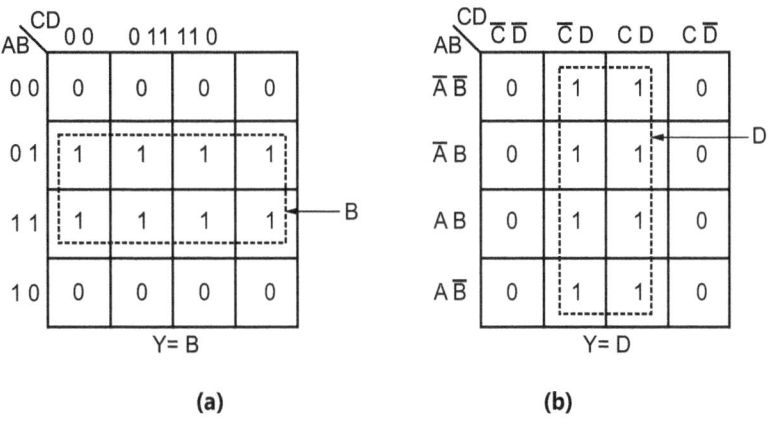

$Y = B$

(a)

$Y = D$

(b)

	$\bar{C}\bar{D}$	$\bar{C}D$	CD	$C\bar{D}$
$\bar{A}\bar{B}$	1	1	1	1
$\bar{A}B$	0	0	0	0
AB	0	0	0	0
$A\bar{B}$	1	1	1	1

$Y = \bar{B}$

(c)

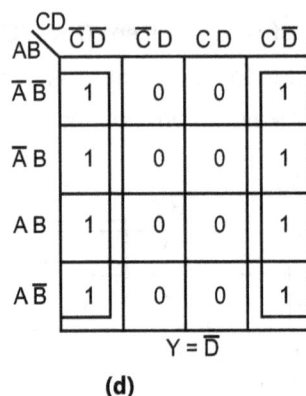

$Y = \bar{D}$

(d)

Fig. 1.16

1.13.1 Prime Implicant and Essential Prime Implicant

Q. What is prime implicant and essential prime implicant ?

- A group of one or more 1's which are adjacent and can be combined on a Karnaough Map is called an implicant.
- The process of simplication involves grouping of minterms and identifying prime implicants (PI) and essential prime implicants (EPI).
- A prime implicant is a group of minters that cannot be combined with any other minterm or groups. An essential prime implicant is a prime implicant in which one or more minterms are unique i.e. it contains at least one minterm which is not contained in any other prime-implicant.
- A prime implicant is a product term which cannot be further simplified by combination with other terms.

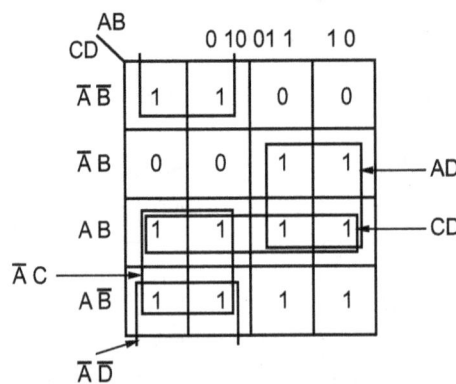

Fig. 1.17

Prime implicant = $\bar{A}\bar{D} + \bar{A}C + AD + CD$

Essential prime implicant = $\bar{A}\bar{D}$

1.13.2 Don't Care Condition

- In some logic circuits, certain input conditions never occur or they are not possible. Therefore, the corresponding output never appears and the output level is not defined. It can be either HIGH or LOW. These output levels are represented as 'Don't Care Conditions' and are indicated by 'X'.
- Don't care conditions can be used to form groups and hence help in simplifying the Boolean expression. See the example below;

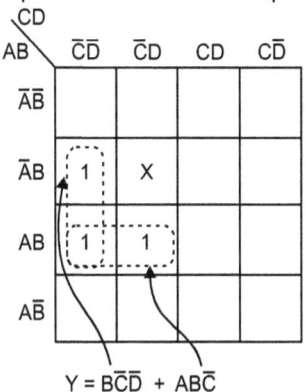
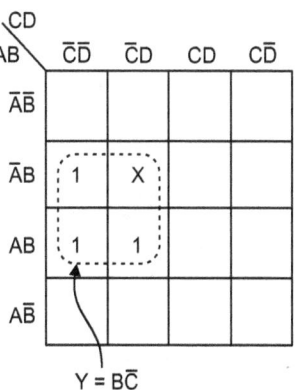

(a) Withoout Don't Care Condition   (b) With Don't Care Condition

Fig. 1.18 : Use of Don't Care Condition in simlifying the Boolean Expression

Example 1.32 :

Simplify the following Boolean expression

$Y(A,B,C,D) = \Sigma m(1,3,7,11,15) + d(0,2,5)$

Solution :

Representing all the minterms and don't care conditions on the K – map

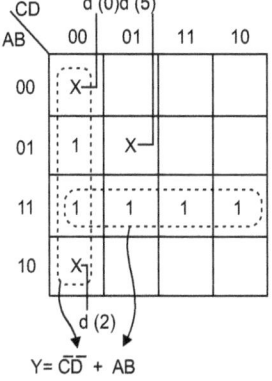

Fig. 1.19

Example 1.33 :

Simplify the Boolean expression Y = π M (4,5,6,7,8,12) · d (0,13,15,14)

Solution :

Represent all the maxterms and don't care conditions in the K – map

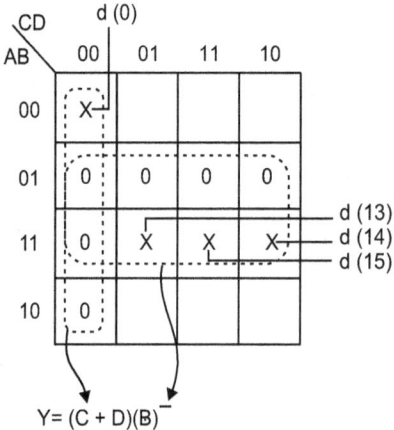

Y= (C + D)(B̄)

Fig. 1.20

1.13.3 Limitations of Karnaugh Map

Q. What is the limitation of K-map?

- The Map method of simplification is convenient as long as for the number of five and six variables. If the number of variables increases the difficultly to make combination of variables in k-map is increases.

Unit - II

SEQUENTIAL LOGIC

2.1 LOGIC CIRCUITS

- Digital circuits or logical circuits are classified into two types : combinational circuits and sequential circuits.
- Sequential circuits are further divided into two groups : synchronous and asynchronous circuits.
- The following diagram shows the classification of logic circuits.

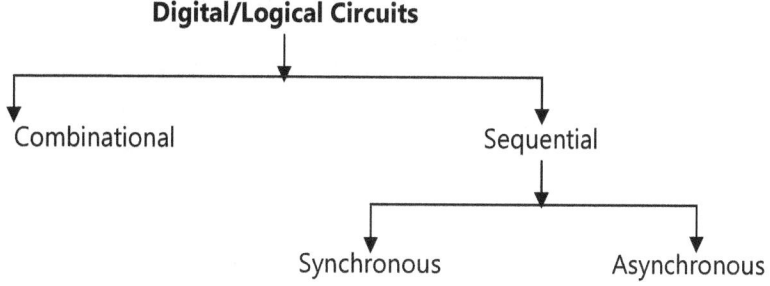

Fig. 2.1

2.1.1 Combinational Circuit

Q. Write short note on combinational circuit ?

- Combinational circuit uses logic gates to implement or satisfy a given Boolean expression.
- The outputs of combinational circuit is a logical function of the input variables. This can be shown as in Fig. 2.2.

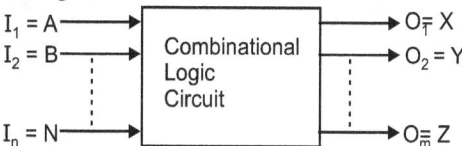

Fig. 2.2 : Block diagram of combinational logic circuit

- The combinational logic circuit has only logic gates and does not require memory. It's operation depends upon the present states of inputs and not on the previous (history) states of the inputs.

2.1.2 Sequential Logic Circuit

Q. Write short note on sequential circuit ?

- Sequential circuit is designed using combinational logic circuit and memory elements. There are requirements in digital applications where the output variables depends on the sequence in which the input variables are received.
- For example, counter, a counter circuits count input pulses and hence it has to remember number of input pulses it has received so far.
- This dependency on previous input conditions needs to be stored in memory.
- Combination logic circuit cannot store data and therefore, we require memory elements along with combinational circuit to design sequential logic circuit.
- This is shown in Fig. 2.3.
- The output of a sequential logic circuit depends upon the present inputs as well as the last state of inputs and outputs.

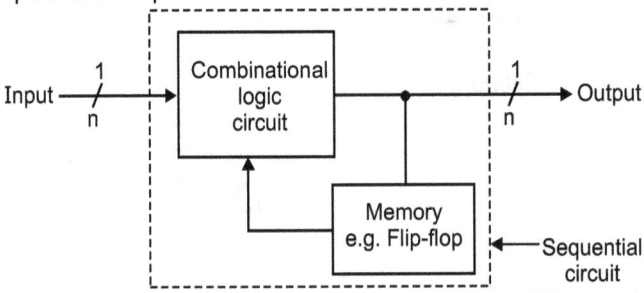

Fig. 2.3 : Block diagram of sequential circuit

- The present state stored in the memory and external inputs are logically evaluated in the combinational block to determine the outputs.

2.1.3 Comparison of Combinational and Sequential Circuit

Q. Explain difference between combinational and sequential circuit. [Dec. 09, 4 M]

Combinational Circuit	Sequential Circuit
1. The outputs depend on the combination of inputs.	1. The outputs depend on the past history of inputs as well as the present input states.
2. Memory is not required.	2. Memory is required to store previous states of the inputs.
3. The delay between outputs and inputs is less, so the combinational circuit is faster.	3. Sequential circuit is slower due to propagational delay of additional memory element.

4. Combinational circuits are concurrent in nature.	4. Sequential circuit is not entirely concurrent.
5. Easier to design.	5. Complex to design. Timings can be critical.
6. Block diagram 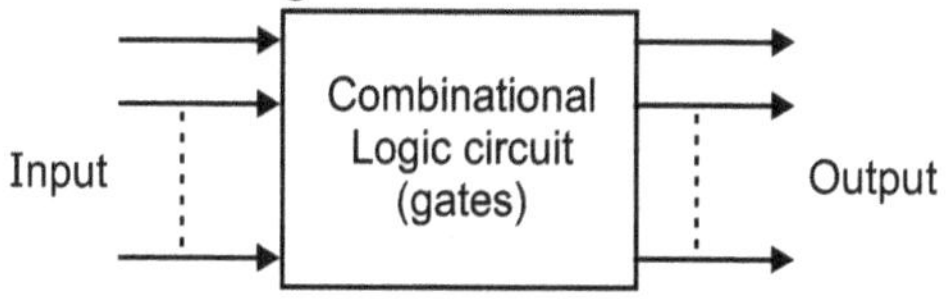 : Fig. 2.4 (a)	6. Block diagram 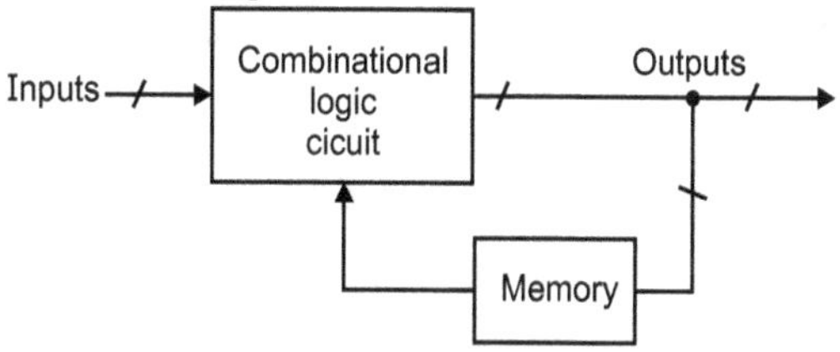 : Fig. 2.4 (b)

2.1.4 Sequential Circuit Types

(A) Synchronous Circuit :

- The change in inputs can affect memory element upon the activation of clock signal.
- Memory elements are clocked flip-flops.
- The maximum operational speed of synchronous circuit is governed by the clock speed, which in turn, is decided by the propagation delays of the logic gates.

(B) Asynchronous Circuit :

- The change in inputs can occur at any instant of time.
- Memory elements are unclocked flip-flops or time delay elements.
- Asynchronous circuits can operate faster than synchronous circuits because the clock is absent.

2.2 LATCH VS FLIP-FLOP

Q. Explain difference between Latch and Flip flop.

- The main difference between latches and flip-flops is the method used for changing their state.
- Latches are controlled by enable signal, and they are level triggered, either positive level triggered or negative level triggered.
- Flip-flops are pulse or clock edge triggered instead of level triggered.

2.3 LEVEL TRIGGERED AND EDGE TRIGGERED

Q. Explain different type of level triggered and edge triggered?

2.3.1 Level Triggered

In level triggering the output state change according to input (s) when active level (i.e. positive or negative) is maintained at the enable input.

Two types of level triggered

1. **Positive level triggered**: The output of flip flop respond to the input changes when its enable input is 1 (high).

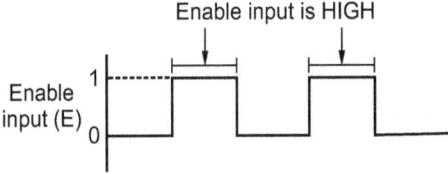

Fig. 2.5 : Positive level triggered

2. **Negative level triggered**: The output of flip-flop respond to the input changes when its input is 0 (low).

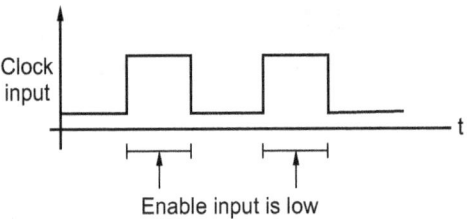

Fig. 2.6 : Negative level triggered

- S-R flip flop and JK flip flop are known as level triggered flip flops as their output changes according to applied inputs as long as clock is present.
- As these flip flops respond when CLK=1 they are further called as positive level triggered flip flops.
- We know that level triggered JK flip flop has the drawback of race around condition. And to overcome that drawback we use master slave JK flip flop which is called as pulse triggered flip flop.
- In a pulse triggered flip flop like MS JK flip flop, output changes according to applied inputs, when a pulse is applied at the clock input. The state of this flip flop changes at the negative transition of the clock.
- Thus, in MS JK flip flop the race around condition is eliminated as the fed back output is blocked at the master when the CLK = 0.

- But in certain systems there is a possibility that the inputs of flip flop may change during the presence of the clock pulse. This causes uncertainty in the output of flip flop. This uncertainty can be eliminated by using edge triggered flip flops.

2.3.2 Edge Triggered

In edge triggered flip flops output changes according to applied inputs only at the positive or negative edge of the clock pulse.

- Based on the type of edge there are two types of edge triggered flip flops : (1) positive edge triggered and (2) negative edge triggered.
- In case of positive edge triggered flip flop output changes only when the clock pulse changes from 0 to 1. While in case of negative edge triggered flip flop output responds only when the clock pulse changes from 1 to 0. The positive and negative edge of the clock is shown in Fig. 2.7.

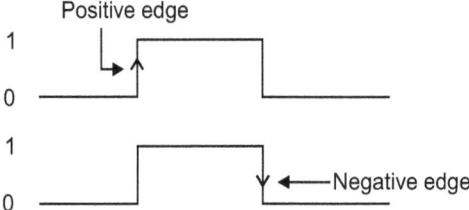

Fig. 2.7 : Positive & negative edge of the clock

- Thus, the state of the flip flop changes during very short interval of time in which clock changes from 0 to 1 or 1 to 0 and the uncertainty in the output gets completely eliminated.
- The logic symbol of positive edge triggered and negative edge triggered JK flip flop is shown in Fig. 2.8.

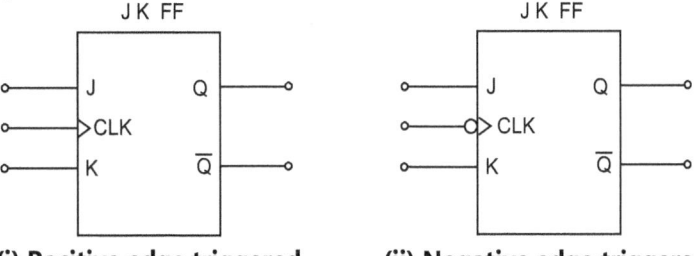

(i) Positive edge triggered   (ii) Negative edge triggered

Fig. 2.8 : Edge triggered JK flip flop

- Note that the logic symbol of negative edge triggered JK flip flop is same as that of MS JK flip flop without preset and clear inputs.
- Also in case of positive edge triggered JK flip flop bubble is absent.

2.4 LATCH

Q. Explain what is mean by latch?

- This circuit is with 2 input NAND gates N_1 and N_2; two additional inverters N_3 and N_4 is as shown in Fig. 2.9.

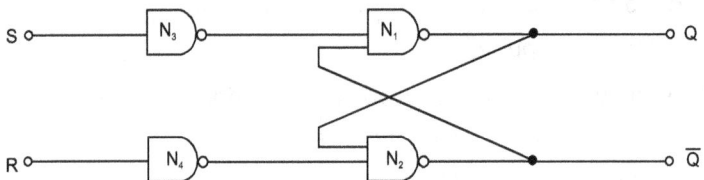

Fig. 2.9 : Memory cell with provision for entering data

- If S = R = 0, the circuit will behave exactly as the previous circuit shown in Fig. 3.7.
- If S = 1 & R = 0 then the output of N_3 will be 0 and the output of N_4 will be 1. As one of the inputs of N_1 is 0, its output will be certainly 1 (Q = 1).
- When Q become 1, both inputs of N_2 become 1 causing its output to go low ($\bar{Q}$ = 0). This is known as 1 state or set state of the circuit, which is achieved with the input pattern S = 1 and R = 0.
- If S = 0 and R = 1, then the output of N_4 will be 0 and the output of N_3 will be 1. As one of the inputs of N_2 becomes 0, its output will be certainly 1 ($\bar{Q}$ = 1).
- When $\bar{Q}$ becomes 1, both inputs of N_1 become 1 causing its output to go low (Q = 0). This is known as 0 state or reset state of the circuit which is achieved with the input pattern S = 0 and R = 1.
- In this way, user can enter desired information in the one bit memory cell.
- Uptil now we have seen that the outputs Q and $\bar{Q}$ are always complementary. If we apply the input S = 1 and R = 1, then the output of N_3 and N_4 become 0. This makes one input of both N_1 and N_2 as 0, which in turn cause both outputs Q and $\bar{Q}$ to become 1.
- Both Q and $\bar{Q}$ getting same state is not allowed and therefore the condition of inputs S = R = 1 is prohibited.

2.4.1 SR Latch using NAND Gate

Q. Explain SR latch using NAND gate?

- The simplest way to make any basic single bit set-reset SR latch is to connect together a pair of cross-coupled 2-input NAND gates as shown, to form a set-reset bistable also known as an active low SR NAND gate latch, so that there is feedback from each output to one of the other NAND gate inputs.

- This device consists of two inputs, one called the Set, S and the other called the Reset, R with two corresponding outputs Q and its inverse or complement $\bar{Q}$ (not-Q) as shown below in Fig. 2.10.

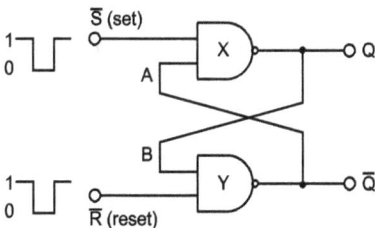

Fig. 2.10 : SR Latch using NAND gate

- **When S = 0, R = 0 :**
  The input R is at logic level "0" (R = 0) and input S is at logic level "1" (S = 1), the NAND gate Y has at least one of its inputs at logic "0" therefore, its output $\bar{Q}$ must be at a logic level "1" (NAND Gate principles). Output $\bar{Q}$ is also fed back to input "A" and so both inputs to NAND gate X are at logic level "1", and therefore its output Q must be at logic level "0".

- **When S = 1, R = 1 :**
  The NAND gate Y inputs are now R = "1" and B = "0". Since one of its inputs is still at logic level "0" the output at $\bar{Q}$ still remains HIGH at logic level "1" and there is no change of state. Therefore, the flip-flop circuit is said to be "Latched" or "Set" with $\bar{Q}$ = "1" and Q = "0".

- **When S = 0, R = 1 :**
  $\bar{Q}$ is at logic level "0", ($\bar{Q}$ = "0") its inverse output at Q is at logic level "1", ($\bar{Q}$ = "1"), and is given by R = "1" and S = "0". As gate X has one of its inputs at logic "0" its output $\bar{Q}$ must equal logic level "1" (again NAND gate principles). Output Q is fed back to input "B", so both inputs to NAND gate Y are at logic "1", therefore, $\bar{Q}$ = "0".

- **When S = 1, R = 1 :**
  If the set input, S now changes state to logic "1" with input R remaining at logic "1", output $\bar{Q}$ still remains LOW at logic level "0" and there is no change of state. Therefore, the flip-flop circuits "Reset" state has also been latched and we can define this "set/reset" action in the following truth table 2.1.

Table 2.1 : Truth table of latch using NAND gate

State	S	R	Q	$\bar{Q}$	Description
Set	1	0	0	1	Set Q » 1
	1	1	0	1	no change
Reset	0	1	1	0	Reset Q » 0
	1	1	1	0	no change
Invalid	0	0	1	1	Invalid Condition

- It can be seen that when both inputs S = "1" and R = "1" the outputs $\bar{Q}$ and $\bar{Q}$ can be at either logic level "1" or "0", depending upon the state of the inputs S or R before this input condition existed. Therefore the condition of S = R = "1" does not change the state of the outputs $\bar{Q}$ and $\bar{Q}$.

- The input state of S=0 and R=0 is an undesirable or invalid condition and must be avoided. The condition of S = R = "0" causes both outputs $\bar{Q}$ and $\bar{Q}$ to be high together at logic level "1" when we would normally want $\bar{Q}$ to be the inverse of $\bar{Q}$. The result is that the flip-flop loses control of $\bar{Q}$, and if the two inputs are now switched "high" again after this condition to logic "1", the flip-flop becomes unstable and switches to an unknown data state based upon the unbalance as shown in the following switching diagram.

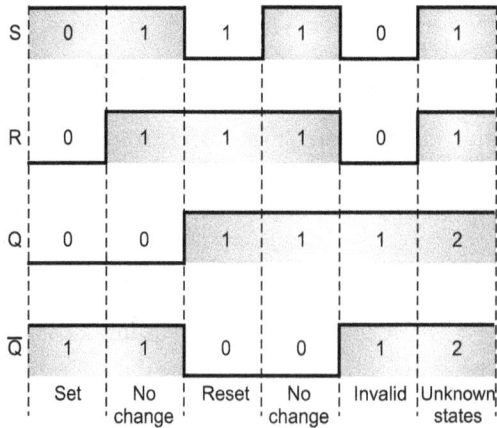

Fig. .2.11 : S-R latch using NAND gate Switching Diagram

- Then, a bistable SR flip-flop or SR latch is activated or set by a logic "1" applied to its S input and deactivated or reset by a logic "1" applied to its R. The SR flip-flop is said to be in an "invalid" condition (Meta-stable) if both the set and reset inputs are activated simultaneously.

2.4.2 SR Latch using NOR Gate

Q. Explain SR latch using NOR gate?

- RS latch have two inputs, S and R. S is called set and R is called reset.
- The S input is used to produce HIGH on Q (i.e. store binary 1 in flip-flop). The R input is used to produce low on Q (i.e. store binary 0 in flip-flop). $\bar{Q}$ is Q complementary output, so it always holds the opposite value of Q.
- The output of the S-R latch depends on current as well as previous inputs or state, and its state (value stored) can change as soon as its inputs change. The circuit and the truth table of RS latch is shown below.

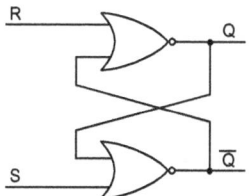

Fig. 2.12

Table 2.2 : Truth table SR latch using NOR gate

S	R	Q	Q+
0	0	0	0
0	0	1	1
0	1	X	0
1	0	X	1
1	1	X	0

- The operation has to be analyzed with the 4 inputs combinations together with the 2 possible previous states.

- **When S = 0 and R = 0 :** If we assume Q = 1 and $\bar{Q}$ = 0 as initial condition, then output Q after input is applied would be Q = 1 and $\bar{Q}$ = 0. Assuming Q = 0 and $\bar{Q}$ = 1 as initial condition, then output Q after the input applied would be Q = 0 and $\bar{Q}$ = 1. So it is clear that when both S and R inputs are low, the output is retained as before the application of inputs. (i.e. there is no state change).

- **When S = 1 and R = 0 :** If we assume Q = 1 and $\bar{Q}$ = 0 as initial condition, then output Q after input is applied would be Q = 1 and $\bar{Q}$ = 0. Assuming Q = 0 and Q = 1 as initial condition, then output Q after the input applied would be $\bar{Q}$ = 1 and $\bar{Q}$ = 0. So in simple words when S is HIGH and R is low, output Q is high.

- **When S = 0 and R = 1 :** If we assume Q = 1 and $\bar{Q}$ = 0 as initial condition, then output Q after input is applied would be Q = 0 and $\bar{Q}$ = 1. Assuming Q = 0 and $\bar{Q}$ = 1 as initial condition, then output Q after the input applied would be Q = = 0 and $\bar{Q}$ = 1. So in simple words when S is LOW and R is HIGH, output Q is LOW.
- **When S = 1 and R =1 :** No matter what state Q and $\bar{Q}$ are in, application of 1 at input of NOR gate always results in 0 at output of NOR gate, which results in both Q and $\bar{Q}$ set to LOW (i.e. Q = $\bar{Q}$). LOW in both the outputs basically is wrong, so this case is invalid.
- The waveform below shows the operation of NOR gates based RS Latch.

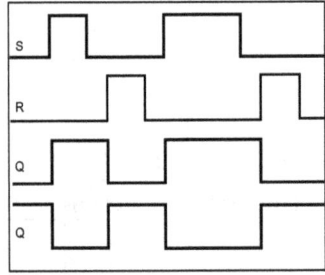

Fig. 2.13 : Waveform of SR latch using NOR gates

2.4.3 D Latch

Q. What is D latch?

- The SR latch seen earlier contains ambiguous state; to eliminate this condition we can ensure that S and R are never equal. This is done by connecting S and R together with an inverter.
- Thus we have D Latch this is same as the RS latch, with the only difference that there is only one input, instead of two (R and S). This input is called D or Data input.
- D latch is called D transparent latch for the reasons explained earlier. Delay flip-flop or delay latch is another name used. Below is the truth table and circuit of D latch.

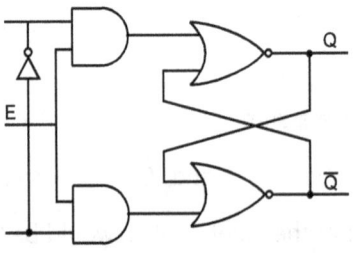

Fig. 2.14 (a)

Table 3.3 : Truth table of D latch

D	Q	Q+
1	X	1
0	X	0

- Below is the D latch waveform, which is similar to the RS latch one, but with R removed.

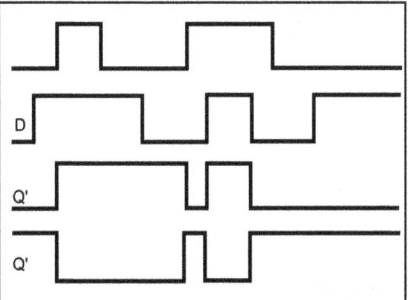

Fig. 2.14 (b) : D latch waveform

2.5 CLOCKED S-R FLIP-FLOP

Q. Explain clocked SR flip flop?

- It is often required to enter the desired digital information in the memory cell, in synchronism with a train of pulses known as clock. The circuit of clocked S-R flip flop is as shown in Fig. 2.15.

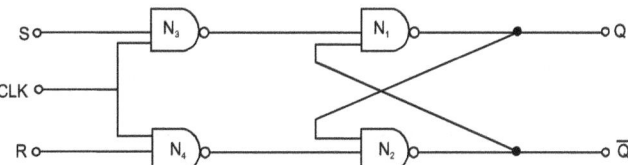

Fig. 2.15 : Clocked S-R flip flop

- In above circuit, when CLK = 0, output of both N_3 and N_4 is certainly 1. In this case, both S and R inputs have no effect on output Q.
- When CLK = 1, the operation of this circuit is exactly the same as that of SR latch.
- For S = R = 0, then output Q does not change i.e. if it is 0 it remains 0 and if it is 1, it remains 1. Thus, there is no change in the output for this input condition.
- For S = 1 and R = 0, the output Q becomes 1 in SR latch. This is known as the set state of the circuit.
- For S = 0 and R = 1 the output Q becomes 0 in SR latch. This is known as the reset state of the circuit.

- For S = R = 1, both the outputs Q and $\bar{Q}$ try to become 1 which is not allowed and therefore this input condition is prohibited.
- Thus, the above circuit responds to S and R inputs, only when CLK = 1.
- The operation of the circuit for CLK = 1 can be tabulated as shown in table 2.3.

Table 2.3 : Truth table of clocked SR flip-flop

Inputs		Output
S	R	Q
0	0	No change
0	1	0 (Reset)
1	0	1 (Set)
1	1	Prohibited

- If we represent Q_n as the output of present state of the circuit and S_n, R_n as the inputs of the present state, then Q_{n+1} becomes the output of the next state of the circuit.
- The above table 2.3 can be redrawn in terms of present state and next state as table 2.4.

Table 2.4 : Truth table of S-R flip flop

Inputs		Output
S_n	R_n	Q_{n+1}
0	0	Q_n
0	1	0
1	0	1
1	1	Prohibited

- The table 2.4 is the truth table of clocked S-R flip flop.
- The truth table of a flip flop is also referred to as the characteristic table as it specifies the operational characteristic of the flip flop.
- Logic symbol of clocked S-R flip flop is as shown in Fig. 2.16.

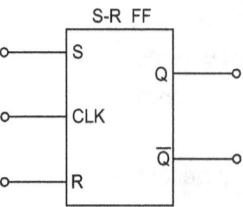

Fig. 2.16 : Logic symbol of clocked S-R flip flop

2.6 CLOCKED S-R FLIP FLOP WITH PRESET AND CLEAR INPUTS

Q. Explain SR flip flop with preset and clear inputs?

- The circuit of clocked S-R flip flop shown in Fig. 2.17 switches to either set state or reset state when the power is turned on i.e. the state of the circuit is uncertain.
- In many applications it is required to define the initial state of the flip flop when the power is turned on.
- This is accomplished by using the preset and clear inputs.
- Preset and clear inputs are known as asynchronous inputs as they do not work in synchronism with the clock.
- Clocked S-R flip flop with preset and clear inputs can be obtained by using N_1 and N_2 NAND gates as 3 input gates as shown in Fig. 2.17.

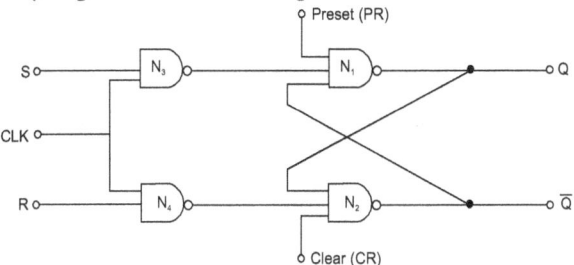

Fig 2.17 : Clocked S-R flip flop with preset and clear inputs.

- In When PR = CR = 1, above circuit operates in accordance with the truth table of clocked S-R flip flop given in table 3.5.
- When CR = 0 and PR = 1, one of the inputs of N_2 is 0, therefore its output is certainly high ($\bar{Q}$ = 1). Consequently all three inputs of N_1 are high which make Q = 0. Thus, CR = 0 resets or clears the flip flop.
- Similarly when CR = 1 and PR = 0, one of the inputs of N_1 is 0, therefore its output is certainly high (Q = 1). Consequently all three inputs of N_2 are high which make $\bar{Q}$ = 0. Thus, PR = 0 sets the flip flop.
- Both preset & clear inputs are known as active low inputs as they perform the intended operation of setting or clearing the flip flop, when they are low.
- Once the desired initial state of the flip flop is achieved using preset & clear inputs, these inputs are connected to logic 1 while the normal operation of the flip flop takes place.
- The condition PR = CR = 0 must not be used, since this leads to an uncertain state.

- The logic symbol of this flip flop is as shown in Fig. 2.18. Preset and clear inputs are shown as bubbled inputs indicating that they are active low inputs.

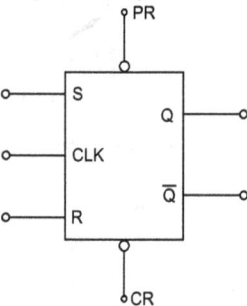

Fig 2.18 : Logic symbol of clocked S-R flip flop with preset and clear inputs.

2.7 JK FLIP FLOP

Q. What is race around condition? Explain with the help of timing diagram how it is removed in basic flip-flop circuit. **[May 05, 8 M]**

Q. Compare race and race around condition. How will you avoid race around condition? Explain? **[Dec. 05, 8 M]**

Q. Draw neat diagram of JK flip-flop using SR flip-flop. Write the truth table and explain what happens if both the inputs are 1 (J = K = 1). **[Dec. 04, 6 M]**

Q. How the race around condition is avoided? **[Dec. 08, 09, 3 M]**

- We know that in case of clocked S-R flip flop, for the input condition S = R = 1 both the outputs Q and $\bar{Q}$ try to become 1, which is not allowed and therefore this input condition is prohibited.
- This drawback can be eliminated by converting S-R flip flop into a JK flip flop.
- The data input J is ANDed with $\bar{Q}$ to obtain S input and the data input K is ANDed with Q to obtain R input as shown in Fig. 2.19.

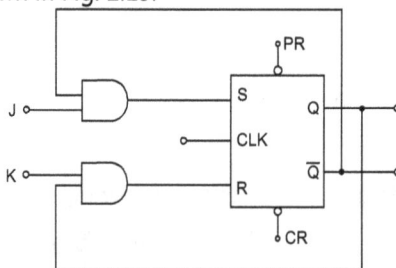

Fig. 2.19 : JK flip flop constructed using S-R flip flop

- When J = K = 0, output of both AND gates is 0. Therefore, S and R both become 0. So next state output Q_{n+1} remains same as that of present state output Q_n.

- When J = 0 & K = 1, the output of upper AND gate is 0, so S = 0. If the present state output Q_n = 0, the output of lower AND gate is also 0 & R becomes 0.
- For the input condition S = R = 0 the next state output remains unchanged. But if the present state output Q_n= 1, the output of lower AND gate becomes 1 i.e. R becomes 1.
- With S = 0 and R = 1 input combination the next state output Q_{n+1} is reset. Thus for J = 0 & K = 1 input condition, irrespective of the present state Q_n, the next state output Q_{n+1} be is 0 i.e. the flip flop is reset.
- Similarly for J = 1 and K = 0 input condition, the next state output Q_{n+1} is certainly 1 i.e. the flip flop is set.

Race around condition

- The race around condition occurs for the input combination J = K = 1.
- Let us assume that initially the output Q is 0. With this the output of lower AND gate becomes 0 and upper AND gate becomes 1. Therefore S becomes 1 & R becomes 0. This input combination of S-R causes output Q to become 1.Thus the output changes from 0 to 1 after the time interval Δt equal to the propagation delay through AND gate and S-R flip flop. Now we have J = K = 1 and output Q = 1.
- After another time interval Δt, the output Q will change back to 0 and the cycle repeats till CLK=1.
- At the end of the clock pulse the output Q is uncertain and this situation is known as race around condition. It is shown in Fig. 2.20.

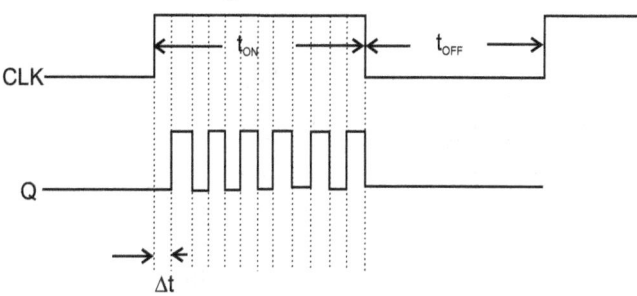

Fig. 2.20 : Timing diagram showing race around condition

- The race around condition can be eliminated if t_{ON} is made smaller than the propagation delay Δt.
- It can also be eliminated using the master slave JK (MS JK) flip flop.
- The operation of JK flip flop can be expressed with the truth table 2.5.

Table 2.5 : Truth table of JK flip flop

Inputs		Output
J_n	K_n	Q_{n+1}
0	0	Q_n
0	1	0
1	0	1
1	1	$\bar{Q}_n$

- The logic symbol of JK flip flop is shown in Fig. 2.21.

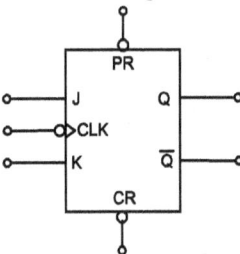

Fig. 2.21 : Logic symbol of JK flip flop

2.7.1 Master Slave JK (MS JK) Flip Flop

> **Q.** What is the advantage of MS JK flip-flop ? Also explain working of MS JK flip-flop.
> **[Dec. 10, 8 M]**
>
> **Q.** What do you mean by master slave JK flip-flop. Explain the advantages of this flip-flop draw suitable circuit diagram and timing diagram. **[Dec. 06, 10 M]**

- Master slave JK flip flop is a cascade of two S-R flip flops as shown in Fig. 2.22.
- As shown in Fig. 2.22, outputs of slave are fed back to the inputs of master. Also clock is directly applied to the master while it is inverted and then applied to the slave.
- When CLK=1, the master is enabled and the slave is disabled. The outputs of master Q_m and $\bar{Q}_m$ respond to the inputs J and K according to the table 3.6. As long as CLK=1, Q & $\bar{Q}$ outputs do not change as the slave is disabled and therefore the fed back inputs of master also do not change.

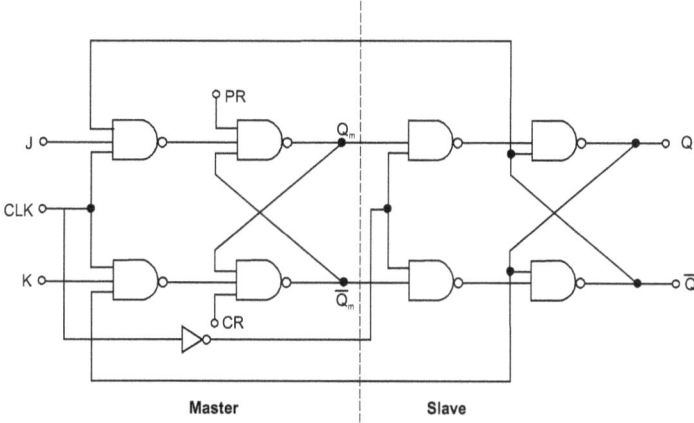

Fig. 2.22 : Master slave JK flip flop

- When CLK= 0, the slave is enabled and the master gets disabled. The outputs Q and $\bar{Q}$ change according to the outputs of the master Q_m and $\bar{Q}_m$. As long as CLK = 0, Q_m and $\bar{Q}_m$ outputs do not change as the master is disabled and therefore Q and $\bar{Q}$ outputs also retain their new values. Thus the race around condition gets eliminated.
- The state of the master slave JK flip flop shown in Fig. 2.23, changes at the negative transition of the clock pulse.
- The logic symbol of master slave JK flip flop is shown in Fig. 2.23.

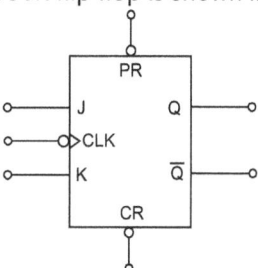

Fig. 2.23 : Logic symbol of MS JK flip flop

- The symbol '>' at the CLK input indicates that output changes when the clock makes a transition.
- The bubble indicates that the output changes when there is a negative transition of the clock (i.e. when the clock changes from 1 to 0).

2.8 D FLIP FLOP

Q. Explain D flip flop with preset and clear input?

- It has only one input called as data input (D).
- It is also known as data flip flop or delay flip flop.

- If we use only middle two rows of the truth table of S-R flip flop or JK flip flop we obtain D flip flop.
- The middle two rows of both truth tables indicate that the two inputs S, R or J, K are always complement of each other.
- Thus a D flip flop can be constructed from S-R flip flop or JK flip flop by connecting a NOT gate in between the two inputs as shown in Fig. 2.24.

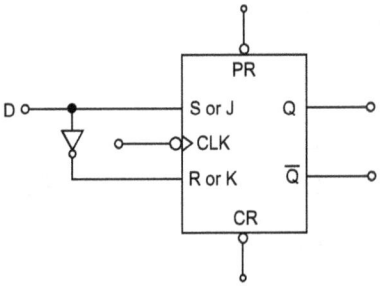

Fig. 2.24 : D flip flop using S-R flip flop or JK flip flop

- The truth table of D flip flop is as shown in table 2.6.

Table 2.6 : Truth table of D flip flop

Input	Output
D_n	Q_{n+1}
0	0
1	1

- Here D_n represents the present state input and Q_{n+1} represents the next state output.
- From truth table, it is clear that output is same as that of input therefore it is known as 'data' flip flop.
- The input data appears at the output at the end of the clock pulse. Thus transfer of data from input to the output is delayed by clock pulse and hence it is also called as 'delay' flip flop.
- The logic symbol of D flip flop is shown in Fig. 2.25.

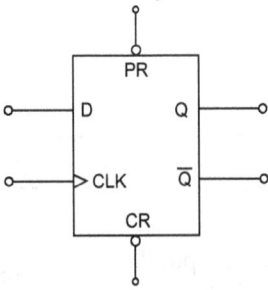

Fig. 2.25 : Logic symbol of D flip flop

2.9 T FLIP FLOP

Q. Explain D flip flop with preset and clear input? [May 07, 2 M]

- It has only one input called as toggle input (T). It is known as toggle flip flop.
- A T flip flop can be constructed from JK flip flop, just by connecting J and K input terminals together as shown in Fig. 2.26.

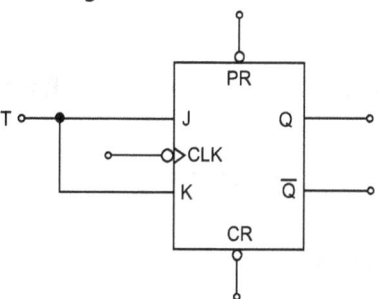

Fig. 2.26 : T flip flop using JK flip flop.

- The truth table of T flip flop is as below.

Table 2.7 : Truth table of T flip flop

Input	Output
T_n	Q_{n+1}
0	Q_n
1	$\bar{Q}_n$

- Here T_n represents the present state input, Q_n represents the present state output and Q_{n+1} represents the next state output.
- From truth table it is clear that, for T = 1, it acts as toggle switch. The output Q changes for every active transition of the clock signal. Therefore it is called as toggle flip flop.
- S-R flip flop can not be converted into T flip flop since S = R = 1 input condition is not allowed.
- The logic symbol of T flip flop is shown in Fig. 2.27.

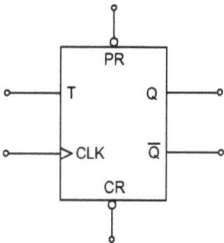

Fig. 2.27 : Logic symbol of T flip flop

2.10 REGISTERS

Q. What is registers? Explain different type of register?

- We have seen that a flip-flop is one bit memory cell, which stores the one bit of digital data. The group of flip-flops stores more than one bit of digital data.
- The N flip-flops store N bits of digital data. The array of flip-flops is known as register. Registers are used for storing digital information.
- D flip flop is used for the construction of registers. S-R flip flop & JK flip flop converted into D flip flop are also used in registers.
- Registers are the inherent part of the architecture of any microprocessor or microcontroller. For example Intel's 8086 microprocessor consist of various 16-bit registers like AX, BX, CX, DX etc.

2.10.1 Buffer Register

- An 'n' bit registers has group of 'n' flip flop and capable to store any binary information, which contains 'n' numbers of bits.
- This type of register is also called storage registers.
- These are used for temporary storage of data.

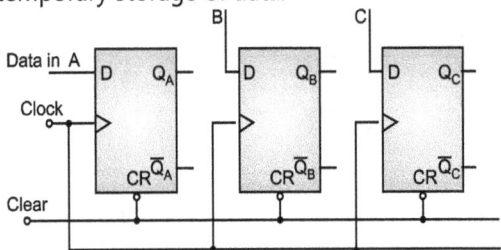

Fig. 2.28 : Buffer register

2.11 SHIFT REGISTER

- The data can be entered in serial or parallel form and can be retrieved in the serial or parallel form. The serial form means bit by bit (one bit at time) and parallel means all the bits are simultaneously retrieved. On the basis of data entered (write) and retrieved (read), the registers are classified as,
- Serial In Serial Out
- Serial In Parallel Out
- Parallel In Serial Out
- Parallel In Parallel Out
- Registers, in which data are entered or/and retrieved in serial form, are referred to as shift register.

2.11.1 Serial In Serial Out Shift Register

> Q. Draw and explain the circuit diagram of 3 bit shift register with serial left shift.
>
> [May 05, 4 M]

- In serial in serial out shift register, data is entered and retrieved in serial fashion with clock.
- The logic diagram of 4-bit serial in serial out shift register using J-K flip-flop is shown Fig. 2.29.

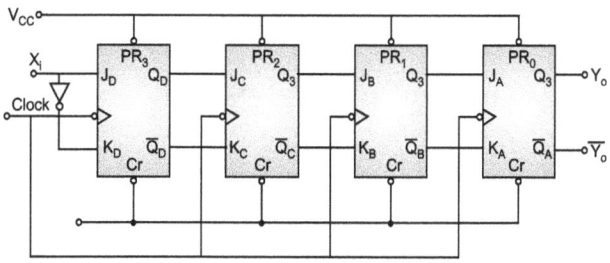

Fig. 2.29

- In Fig. 2.29, X_i is input and Y_o is output of serial in serial out shift register.
- The process of entering the digital data starts with the least significant bits. The data input is entered with falling edge of clock pulse, hence number of clock pulses required to enter the data is equal to the length of digital data or size of shift register. The data is read, bit by bit at output Y_o with clock pulse.
- Let us consider the data 0111 is applied to the input. How the data was entered in shift register is given in Table 2.8 and waveforms of shift register for serial input are shown in Fig. 2.30.

Table 2.8

CLK No.	X_i	Q_D	Q_C	Q_B	Q_A
0	1 (LSB)	0	0	0	0
1	1	1	0	0	0
2	1	1	1	0	0
3	0	1	1	1	0
4		0	1	1	1

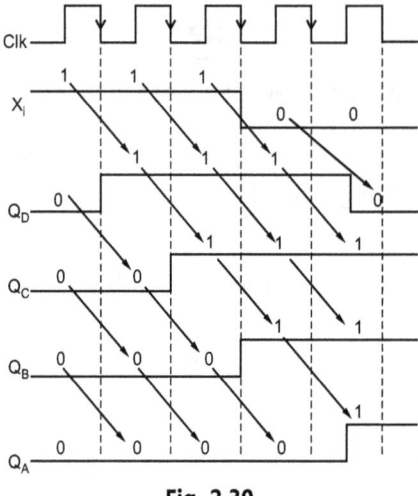

Fig. 2.30

Operation :

The input of flip-flop D is Xi, flip-flop of C is Q_D, flip-flop of B is Q_C and flip-flop of A is Q_B. All flip-flops operate as D flip-flop and input applied is 0111.

Initially shift register is cleared.

$$Q_D\ Q_C\ Q_B\ Q_A = 0000 \text{ and input } X_i = 1$$

- At negative edge of first clock pulse, the input data is entered into the flip-flop and at the end of first clock pulse,

$$Q_D\ Q_C\ Q_B\ Q_A = 1000 \text{ and input } X_i = 1$$

- At negative edge of second clock pulse, the inputs are entered and at the end of second clock pulse,

$$Q_D\ Q_C\ Q_B\ Q_A = 1100 \text{ and input } X_i = 1$$

- At negative edge of third clock pulse, the inputs are entered and at the end of third clock pulse,

$$Q_D\ Q_C\ Q_B\ Q_A = 1110 \text{ and input } X_i = 0$$

- At negative edge of fourth clock pulse, the inputs are entered and at the end of fourth clock pulse,

$$Q_D\ Q_C\ Q_B\ Q_A = 0111$$

Disadvantages :

- n clock pulses are required to enter the n-bit data.
- n clock pulses are required to read the n-bit data.
- Once the data is read, it will be lost.

2.11.2 Serial in Parallel Out Shift Register

- In serial in parallel out shift register, data is entered into the register in serial fashion same as serial in serial out shift register and read from the shift register in parallel fashion. In serial output shift register, clock pulses are required to read the data and once the data is read, it will be lost, but in parallel out shift register, clock pulse(s) is not required to read the data and data is not lost after the read operation.

- The logic diagram of four-bits serial in parallel out shift register using D flip-flop is shown in Fig. 2.31.

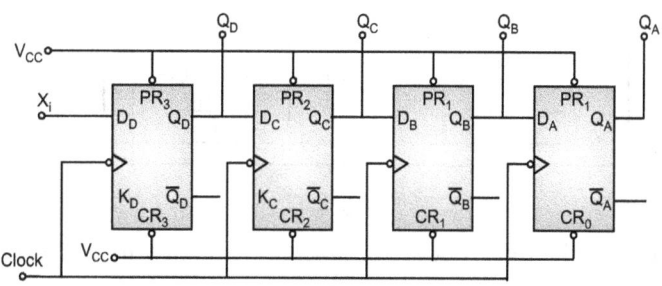

Fig. 2.31

where X_i is serial input for shift register and Q_D Q_C Q_B Q_A are the parallel outputs of shift register.

2.11.3 Parallel In Serial Out Shift Register

Q. Draw and explain the circuit diagram of 3 bit shift register with the following facility parallel in serial out and reset. **[Dec. 08, 6 M]**
Q. Explain with a neat diagram working of parallel in serial out 4-bit shift register. Draw necessary timing diagram. **[May 10, 6 M]**
Q. How will you design parallel in serial out 4bit register having both shift right and shift left facility. **[Dec. 07, 8 M]**

- In parallel in serial out shift register, the data is entered in parallel fashion and data is read in serial fashion. There are two types of parallel loading :
  1. Asynchronous loading,
  2. Synchronous loading.

2.11.3.1 Asynchronous loading

- In asynchronous loading, the preset inputs are used to load the data simultaneously. The logic diagram of four bit parallel in serial out shift register with asynchronous loading is shown in Fig. 2.32.

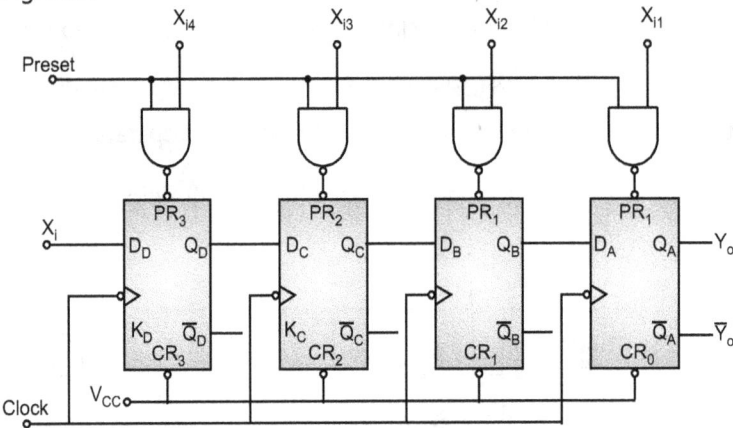

Fig. 2.32

- Initially, connecting the clear input to ground clears the flip-flops. The inputs are given to the parallel inputs (X_{i1}, X_{i2}, X_{i3} and X_{i4}) and preset is connected to logic '0', the output of NAND gate is complement of input, the preset input is active low, flip-flop is set for '0' and unchanged for '1'. The data are written into the registers. The inputs are written into the registers without clock pulse. Such parallel loading is known as asynchronous loading. The data is read from output lines Y_O bit by bit by applying the clock pulse. Once, data is read, it will be lost.

- For example, let us assume the data stored in a shift register is 0101 and it will be read from the output line Y_O. How the data is read from the shift register is given in Table 2.9 and waveforms of shift register for serial out are shown in Fig. 2.33.

Table 2.9

CLK No.	Q_D	Q_C	Q_B	Q_A	Y_O
0	1	1	0	1	1
1	0	1	1	0	0
2	0	0	1	1	1
3	0	0	0	1	1
4	0	0	0	0	0

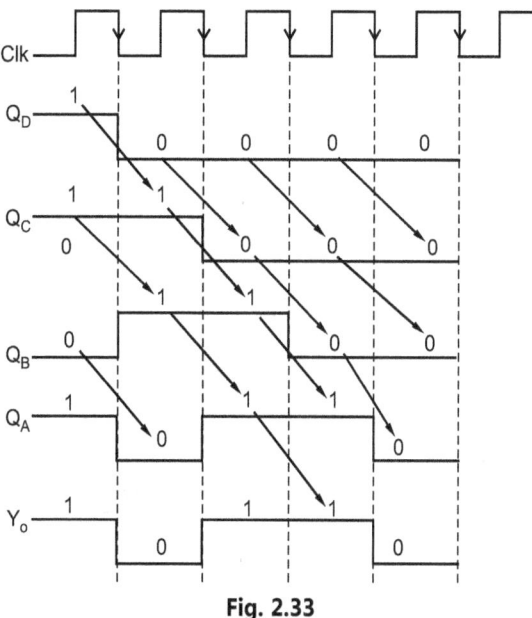

Fig. 2.33

Operation :

The input of flip-flop D is '0', flip-flop of C is Q_D, flip-flop of B is Q_C and flip-flop of A is Q_B. All flip-flops operate as D flip-flop.

Initially data stored in a shift register is 1101.

$$Q_D\ Q_C\ Q_B\ Q_A = 1101 \text{ and output } Y_O = 1$$

- At negative edge of first clock pulse,

$$Q_D\ Q_C\ Q_B\ Q_A = 0110 \text{ and output } Y_O = 0$$

- At negative edge of second clock pulse,

$$Q_D\ Q_C\ Q_B\ Q_A = 0011 \text{ and output } Y_O = 1$$

- At negative edge of third clock pulse,

$$Q_D\ Q_C\ Q_B\ Q_A = 0001 \text{ and output } Y_O = 1$$

- At negative edge of fourth clock pulse,

$$Q_D\ Q_C\ Q_B\ Q_A = 0000 \text{ and output } Y_O = 0$$

In n-bit parallel in parallel out shift register, n clock pulses are required to read the data and once the data is read, it will be lost.

2.11.3.2 Synchronous loading

- In synchronous loading, the input data is entered in parallel form with clock pulse. The logic diagram of four bit parallel in serial out shift register in synchronous mode is shown in Fig. 2.34.

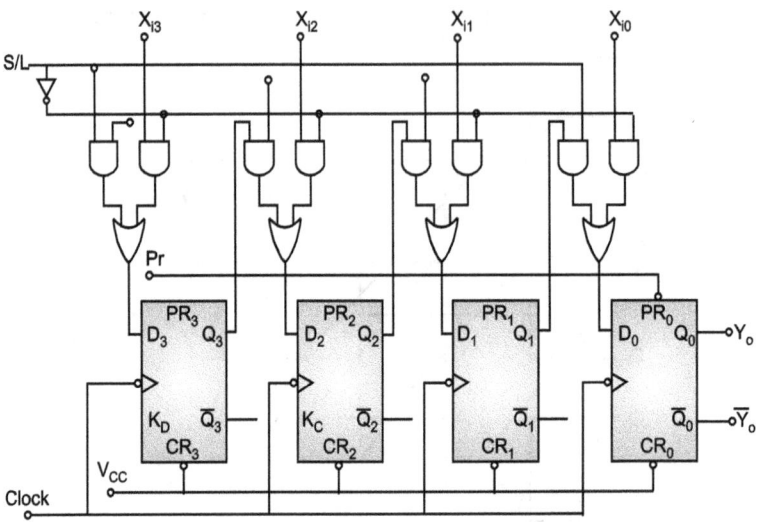

Fig. 2.34

- Shift/ $\overline{\text{Load}}$ control signal is used to control the operation of the shift register. When Shift/ $\overline{\text{Load}}$ is at logic '1', the data is read from Y_O bit-by-bit with clock pulse. When Shift/ $\overline{\text{Load}}$ is at logic '0', the data inputs X_{i1}, X_{i2}, X_{i3} and X_{i4} load simultaneously with clock pulse. Such type of loading is referred as synchronous loading.
- For example : Consider data inputs are 0101.
- When Shift/ $\overline{\text{Load}}$ signal is 0, the outputs of gates G_1, G_3, G_5 and G_7 are 0 and outputs of gates G_2, G_4, G_6 and G_8 are same to the inputs 0101. The outputs of OR gates are 0101, and these are inputs to D flip-flops. It is loaded into register with falling of the clock pulse.
- When Shift/ $\overline{\text{Load}}$ is 0, the outputs of gates G_2, G_4, G_6 and G_8 are 0 and the outputs of gates G_1, G_3, G_5 and G_7 are 0 Q_3 Q_2 Q_1. The outputs of OR gates are 0 Q_3 Q_2 Q_1, and these are the input to D flip-flops. It is loaded into the register with falling edge of clock pulse. It shows that data is shifted in register and we get output at Y_O.

2.11.4 Parallel In Parallel Out Shift Register

- In parallel in parallel out shift register, data is entered as well as read in parallel fashion. There are two types of parallel loading : (1) Asynchronous loading and (2) Synchronous loading. The logic diagram of four-bit asynchronous loading parallel in and parallel out is shown in Fig. 2.35 and synchronous loading parallel in parallel out is shown in Fig. 2.36.

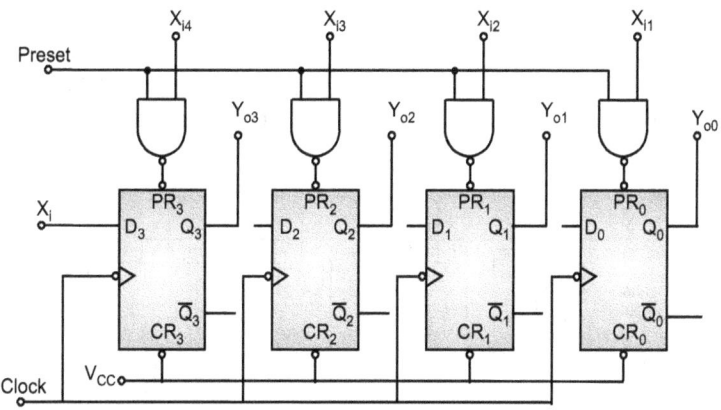

Fig. 2.35

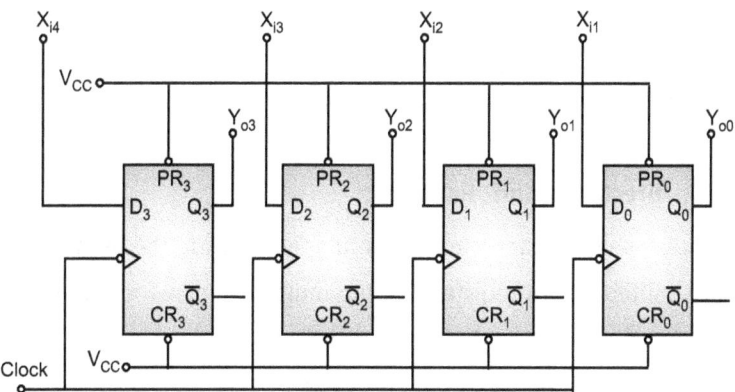

Fig. 2.36

2.11.5 Bi-directional Shift Register

Q. Draw and explain 4 bit bidirectional shift register.	[Dec. 11, 8 M]
Q. Draw the circuit of 3-bit bidirectional shift register.	[Dec. 05, 6 M]
Q. Draw and explain 4-bit shift register having shift and right. Explain any one application of such register.	[May 06, 6 M]

- In bi-directional shift register, the data is shifted to left as well as to right direction. The direction is controlled by the control input $R/\overline{L}$. The four-bit bi-directional shift register is shown in Fig. 2.37.

- When $R/\overline{L}$ control signal is high, the gates G_1, G_3, G_5 and G_7 are enabled. The output of flip-flop A is input for flip-flop B, the output of flip-flop B is input for flip-flop C, the output of flip-flop C is input for flip-flop D and X_{iR} is input for flip-flop. Data is shifted right with clock pulse.

- When R/L̄ control signal is low, the gates G_2, G_4, G_6 and G_8 are enabled. The output of the flip-flop D is input for flip-flop C, the output of the flip-flop C is input for flip-flop B, the output of the flip-flop B is input for flip-flop A and X_{iL} is input for flip-flop D. Data is shifted left with clock pulse.

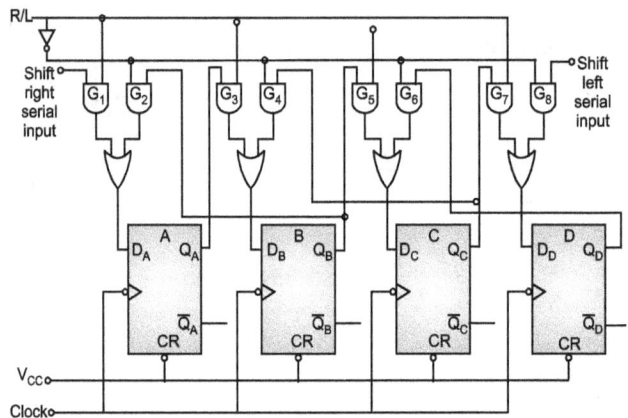

Fig. 2.37

Application of Bi-Directional Shift Register :

- The bi-directional shift register is used to multiply or divide the number by 2^n, provided that '1' is not shifted out of register. For the multiplication of number by 2^n, the data is shifted in left side by the amount of n bits with $X_{iL} = 0$.

- For example : Consider the number is loaded in shift register 0001 and we have to multiply number by $4 = 2^2$.

$$0 0 0 1$$
$$0 0 0 1 \times 2 = 0 0 1 0 \text{ shifted left by 1 bit with } X_{iL} = 0$$
$$0 0 0 1 \times 2^2 = 0 1 0 0 \text{ shifted left by 2 bits with } X_{iL} = 0$$

- In this process the most significant bit is lost.
- For the division of number by 2^n, the data is shifted in right by the amount of n bits with $X_{iR} = 0$. For example, consider the number is loaded in shift register 1000 and we have to divide the number by 2^2.

$$1 0 0 0$$
$$1 0 0 0 / 2 = 0 1 0 0 \qquad \text{shifted right by 1 bit with } X_{iR} = 0$$
$$1 0 0 0 / 2^2 = 0 0 1 0 \qquad \text{shifted right by 2 bits with } X_{iR} = 0$$

In this process the least significant bit is lost.

2.11.6 Universal Register

- The universal shift register operates in all possible four modes (SISO, SIPO, PISO, PIPO) and also as bi-directional shift registers. Logic diagram of four-bit shift register operates in all four modes as shown in Fig. 2.38.

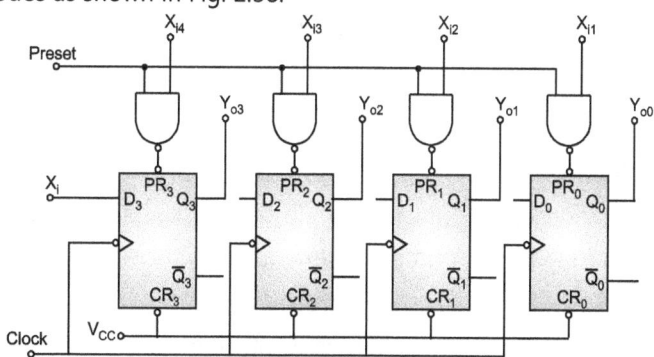

Fig. 2.38

where, X_i is serial input of shift register

$X_{i3}, X_{i2}, X_{i1}, X_{i0}$ are four parallel inputs of shift register

Y_O is serial output of shift register

$Y_{O3}, Y_{O2}, Y_{O1}, Y_{O0}$ are four parallel outputs of shift register.

2.12 COUNTERS

- Counter are used for counting the number of events occurred.
- A circuit that counts electrical pulses, applied as input to it is known as counter.
- In practice these circuits are used as event counters i.e. to count number of event occurred. Electrical pulses are generated corresponding to the occurrence of an event and these pulses are given as input to the counters.
- Flip-flops are used for the construction of counters an N-bit counter consists of N flip-flops.
- A counter with n flip-flops has 2^n possible states. Therefore a 3 bit up counter can count from 0 to 7 while 4-bit down counter can count from 15 down to 0.
- Number of distinct states in the operation of counter is known as modulus of that counter and that counter is called mod 2^n counter.
  e.g. 3-bit counter, the number of states is $2^3 = 8$. Thus modulus of three bit counter is 8 and it is also called as modulo 2^3 i.e. mod 8 counter.

2.12.1 Classification of Counters

- Basically counters are divided into types

(a) Synchronous counter : In synchronous counters all the flip-flops receive the external clock pulse simultaneously e.g. ring and Johnson counter.

(b) Asynchronous counter : For asynchronous counters the external clock signal is applied to one flip-flop and then the output of preceding flip-flop is connected to the clock of next flip-flop.

- Based upon output sequence the counters are also classified into three categories.

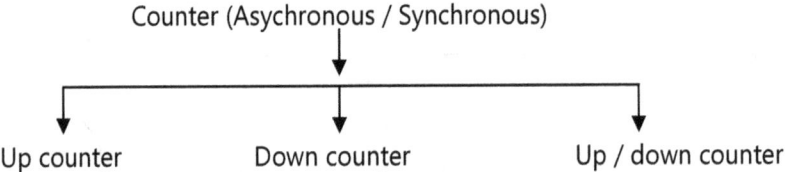

- **Up counter-** If the decimal equivalent of the counter output increases with successive clock pulses, it is called as up counter. For example in a three bit up counter output goes from 0 to 7.
- **Down counter-** If the decimal equivalent of the counter output decreases with successive clock pulses, it is called as down counter. For example in a four bit down counter output goes from 15 down to 0.
- **Up/Down counter-** A counter which can count in any direction i.e. up or down, depending upon direction control input is called as up/down counter.

2.13 ASYNCHRONOUS (RIPPLE) COUNTERS

- A two-bit asynchronous counter is shown in Fig. 2.39 (a). The external clock is connected to the clock input of the first flip-flop (FF_0) only. So, FF_0 changes state at the falling edge of each clock pulse, but FF_1 changes only when triggered by the falling edge of the Q output of FF_0.
- Because of the inherent propagation delay through a flip-flop, the transition of the input clock pulse and a transition of the Q output of FF0 can never occur at exactly the same time. Therefore, the flip-flops cannot be triggered simultaneously, producing an asynchronous operation.

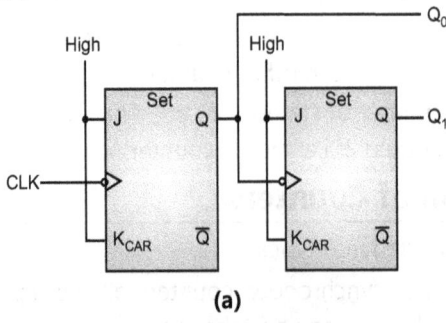

(a)

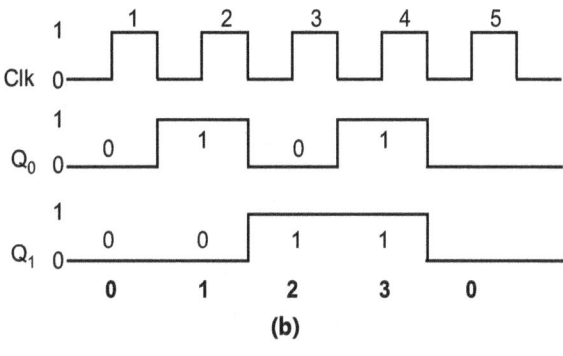

(b)

Fig. 2.39

- Note that for simplicity, the transitions of Q_0, Q_1 and CLK in the timing diagram above are shown as simultaneous even though this is an asynchronous counter. Actually, there is some small delay between the CLK, Q_0 and Q_1 transitions.
- Usually, all the CLEAR inputs are connected together, so that a single pulse can clear all the flip-flops before counting starts. The clock pulse fed into FF_0 is rippled through the other counters after propagation delays, like a ripple on water, hence the name Ripple Counter.
- The 2-bit ripple counter circuit above has four different states, each one corresponding to a count value. Similarly, a counter with n flip-flops can have 2 to the power n states. The number of states in a counter is known as its mod (modulo) number. Thus a 2-bit counter is a mod-4 counter.
- A mod-n counter may also described as a divide-by-n counter. This is because the most significant flip-flop (the furthest flip-flop from the original clock pulse) produces one pulse for every n pulses at the clock input of the least significant flip-flop (the one triggers by the clock pulse).

2.13.1 3-Bit Asynchronous Up (Ripple) Counter

| Q. Draw and explain 3-bit asynchronous up-counter. Also draw the necessary timing diagram. [May 07, Dec. 12, 6 M] |
| Q. Draw 3-bit asynchronous counter. Explain with timing diagram. [Dec. 09, 8 M] |

- For the implementation of 3-bit counter, three flip flops are required.
- The number of distinct states in the operation of this counter is $2^3 = 8$. Therefore, it is also called as mod-8 counter.
- In case of 3-bit up counter, the output goes from 0 to 7.
- Let Q_2, Q_1 and Q_0 be the outputs of the three flip flops used for the design. The count sequence is as shown in the table 2.10.

Table 2.10 : Count sequence of 3-bit up counter

Q_2	Q_1	Q_0	State of the counter
0	0	0	0
0	0	1	1
0	1	0	2
0	1	1	3
1	0	0	4
1	0	1	5
1	1	0	6
1	1	1	7

- From the table 2.10 it is clear that the output Q_0 of the least significant flip flop changes for every clock pulse applied to it. So it can be implemented using a T type flip flop with $T_0 = 1$.
- Also, the output Q_1 changes from 0 to 1 or 1 to 0, only when in the corresponding states Q_0 changes from 0 to 1. So it can be implemented using a T-type flip flop with $T_1 = 1$ and Q_0 is connected as its clock input.
- Similarly the output Q_2 changes only when Q_1 changes from 0 to 1. So it can be implemented using a T-type flip flop with $T_2 = 1$ and Q_1 is connected as its clock input. This completes the design and the resulting circuit is as shown as Fig. 2.40(a).

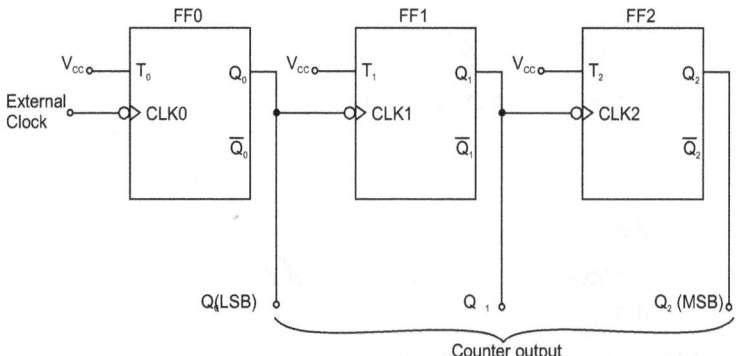

Fig. 2.40 (a) : 3-bit ripple up counter

- The waveforms of the outputs are shown in Fig. 2.40.

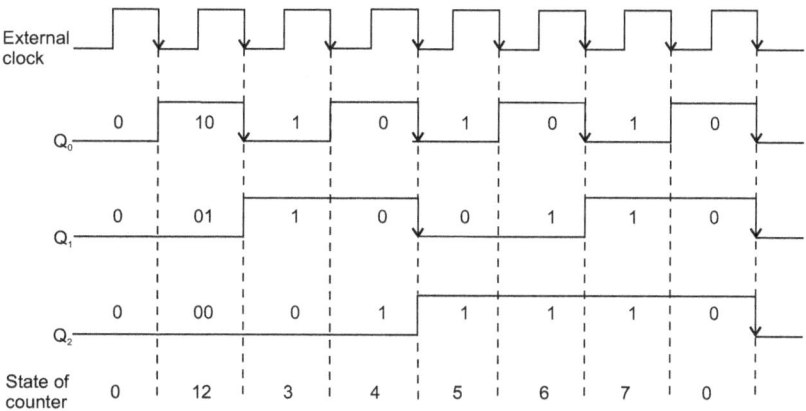

Fig. 2.40 (b) : Waveforms/Timing diagram of 3 bit ripple up counter

- From the waveform of external clock and Q_0, it is clear that two clock periods are required for the completion of one cycle of Q_0. Therefore, clock frequency is twice to that of Q_0 output. In other words the Q_0 is the divide by 2 ($\div$ 2) output with respect to clock frequency. Similarly Q_1 is the divide by 4 ($\div$ 4) output and Q_2 is divide by 8 ($\div$ 8) output with respect to clock frequency.

- Therefore this mod - 8 counter is also known as divide by 8 ($\div$ 8) counter.

2.13.2 4-Bit Asynchronous Up Counter

Q. Draw 4-bit asynchronous counter. Also explain timing diagram for the same.
Q. Draw and explain 4-bit binary up counting with this concept. Also draw the necessary timing diagram. Is there any frequency division concept in it? Comment on frequency generated at the output of each flip-flop. **[May 08, 4 M]**

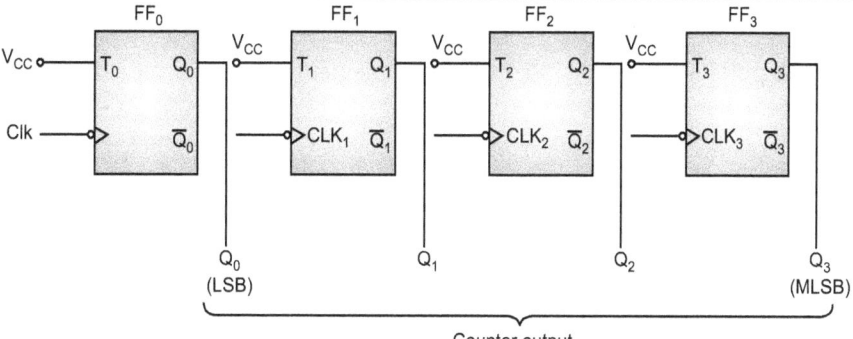

Fig. 2.41 (a) : 4-bit (asynchronous ripple) counter

Fig. 2.41 shows the circuit diagram of 4-bit asynchronous counter using the T flip-flops.

- Since it is 4 bit asynchronous up counter, we need to use four flip-flops number of distinct states in the operation of this counter is $2^4 = 16$.

Therefore, it is called as mod-16 counter.
- Let Q_0, Q_1, Q_2 and Q_3 be the outputs of the three flip-flops used for the design. The count sequence is as shown in the table.
- Table 2.11 count sequence of 4-bit up counter.

Table 2.11

Q_3	Q_2	Q_1	Q_0	State of the counter
0	0	0	0	0
0	0	0	1	1
0	0	1	0	2
0	0	1	1	3
0	1	0	0	4
0	1	0	1	5
0	1	1	0	6
0	1	1	1	7
1	0	0	0	8
1	0	0	1	9
1	0	1	0	10
1	0	1	1	11
1	1	0	0	12
1	1	0	1	13
1	1	1	0	14
1	1	1	1	15

- From the table it is clear that the output Q_0 of the least significant flip-flop changes for every clock pulse applied to it. So it can be implemented using at type flip-flop with $T_0 = 1$.
- Also the output Q_1 changes from 0 to 1 or 1 to 0, only when in the corresponding states Q_0 changes from 0 to 1. So it can be implemented using a T-type flip flop with $T_1 = 1$ and Q_0 is connected as its clock input.
- Similarly the output Q_2 changes only when Q_1 changes from 0 to 1 so it can be implemented using a T-type flip-flop with $T_2 = 1$ and Q_1 is connected as its clock input.
- Similarly the output Q_3 changes only when Q_2 changes from 0 to 1 so it can be complemented using at type flip-flop with $T_3 = 1$ and Q_2 is connected as its clock input.
- Waveform of output shown below for 4 bit asynchronous (ripple) counter.

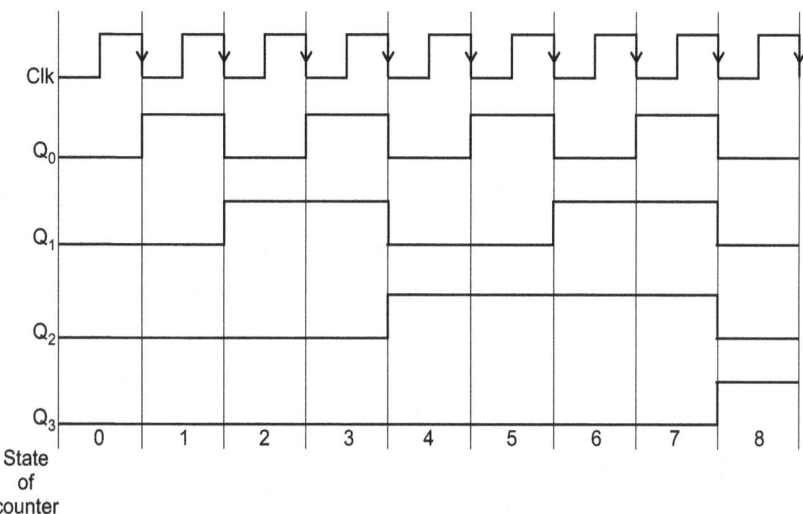

Fig. 2.41 (b)

2.13.3 3-bit Asynchronous Down Counter

Example 2.1 : Design 3 bit down ripple counter. Draw waveforms. [Dec. 2007, 4 M]

Solution :

- 3 bit ripple down counter requires three flip flops. The counter output goes from 7 down to 0. The count sequence is as shown in table 2.12.

Table 2.12 : Count sequence of 3-bit down counter

Q_2	Q_1	Q_0	State of the counter
1	1	1	7
1	1	0	6
1	0	1	5
1	0	0	4
0	1	1	3
0	1	0	2
0	0	1	1
0	0	0	0

- As like previous example, the least significant stage can be implemented using T flip flop with $T_0 = 1$.
- Output Q_1 changes whenever there is 0 to 1 transition of Q_0, in the corresponding states. So we can realize it with a flip flop which is positive edge triggered. The Q_0 output needs to be connected to the clock input and $T_1 = 1$.

- When Q_0 makes transition from 0 to 1, $\bar{Q}_0$ changes from 1 to 0. So we can realize the second stage by using a negative edge triggered flip flop as shown in Fig. 2.42 with $T_1 = 1$. $\bar{Q}_0$ output needs to be connected as clock input.
- Similarly, the most significant stage can be realized with a negative edge triggered T flip flop with $T_2 = 1$ and $\bar{Q}_1$ connected as its clock input. This completes the design and the resulting circuit is as shown in Fig. 2.42. Also the waveforms of the outputs are shown in Fig. 2.43.

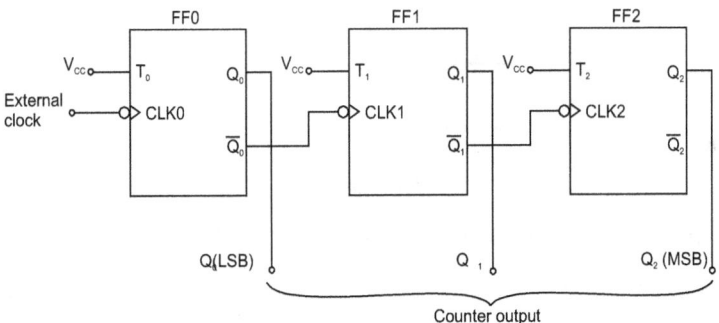

Fig. 2.42 : 3 bit ripple down counter

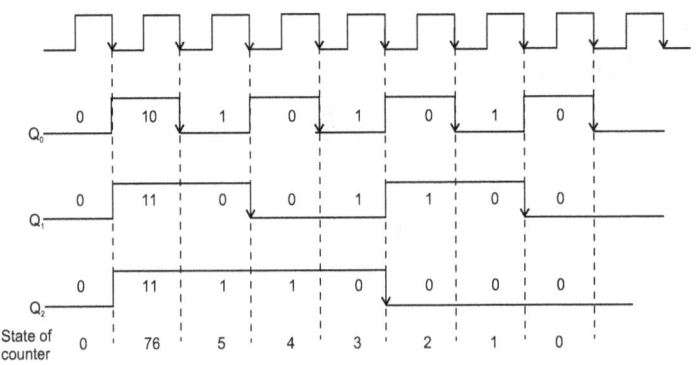

Fig. 2.43 : Waveforms/Timing diagram of 3 bit ripple down counter

2.13.4 4 Bit up / down Ripple Counter

Example 2.4 :
Design a 4-bit binary Up/Down ripple counter with a control for Up/Down counting. Also draw timing diagram. **[Dec. 2004, 8 M]**

Solution :
- A ripple up counter Q output of the preceding stages are to be connected to the clock inputs of next stages.

- Similarly from example we know that for a ripple down counter $\bar{Q}$ outputs of preceeding stages are to be connected to the clock input of next stages.
- Therefore to design a Up/Down counter, AND-OR gates are used between flip flops as shown in Fig. 2.44 (a).
- The upper AND gates are enabled when UP/Down input is at logic 1 which connect Q outputs to the inputs. While the lower AND gates are enabled when UP/Down input is 0 which connect $\bar{Q}$ outputs to the clock inputs. For 4-bit counter, 4 four flip flops are required.

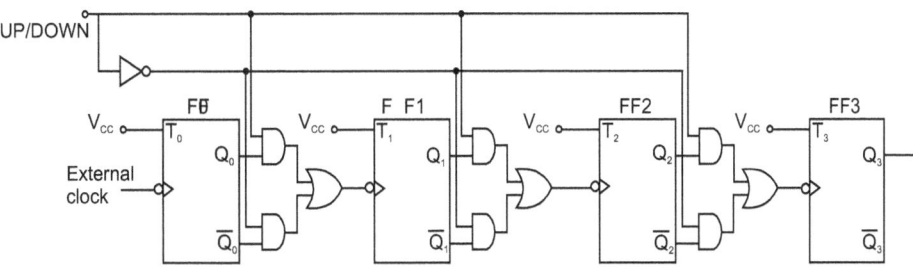

Fig. 2.44 (a) : 4-bit ripple Up/Down counter

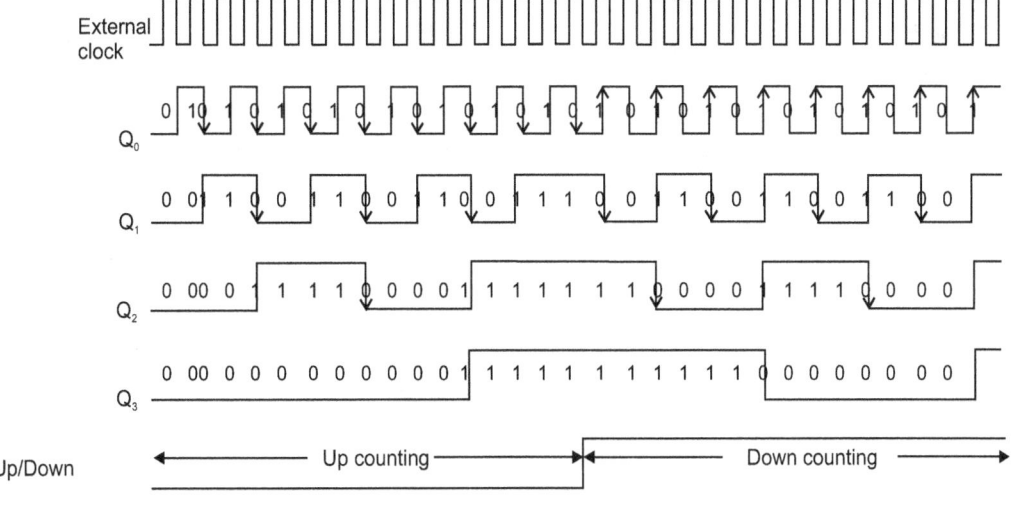

Fig. 2.44 (b) : Timing diagram of 4-bit Up/Down counter

2.13.5 MOD-N counter (Modulus of the counter)

Q. What is Mod counter ?

- N bit ripple counter is called as modulus N counter.
- Modulus of counter = 2^n
- From the modulus we can conclude the number of states of counter.

Table 2.13

Sr. No.	Counter type	Modulus
1	2 bit	MOD – 4
2	3 bit	MOD – 8
3	4 bit	MOD - 16

Example 2.2 : Design mod 5 ripple up counter.

Solution :

- It is given that modulus of counter is 5. So number of distinct states in the operation of the counter are 5. The number of flip flops required can be obtained using the following ineqality.

$$2^N \geq \text{Modulus of counter} \quad \ldots(3.9)$$

Where N = number of flip flops.

For N = 1 & N = 2 the inequality is not satisfied.

Putting N = 3, we get,

$$2^3 \geq 5$$
$$\Rightarrow 8 \geq 5$$

- The inequality is satisfied. Therefore for the implementation of mod 5 counter three flip flops are required.
- As ripple up counter is to be designed, we have to use three T flip flops with the T inputs connected to V_{CC}. Also Q_0 and Q_1 outputs are to be connected as the clock input of the respective next stages.
- The count sequence is shown in table 2.14.

Table 2.14 : count sequence of mod 5 ripple up counter

Q_2	Q_1	Q_0	State of the counter
0	0	0	0
0	0	1	1
0	1	0	2
0	1	1	3
1	0	0	4
0	0	0	0

- The counter output goes from 0 to 4. Therefore, it is a truncated counter. So we need to design 'reset logic'.
- From the table it is clear that after the state 4 the counter should be reset i.e. The state 5 should not occur.

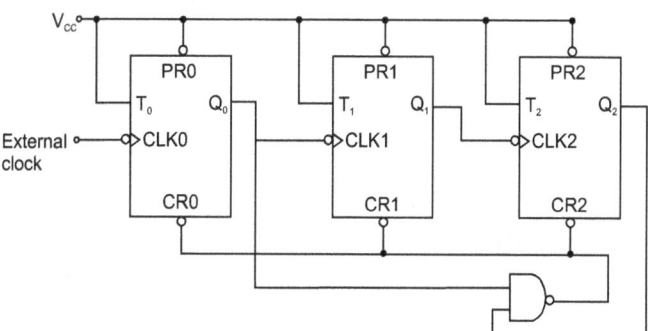

Fig. 2.45 : Mod-5 ripple up counter

- For state 5, $Q_2 Q_1 Q_0$ = 101. Therefore whenever both Q_2 & Q_0 become 1, at that instant the counter should be reset. It can be achieved with a simple 2 input NAND gate. The output of the NAND gate must be connected to the clear input of all flip flops, so that the counter gets reset after the state 4. The resulting circuit diagram is as shown in Fig. 2.45.

2.14 SYNCHRONOUS COUNTER

Q. What is synchronous counter?

- The Synchronous Counter, the external clock signal is connected to the clock input of every individual flip-flop within the counter so that all of the flip-flops are clocked together simultaneously (in parallel) at the same time giving a fixed time relationship.

- In the synchronous counter the individual output bits changing state at exactly the same time in response to the common clock signal with no ripple effect and therefore, no propagation delay.

- Synchronous Counters use edge-triggered flip-flops that change states on either the "positive-edge" (rising edge) or the "negative-edge" (falling edge) of the clock pulse on the control input resulting in one single count when the clock input changes state.

- Synchronous counters count on the rising-edge which is the low to high transition of the clock signal and asynchronous ripple counters count on the falling-edge which is the high to low transition of the clock signal.

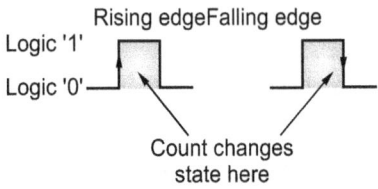

Fig. 2.46

- It may seem unusual that ripple counters use the falling-edge of the clock cycle to change state, but this makes it easier to link counters together because the most significant bit (MSB) of one counter can drive the clock input of the next.

- This works because the next bit must change state when the previous bit changes from high to low – the point at which a carry must occur to the next bit. Synchronous counters usually have a carry-out and a carry-in pin for linking counters together without introducing any propagation delays.

Design steps of synchronous counter

- In synchronous counter all the flip flops are clocked simultaneously. Therefore it is faster in operation.
- It can be designed for any count sequence which need not be always straight binary.
- For the design of synchronous counter, first find out the number of flip flops required.
- Then prepare a table consisting of present state, next state and determine the flip flop inputs which must be present to obtain the next state using the excitation table of the flip flop.
- Prepare k-map for each flip flop input and obtain the simplified expressions from which complete the circuit diagram.

2.14.1 3-bit Synchronous Counter

Example 2.3 :

Design 3-bit synchronous counter using JK flip flop and explain. [May 2006, 8 M]

Solution :

- We know that for 3 bit counter three flip flops are required.
- The table consisting of present state, next state and the required inputs of flip flop is as shown in table 2.15. Here Q_2, Q_1 and Q_0 represent the present state variables with Q'_2 Q'_1 and Q'_0 represent the next state variables.

Table 2.15

Present state			Next state			Flip flip inputs					
Q_2	Q_1	Q_0	Q'_2	Q'_1	Q'_0	J_2	K_2	J_1	K_1	J_0	K_0
0	0	0	0	0	1	0	×	0	×	1	×
0	0	1	0	1	0	0	×	1	×	×	1
0	1	0	0	1	1	0	×	×	0	1	×
0	1	1	1	0	0	1	×	×	1	×	1
1	0	0	1	0	1	×	0	0	×	1	×
1	0	1	1	1	0	×	0	1	×	×	1
1	1	0	1	1	1	×	0	×	0	1	×
1	1	1	0	0	0	×	1	×	1	×	1

- Observe the first row of the table 2.15. Present state is $Q_2 Q_1 Q_0 = 0\ 0\ 0$ and next state $Q'_2 Q'_1 Q'_0 = 0\ 0\ 1$. For flip flop 2, $Q_2 = Q'_2 = 0$. Therefore, from first row of excitation table of JK flip flop we get the $J_2 K_2$ input combination as 0 X.

- Similarly for flip flop 1 as $Q_1 = Q'_1 = 0$, the $J_1 K_1$ input combination is 0 X.

- For flip flop 0, present state = $Q_0 = 0$ while the next state = $Q'_0 = 1$. Therefore from the second row of excitation table of JK flip flop we get $J_0 K_0$ input combination as 1 X.

- This completes the first row of the table 2.15. Proceeding in a similar manner, the remaining rows of the table are completed.

- Now we represent each individual input in a k map and obtain the simplified expressions.

K-map for $J_2 \Rightarrow$

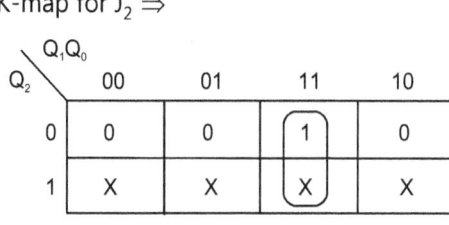

$\therefore J_2 = Q_1 Q_0$

K-map for $K_2 \Rightarrow$

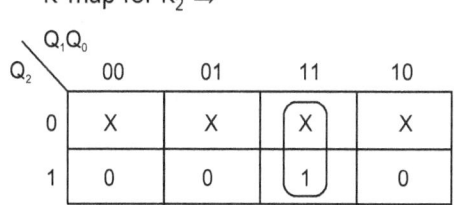

$\therefore K_2 = Q_1 Q_0$

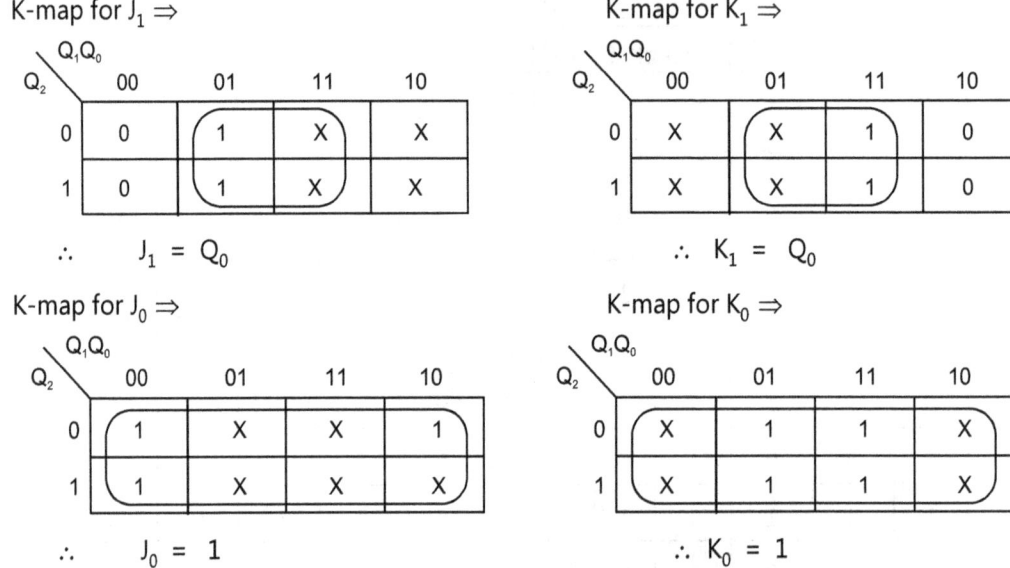

∴ $J_1 = Q_0$

∴ $K_1 = Q_0$

∴ $J_0 = 1$

∴ $K_0 = 1$

- Based on above expressions, the resulting circuit diagram is drawn in Fig. 2.47.

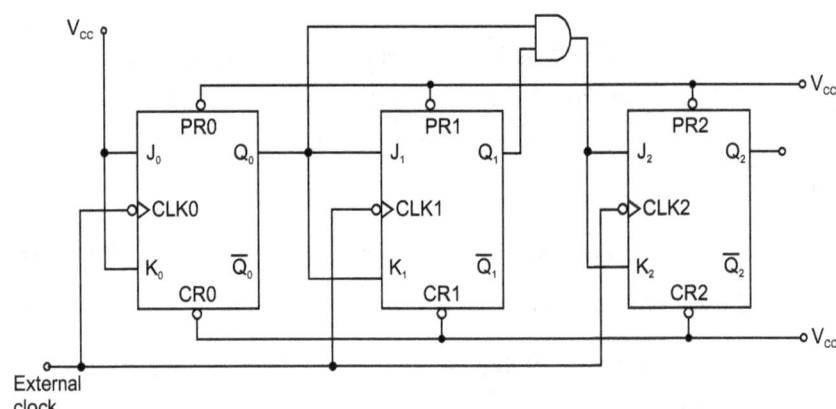

Fig. 2.47 : 3-bit synchronous up counter

2.14.2 4-bit Synchronous Counter

- It can be seen that the external clock pulses (pulses to be counted) are fed directly to each J-K flip-flop in the counter chain and that both the J and K inputs are all tied together in toggle mode, but only in the first flip-flop, flip-flop A (LSB) are they connected HIGH, logic "1" allowing the flip-flop to toggle on every clock pulse.
- Then the synchronous counter follows a predetermined sequence of states in response to the common clock signal, advancing one state for each pulse.

- The J and K inputs of flip-flop B are connected to the output "Q" of flip-flop A, but the J and K inputs of flip-flops C and D are driven from AND gates which are also supplied with signals from the input and output of the previous stage.

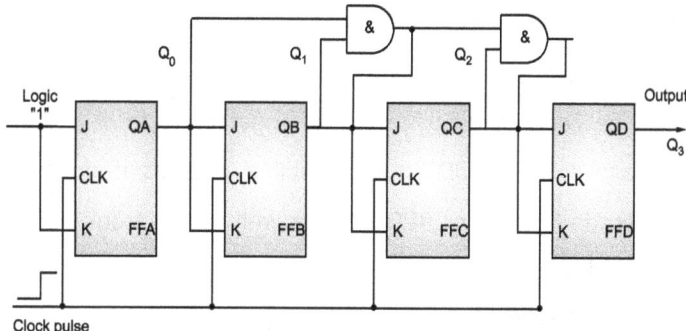

Fig. 2.48

- If we enable each J-K flip-flop to toggle based on whether or not all preceding flip-flop outputs (Q) are "HIGH" we can obtain the same counting sequence as with the asynchronous circuit but without the ripple effect, since each flip-flop in this circuit will be clocked at exactly the same time.
- Then as there is no inherent propagation delay in synchronous counters, because all the counter stages are triggered in parallel at the same time, the maximum operating frequency of this type of frequency counter is much higher than that for a similar asynchronous counter circuit.

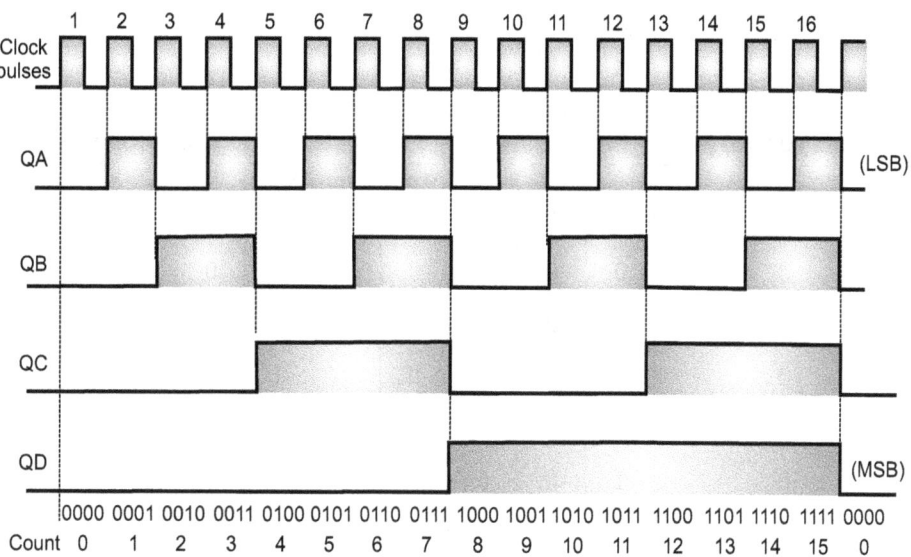

Fig. 2.49 : 4-bit synchronous counter waveform timing diagram

- Because this 4-bit synchronous counter counts sequentially on every clock pulse the resulting outputs count upwards from 0 ("0000") to 15 ("1111").
- Therefore, this type of counter is also known as a 4-bit Synchronous Up Counter.
- As synchronous counters are formed by connecting flip-flops together and any number of flip-flops can be connected or "cascaded" together to form a "divide-by-n" binary counter, the modulo's or "MOD" number still applies as it does for asynchronous counters so a Decade counter or BCD counter with counts from 0 to 2n-1 can be built along with truncated sequences.

2.14.3 3-bit Up/Down Synchronous Counter

Q. Design and implement 3-bit up/down synchronous counter using MS-JK flip-flop with its truth table. Also draw timing diagram. **[Dec. 08, 12 M]**
Q. Explain with a neat diagram working of 3-bit up-down synchronous counter. Draw necessary timing diagram. **[May 10, 10 M]**

- We know that for 4 bit counter four flip-flop are required.
- The table consisting of present state, next state and the required inputs of flip-flop is as shown in table. Here Q_2, Q_1 and Q_0 are present state variable and Q_2', Q_1' and Q_0' represents the next state variables.

Table 2.16

Mode control M	Present state			Next state			Flip-flop inputs		
	Q_2	Q_1	Q_0	Q_2'	Q_1'	Q_0'	T_2	T_1	T_0
0	0	0	0	0	0	1	0	0	1
0	0	0	1	0	1	0	0	1	1
0	0	1	0	0	1	1	0	0	1
0	0	1	1	1	0	0	1	1	1
0	1	0	0	1	0	1	0	0	1
0	1	0	1	1	1	0	0	1	1
0	1	1	0	1	1	1	0	0	1
0	1	1	1	0	0	0	1	1	1

Table 2.17 : For down counting

Mode control M	Present state			Next state			Flip-flop inputs		
	Q_2	Q_1	Q_0	Q_2'	Q_1'	Q_0'	T_2	T_1	T_0
1	0	0	0	1	1	1	1	1	1
1	0	0	1	0	0	0	0	0	1
1	0	1	0	0	0	1	0	1	1
1	0	1	1	0	1	0	0	0	1
1	1	0	0	0	1	1	1	1	1
1	1	0	1	1	0	0	0	0	1
1	1	1	0	1	0	1	0	1	1
1	1	1	1	1	1	0	0	0	1

- Now we represent each individual input in a K-map and obtain the simplified expression.

$$T_2 = \overline{M}Q_1Q_0 + M\,\overline{Q_1}\overline{Q_0}$$

$$T_1 = \overline{M}Q_0 + M\overline{Q_0}$$

$$T_1 = 1$$

- So logic diagram for 3-bit synchronous up down counter is given below :

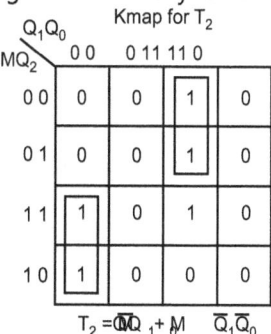

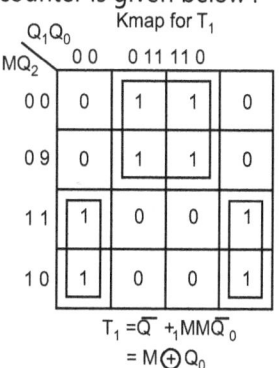

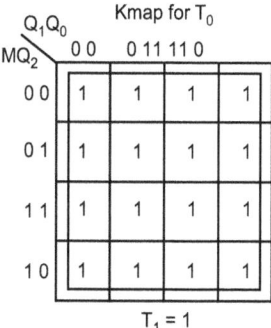

Fig. 2.50 : K-map for 3-bit synchronous up / down counter

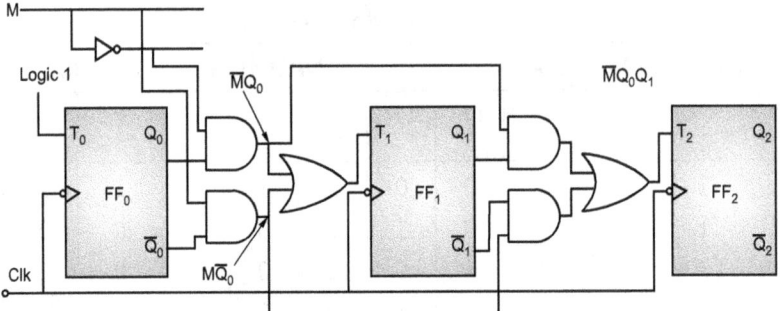

Fig. 2.51 : 3-bit synchronous up / down counter

2.14.4 Modulo N Synchronous Counter

Decade 4-bit Synchronous Counter

- A 4-bit decade synchronous counter can also be built using synchronous binary counters to produce a count sequence from 0 to 9.
- A standard binary counter can be converted to a decade (decimal 10) counter with the aid of some additional logic to implement the desired state sequence.
- After reaching the count of "1001", the counter recycles back to "0000". We now have a decade or Modulo-10counter.

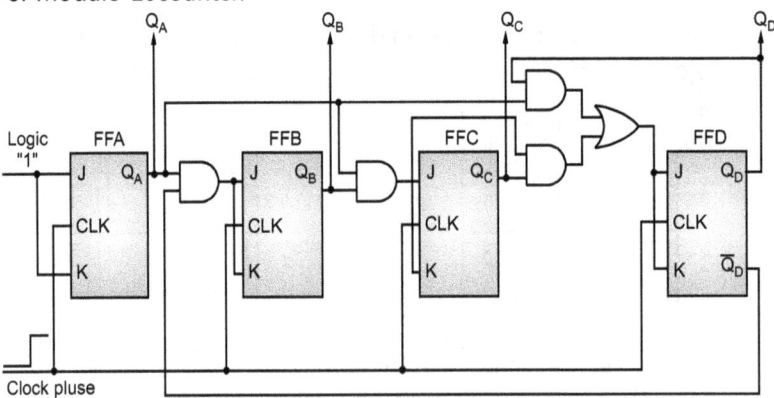

Fig. 2.52 : decade 4-bit synchronous counter

- The additional AND gates detect when the counting sequence reaches "1001", (Binary 10) and causes flip-flop FF3 to toggle on the next clock pulse. Flip-flop FF0 toggles on every clock pulse. Thus, the count is reset and starts over again at "0000" producing a synchronous decade counter.
- We could quite easily re-arrange the additional AND gates in the above counter circuit to produce other count numbers such as a Mod-12 counter which counts 12 states from"0000" to "1011" (0 to 11) and then repeats making them suitable for clocks, etc.

ANALOG AND DIGITAL ELECTRONICS (S.E.ELECTRICAL)   SEQUENTIAL LOGIC

Example 2.4 :

Design mod-12 synchronous counter using D flip flop.   **[May 2008, 8 M]**

Solution :

- For the implementation of MOD-12 counter four D flip flops are required.
- It is also a truncated counter. 0 to 11 are used states while 12 to 15 are unused states.
- Next state of unused state is unknown. Let it be don't care. Therefore the corresponding flip flop input is also don't care.
- The table 2.18 consists of present state, next state & the required input of flip flop.

Table 2.18

Present state				Next state				Flip flop input			
Q_3	Q_2	Q_1	Q_0	Q'_3	Q'_2	Q'_1	Q'_0	D_3	D_2	D_1	D_0
0	0	0	0	0	0	0	1	0	0	0	1
0	0	0	1	0	0	1	0	0	0	1	0
0	0	1	0	0	0	1	1	0	0	1	1
0	0	1	1	0	1	0	0	0	1	0	0
0	1	0	0	0	1	0	1	0	1	0	1
0	1	0	1	0	1	1	0	0	1	1	0
0	1	1	0	0	1	1	1	0	1	1	1
0	1	1	1	1	0	0	0	1	0	0	0
1	0	0	0	1	0	0	1	1	0	0	1
1	0	0	1	1	0	1	0	1	0	1	0
1	0	1	0	1	0	1	1	1	0	1	1
1	0	1	1	0	0	0	0	0	0	0	0

- Now we represent each individual input in a K-map & obtain the simplified expressions.

K-map for D_3 ⇒

Q_3Q_2 \ Q_1Q_0	00	01	11	10
00	0	0	0	0
01	0	0	1	0
11	X	X	X	X
10	1	1	0	1

$D_3 = Q_3\bar{Q_1} + Q_3\bar{Q_0} + Q_2 Q_1 Q_0$

K-map for D_2 ⇒

Q_3Q_2 \ Q_1Q_0	00	01	11	10
00	0	0	1	0
01	1	1	0	1
11	X	X	X	X
10	0	0	0	0

$D_2 = Q_2\bar{Q_1} + Q_2\bar{Q_0} + \bar{Q_3}\bar{Q_2} Q_1 Q_0$

K-map for D_1 ⇒

Q_3Q_2 \ Q_1Q_0	00	01	11	10
00	0	1	0	1
01	0	1	0	1
11	X	X	X	X
10	0	1	0	1

$D_1 = \bar{Q_1} Q_0 + Q_1 \bar{Q_0} = Q_1 \oplus Q_0$

K-map for D_0 ⇒

Q_3Q_2 \ Q_1Q_0	00	01	11	10
00	1	0	0	1
01	1	0	0	1
11	X	X	X	X
10	1	0	0	1

$D_0 = \bar{Q_0}$

- Based on above expressions the resulting circuit diagram is shown in Fig. 2.53.

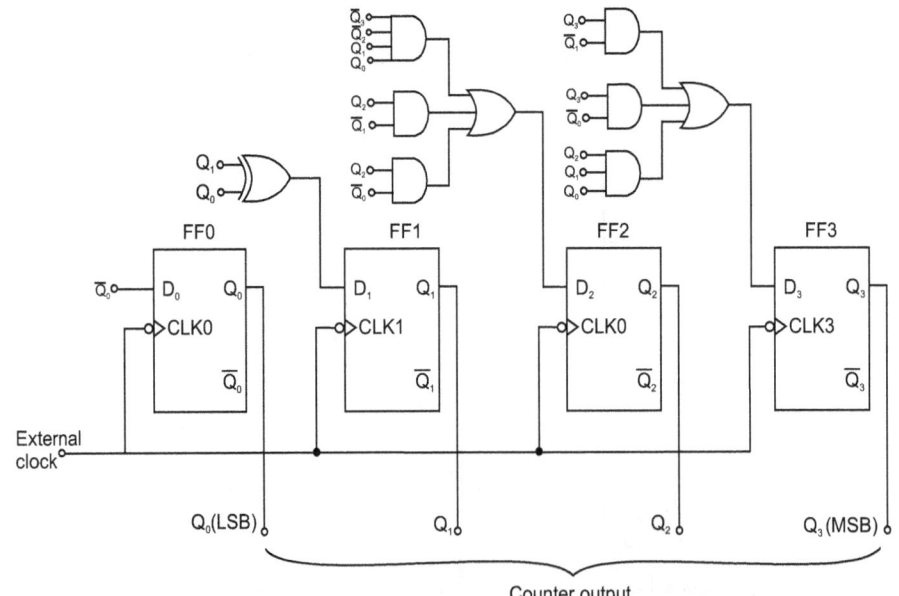

Fig. 2.53

2.14.5 BCD Synchronous Counter

Example 2.5 :

Design and implement synchronous BCD counter using T flip flops. **[May 2005, 8 M]**

Solution :

- From example, we know that a BCD counter requires four flip flops.
- BCD counter is a truncated counter. In BCD up counter 0 to 9 are used states while 11 to 15 are unused states. Next state of unused state is unknown. Let it be don't care. Therefore the corresponding flip flop input is also don't care.
- The table 2.19 consist of present state, next state & the required input of flip flop.

Table 2.19

Present state				Next state				Flip flip input			
Q_3	Q_2	Q_1	Q_0	Q'_3	Q'_2	Q'_1	Q'_0	T_3	T_2	T_1	T_0
0	0	0	0	0	0	0	1	0	0	0	1
0	0	0	1	0	0	1	0	0	0	1	1
0	0	1	0	0	0	1	1	0	0	0	1
0	0	1	1	0	1	0	0	0	1	1	1
0	1	0	0	0	1	0	1	0	0	0	1
0	1	0	1	0	1	1	0	0	0	1	1
0	1	1	0	0	1	1	1	0	0	0	1
0	1	1	1	1	0	0	0	1	1	1	1
1	0	0	0	1	0	0	1	0	0	0	1
1	0	0	1	0	0	0	0	1	0	0	1

- Now we represent each individual input in a K-map and obtain the simplified expressions.

K-map for $T_3 \Rightarrow$

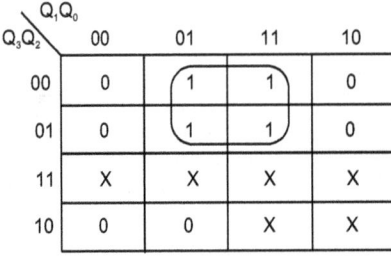

$$\therefore T_3 = Q_3 Q_0 + Q_2 Q_1 Q_0$$

K-map for $T_2 \Rightarrow$

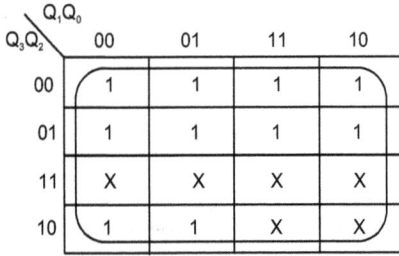

$$\therefore T_2 = Q_1 Q_0$$

K-map for $T_1 \Rightarrow$

$Q_3Q_2 \backslash Q_1Q_0$	00	01	11	10
00	0	1	1	0
01	0	1	1	0
11	X	X	X	X
10	0	0	X	X

$$\therefore T_1 = \bar{Q_3} Q_0$$

K-map for $T_0 \Rightarrow$

$Q_3Q_2 \backslash Q_1Q_0$	00	01	11	10
00	1	1	1	1
01	1	1	1	1
11	X	X	X	X
10	1	1	X	X

$$\therefore T_0 = 1$$

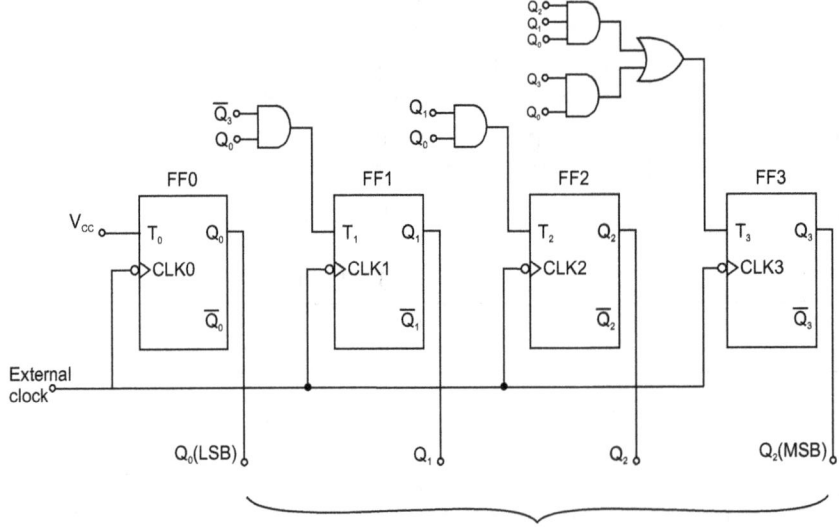

Fig. 2.54

Based on the above expressions the resulting circuit diagram is shown in Fig. 2.54.

2.15 RING COUNTER

Q. Write short note on Ring counter. [Dec. 08]

Q. Explain ring counter design having initial state 01011 from initial state explain all possible states in the ring. [Dec. 10, 10 M]

Q. Explain Ring counter design having initial state 10110. [May 11, 4 M]

- The shift register acts as ring counter, if the serial output is connected back to the serial input as shown in Fig. 2.55.

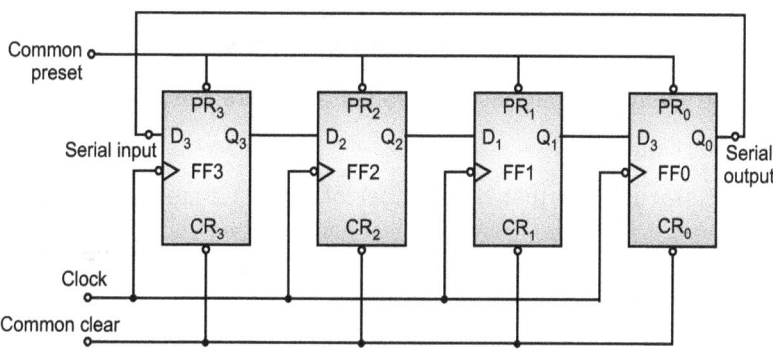

Fig. 2.55 : Ring counter

- Let us consider the initial state of the circuit as $Q_3 Q_2 Q_1 Q_0 = 1000$.
- The output of each flip flop after every clock pulse will be as shown in the table 2.20.

Table 2.20

Clock pulse Number	Q_3	Q_2	Q_1	Q_0
Initially	1	0	0	0
1	0	1	0	0
2	0	0	1	0
3	0	0	0	1
4	1	0	0	0

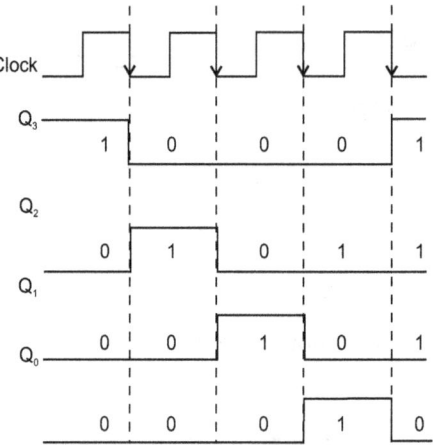

Fig. 2.56 : Waveforms of ring counter

- The n-bit ring counter counts n clock pulses, therefore the circuit shown in Fig. 2.56 counts four clock pulses.
- From table 2.20 it is clear that the number of distinct states in the operation of this counter is four. Therefore, it is a mod - 4 counter. In general n-bit ring counter is mod- n counter. The waveforms are as shown in Fig. 2.56.
- From the waveforms it is clear that, frequency of pulses obtained at any output is equal to frequency of clock pulses divided by four. Therefore this counter is a divide by four ($\div 4$) counter.
- In general n-bit ring counter is a divide by n ($\div$ n) counter.
- The outputs Q_3, Q_2, Q_1 & Q_0 are sequential non-overlapping pulses which can be used to excite the stepper motor.

Example 2.6 :

Explain ring counter design having initial state 01011.

- There are 5 bits in the given initial state, so we have to use 5 flip flops as shown in Fig. 2.57.
- When apply clear (CLR) pulse then flip flop will preset to 1 output and 4 and 2 are reset to 0 output.

$$Q_4\ Q_3\ Q_2\ Q_1 = 01011$$

Fig. 2.57 shows the arrangement of 5 bit ring counter.

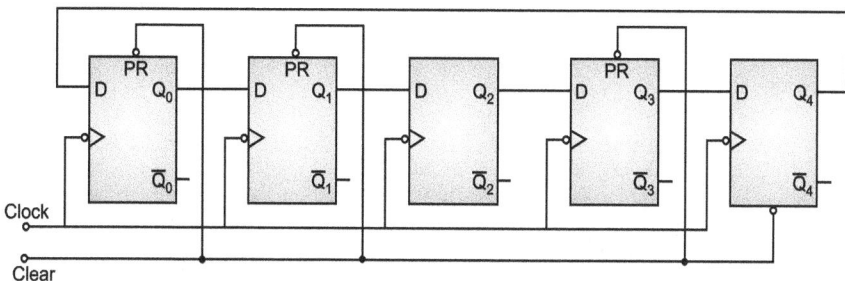

Fig. 2.57

Table 2.21 : 5-bit ring counter table

CLR	CLK	Q₀	Q₁	Q₂	Q₃	Q₄
0	1	1	1	0	1	0
1	1	0	1	1	0	1
1	1	1	0	1	1	0
1	1	0	1	0	1	1
1	1	1	0	1	0	1
1	1	1	1	0	1	0

2.15.1 Johnson Counter

Q. Explain the Johnson's counter design for initial state 0110. From initial state explain and draw all possible state. **[Dec. 09, 8 M]**

- It is also known as twisted ring counter or moebius counter.
- The shift register acts as a Johnson counter if the $\bar{Q}_0$ output is connected to the serial input as shown in Fig. 2.58.

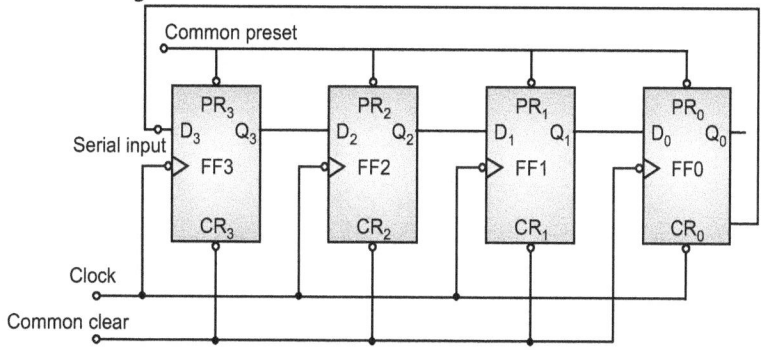

Fig. 2.58 : Johnson counter

- Initially all the flip flops are cleared using the common clear input ie. the initial state of the circuit is $Q_3 Q_2 Q_1 Q_0 = 0000$.
- The output of each flip flop after clock pulse will be as shown in the table 2.22.

Table 2.22

Clock pulse Number	Q_3	Q_2	Q_1	Q_0
Initially	0	0	0	0
1	1	0	0	0
2	1	1	0	0
3	1	1	1	0
4	1	1	1	1
5	0	1	1	1
6	0	0	1	1
7	0	0	0	1
8	0	0	0	0

- From table 2.22 it is clear that the number of distinct states in the operation of this counter is eight. Therefore it is a mod 8 counter. In general, every n-bit Johnson counter is a mod 2n counter. The waveforms are as shown in Fig. 2.59.

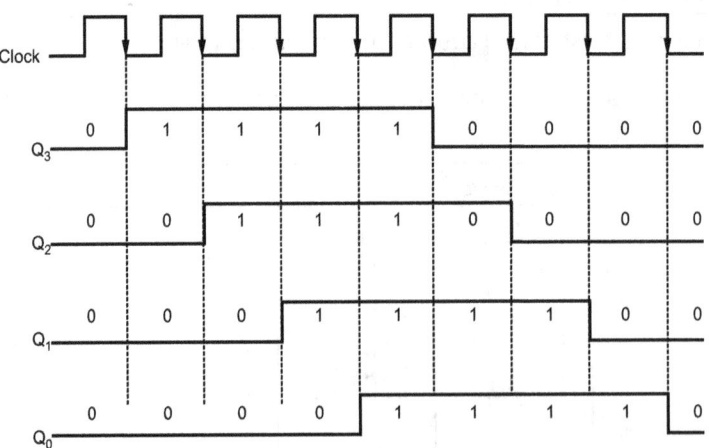

Fig. 2.59 : Waveforms of Johnson counter

- As shown in Fig. 2.59 square waveforms are obtained at each flip flop output.
- Also for completion of one cycle, each output requires eight clock pulses therefore it is a divide by 8 (÷ 8) counter.
- In general, n-bit Johnson counter is a divide by 2n (÷ 2n) counter.

Example 2.7 :

Design Johnson counter using 2-bit shift register.

Draw waveforms. [PU 2007, 4 M]

Solution :

- A 2-bit Johnson counter can be designed using two flip flops. When the output of FF0 is connected to the D_1 input of FF1 as shown in Fig. 2.60 we get the 2 bit Johnson counter.

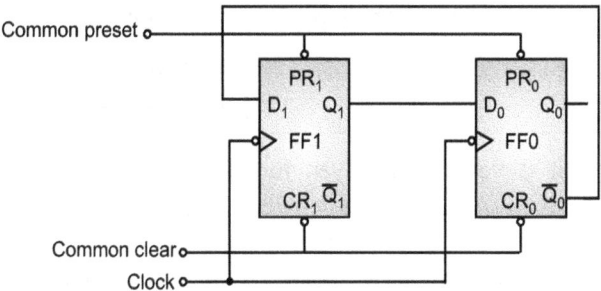

Fig. 2.60 : 2-bit Johnson counter

- The waveforms are shown in Fig. 2.61.

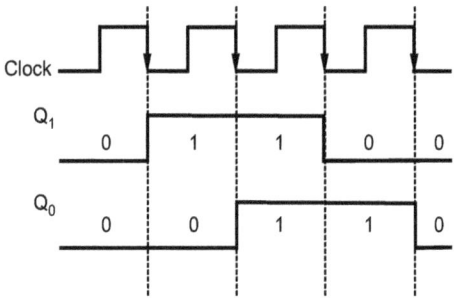

Fig. 2.61 : Waveforms of 2-bit Johnson counter

2.16 DIFFERENCE BETWEEN SYNCHRONOUS AND ASYNCHRONOUS COUNTERS

Table 2.23 : Synchronous Vs asynchronous counters

Sr. No.	Asynchronous counters	Synchronous counters
1.	In this type of counter flip-flops are connected in such a way that output of first flip-flop drives the clock for the next flip-flop.	In this type there is no connection between output of first flip-flop and clock input of the next flip-flip.
2.	Main drawback of these counters is their low speed as the clock is propagated through number of flip-flips before it reaches last flip-flop.	As clock is simultaneously given to all flip-flop there is no problem of propagation delay. Hence they are high speed counters and are preferred when number of flip-flop increase in the given design.
3.	Logic circuit is very simple even for more number of states.	Design involves complex logic circuit as number of state increases.
4.	All the flip-flops are not clocked simultaneously.	All the flip-flops are clocked simultaneously.

Unit - III

OPERATIONAL AMPLIFIER

3.1 INTRODUCTION

- The term operational amplifier or op-amp was first used by John R. Ragazzini in 1947. The op-amp is a multistage amplifier which has number of amplifier stages interconnected to each other.
- The first operational amplifier or op-amp was introduced in the market by Fairchild company as µA 741. The op-amp is used in number of applications.

3.2 BLOCK DIAGRAM OF AN OPERATIONAL AMPLIFIER

Q. Explain the block diagram of IC 741 Op-Amp. [Dec. 11, 4 M]

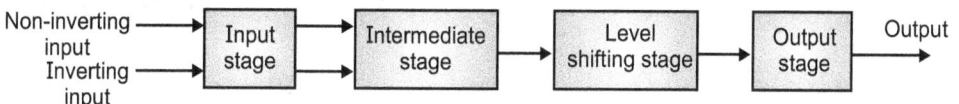

Fig. 3.1 : Block diagram of an operational amplifier

- The input stage is the dual input balanced output differential amplifier. This stage provides most of the gain of the amplifier and also sets the input resistance of the op-amp.
- The second stage is the intermediate stage i.e. another differential amplifier which is driven by the output of the first stage. In most amplifiers second stage is dual input - unbalanced output. Due to direct coupling between all the stages, the dc voltage at the output of intermediate stage goes above the ground level.
- To shift that dc level back to the ground, a level shifting or level translator circuit is used.
- The final stage is the output stage. The output stage is usually a push-pull complementary amplifier. The output stage increases the output voltage swing and raises the current supplying capability of the op-amp. Output stage also provides low output resistance.
- An operational amplifier is a direct coupled, high gain amplifier which consists of one or more differential amplifiers and a level translator and an output stage. The output stage is a push-pull or push-pull complementary symmetry pair.

- The operational amplifier is a versatile device that can be used to amplify DC as well as AC input signals. It was originally designed for computing mathematical functions as addition, subtraction, multiplication and integration.
- If the suitable feedback components are added, the modern day op-amp can be used for a variety of applications such as ac and dc signal amplification, active filters, oscillators, comparators, regulators and others.

3.3 EQUIVALENT CIRCUIT OF AN OP-AMP

Q. Draw the equivalent circuit of an op-amp. **[May 11, 4 M]**

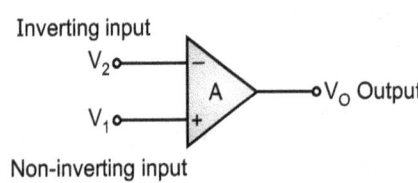 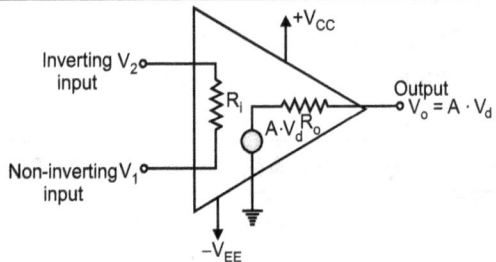

(a) Symbol for op-amp (b) Equivalent circuit of an op-amp

Fig. 3.3

Fig. 3.3 (b) shows the equivalent circuit of an op-amp. The equivalent circuit is useful in analyzing the basic operating principles of op-amps as well as to observe the effects of feedback arrangement. For the circuit shown above, the output voltage is

$$V_O = AV_d = A(V_1 - V_2)$$

where,
- A = Large signal voltage gain
- V_d = Difference input voltage
- V_1 = Voltage at the inverting input terminal
- V_2 = Voltage at the non-inverting input terminal.

3.4 IDEAL OP-AMP CHARACTERISTICS

Q. Explain briefly the parameters of ideal operational amplifier.

[Dec. 11, 4 M, Dec. 12, 2 M]

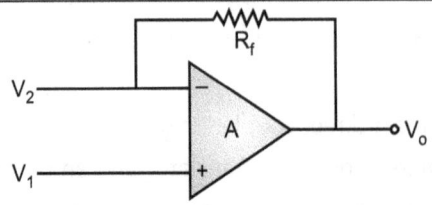

Fig. 3.4 : Ideal op-amp

The ideal amplifier is assumed to have the following characteristics :

1. **Infinite input impedance** : It ensures that no current flows into the amplifier input terminals. Fig. 5.7 shows $I1 = I2 = 0$. Any source can drive it and there is no loading on the driver stage.

2. **Zero output impedance** : The output impedance is denoted as Zo and is zero for an ideal op-amp. This ensures that the output voltage of the op-amp remains same, irrespective of the value of load resistance connected.

3. **Infinite voltage gain** : The gain of an ideal op-amp is infinite (∞), hence the differential input $Vd = V1 - V2$ is essentially zero for the finite output voltage Vo.

4. **Zero voltage and current offset** : It ensures that when the input signal voltage is zero, the output signal will also be zero regardless of the input source resistance.

5. **Infinite bandwidth** : The range of frequency over which the amplifier performance is satisfactory is called its bandwidth. The bandwidth of an ideal op-amp is infinite. This ensures that the gain of op-amp will be constant over the frequency range from zero to infinity. So op-amp can amplify d.c. as well as a.c. signals.

6. **Infinite CMRR** : The ratio of differential gain and common mode gain is defined as common mode rejection ratio (CMRR). An ideal op-amp has infinite CMRR which ensures zero common mode gain. Due to this common mode, noise output voltage is zero for an ideal op-amp.

7. **Infinite slew rate** : Slew rate (SR) is defined as the maximum rate of change of output voltage per unit time and is expressed in volt per microsecond (V/µs).

$$SR = \left.\frac{dV_o}{dt}\right|_{maximum} \quad V/\mu s$$

This is important parameter of op-amp. When the input voltage applied is step type which changes instantaneously then the output also must change rapidly as input changes. If output does not change with the same rate as input then there occurs distortion in the output. Such a distortion is not desirable.

Infinite slew rate indicates that output changes simultaneously with the changes in the input voltage.

8. **Power supply rejection ratio (PSRR)** : Changing the supply voltages alters the operating point of the internal transistors, and this in turn induces a change in V_{OS}.

Supply voltage change is expressed in terms of the power supply rejection ratio.

$$PSRR = \frac{\Delta V_{OS}}{\Delta V_{supply}}$$

Some manufacturers give separate PSRR ratings for change in v_{CC} and v_{EE}.

$$PSRR = \left.\frac{\Delta V_{OS}}{\Delta V_{CC}}\right|_{V_{EE} \text{ constant}}$$

or

$$PSRR = \left.\frac{\Delta V_{OS}}{\Delta V_{EE}}\right|_{V_{CC} \text{ constant}}$$

It is expressed in mV/V or µV/V and ideal value is zero.

These are ideal characteristics of op-amp which are summarized in the following Table 3.1.

Table 3.1

Characteristics	Symbol	Ideal value
Open loop voltage gain	A_{OL}	∞
Input impedance	Z_{in}	∞
Output impedance	Z_o	0
Offset voltage	V_{OS}	0
Bandwidth	BW	∞
CMRR	ρ	∞
Slew rate	SR	∞
Power supply rejection ratio	PSRR	0

3.5 PRACTICAL OP-AMP CHARACTERISTICS

- The characteristics of an ideal op-amp can be approximated closely enough, for many practical op-amps. Practically, they have an open loop gain which is very large (in the region of 10^5 to 10^6) but the gain is not infinite. They have large but finite input impedance. They draw small currents at their input terminal. This can cause a marked effect on the performance of op-amp application, particularly when it is used in application involving frequency dependent performance parameter.

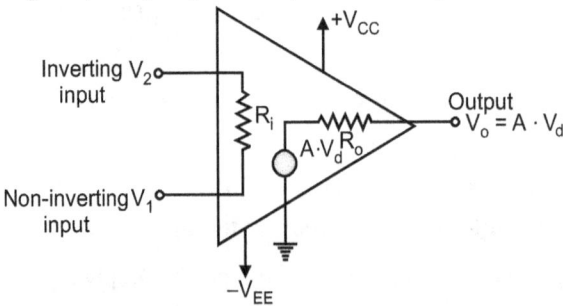

Fig. 3.5 : Practical op-amp

The Fig. 3.5 shows the equivalent circuit of a practical op-amp.

The various characteristics of practical op-amp can be described as below :

(a) Input impedance : It is finite and typically greater than 1 MΩ. But using FETs for the input stage, it can be increased upto several hundred MΩ.

(b) Output impedance : It is typically few hundred ohms. With the help of negative feedback, it can be reduced to very small value like 1 or 2 ohms.

(c) Open loop gain : Ideally, open loop gain is infinite, means when no feedback is applied. Practically, it is of the range of several thousands.

(d) Input offset voltage : Whenever both input terminals (i.e. INV and NON-INV) of the op-amp are grounded, ideally the output voltage should be zero. However, practical op-amp shows a small non-zero output voltage. To make this output voltage zero, a small voltage in the range of mV is required to be applied to one of the input terminals. Such voltage makes the output zero. This d.c. voltage, which makes the output voltage zero, when other terminal is grounded is called input offset voltage (V_{os}). How much voltage (V_{os}) is required is specified by the manufacturer in the data sheet.

(e) Input bias current : Ideally, no current flows into the input terminal. Practical op-amp have some input currents which are very small, of the order of 10^{-6} to 10^{-14} A.

Most of the op-amps use differential amplifier as the input stage. The two transistors of the differential amplifier must be biased correctly. But practically, it is not possible to get exact matching of the two transistors. Thus, the input terminals which are the base terminals of two transistors, do conduct the small d.c. current. These currents of two transistors are denoted as I_{b_1} and I_{b_2}.

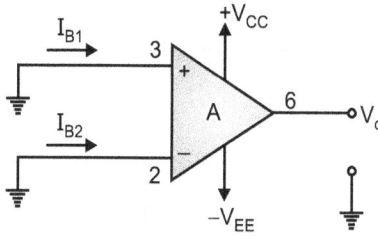

Fig. 3.6 : Input bias currents

So input bias current can be defined as 'the current flowing into each of the two input terminals when they are biased to the same voltage level i.e. when the op-amp is balanced'.

Input bias current I_B is the average of currents that flow into the inverting and non-inverting input terminals of the op-amp.

In the equation form, it is expressed as,

$$\text{Input bias current, } I_B = \frac{|I_{b_1}| + |I_{b_2}|}{2}$$

Ideally, input bias current is zero but practically it is in the range of nA.

For example, for 74IC, $I_b = \pm 7$ nA, for LM74IC it is 80 nA typically.

(f) Input offset current : The algebraic difference between the I_{b_1} and I_{b_2} is called input offset current and denoted as I_{io}.

$$I_{io} = |I_{b_1} - I_{b_2}|$$

Ideally, I_{io} is zero. But practically the magnitude of this current is very small, of the order of 20 to 60 nA. It is measured under the condition that input voltage to op-amp is zero. If we supply equal d.c. currents to the two inputs, output voltage of op-amp must be zero. But practically, there exists some voltage at the output. To make it zero, the two input currents are made to differ by small amount. The difference is treated as input offset current.

(g) Slew rate : Slew rate (SR) is defined as the maximum rate of change of output voltage per unit of time and is expressed in volt per microsecond. The slew rate of op-amp is high but not infinite. Higher the value of slew rate, better is the performance of the op-amp. The slew rate of IC 741 op-amp is 0.5 V/μs.

(h) Power supply rejection ratio : The PSRR for practical op-amp is very small but not zero. The typical value of PSRR for IC 741 op-amp is 30 μV/V.

3.5.1 Comparison of Ideal and Practical Characteristics

Let us compare the ideal and practical characteristics for a popular general purpose op-amp IC 741.

Table 3.2 : Ideal and Practical Parameters of IC 741

Parameter	Symbol	Ideal	Typical for 741 IC
Open loop voltage gain	A_{OL}	∞	200,000
Output impedance	Z_{out}	0	75 Ω
Input impedance	Z_{in}	∞	2 MΩ
Input offset current	I_{ios}	0	20 nA
Input offset voltage	V_{ios}	0	2 mV
Bandwidth	BW	∞	1 MHz
CMRR	ρ	∞	90 dB
Slew rate	S	∞	0.5 V/μsec
Input bias current	I_b	0	80 nA
Power supply rejection ratio	PSRR	0	30 μV/V
Power consumption	–	–	50 mV

3.6 OP-AMP CONFIGURATION

3.6.1 Open Loop Configuration of Op-Amp

Q. Explain open loop configuration of op-amp. [Dec. 10, 4 M]

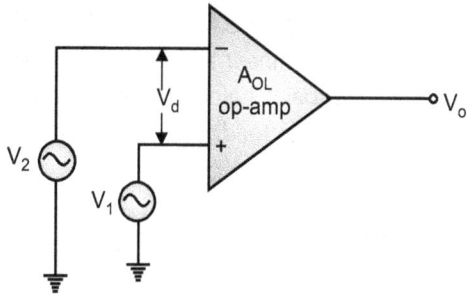

Fig. 3.7 : Open loop configuration of op-amp

- The simple way to use an op-amp is in the open-loop mode. The output voltage of op-amp varies linearly only between the two supply voltages applied to the op-amp that is V_{CC} and $-V_{EE}$.

- Due to the very large gain in open-loop condition, the output voltage is either at $+V_{sat}$ and $-V_{sat}$ as $V_1 > V_2$ or $V_2 > V_1$ respectively. Therefore, very small noise voltage present at the input also gets amplified due to its high open-loop gain and op-amp operates in saturation.

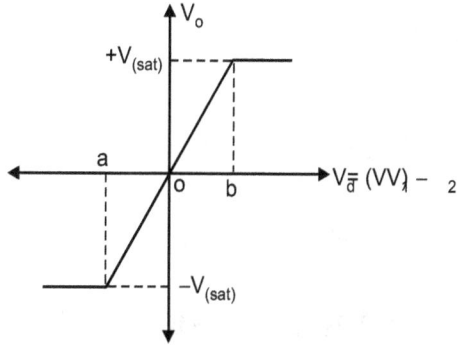

Fig. 3.8 : Transfer characteristics of open-loop op-amp

Fig. 3.8 shows the transfer characteristics of open-loop op-amp. It is clear that output is linear only for a small range of input i.e. from point a to b. This range is very small. This indicates the inability of op-amp to work as a linear small signal amplifier in the open-loop mode. Therefore, op-amp is generally not used in open-loop configuration.

3.6.2 Closed Loop Operation of Op-amp

Q. Explain close loop configuration of op-amp. [Dec. 10, 4 M]

As seen earlier, the op-amp cannot operate linearly in open-loop mode. But the utility of an op-amp can be increased by operating it in closed loop mode. The closed loop operation of an op-amp is possible with the help of feedback. The feedback allows to feed some part of the output back to input terminals. In the linear applications, the op-amp is always used with negative feedback. The negative feedback helps to control gain of the op-amp. The –ve feedback is possible by adding a resistor in feedback path as shown in Fig. 3.9.

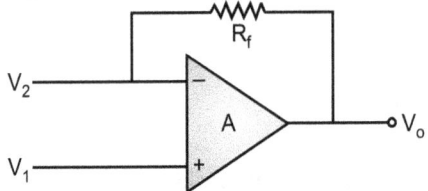

Fig. 3.9 : Closed loop configuration of op-amp

The gain resulting with feedback is called closed loop gain of the op-amp. Due to feedback resistance, there is a reduction in the gain. The closed loop gain is much less than the open-loop gain.

Most of the linear circuits use op-amp in a closed loop mode with negative feedback with R_f. This is because due to reduction in gain, the output is not driven into the saturation and the circuit behaves in a linear manner.

The advantages of negative feedback are :

- It reduces the gain and makes it controllable.
- It reduces the possibility of distortion.
- It increases the bandwidth i.e. frequency range.
- It increases the input resistance of the op-amp.
- It decreases the output resistance of the op-amp.
- It reduces the effect of temperature, power supply on the gain of the circuit.

3.7 COMPARISON OF IDEAL VS PRACTICAL CHARACTERISTICS OF IC 741C

Parameter	Symbol	Ideal	Typical for IC 741C
Open loop voltage gain	A_{OL}	∞	2×10^5
Input offset voltage	V_{io}	0	6 mV
Input offset current	I_{io}	0	20 nA
Input bias current	I_B	0	80 nA

Input impedance	R_i	∞	2 MΩ
Output resistance	R_o	0	75 Ω
Power Supply Rejection Ratio	PSRR	0	30 µV/V
Common Mode Rejection Ratio	CMRR	∞	90 dB
Bandwidth	BW	∞	1 MHz
Slew Rate	SR	∞	0.5 V/µs
Power consumption	P_C	0	50 mw

3.8 APPLICATIONS OF OP-AMP

3.8.1 Op-amp Comparators

Q. Explain the application of OP-AMP as a comparator. [Dec. 11, 5 M]

- A comparator is a circuit which compares a signal voltage which is applied to one of the terminal of op-amp with a known reference voltage at another terminal of the op-amp.

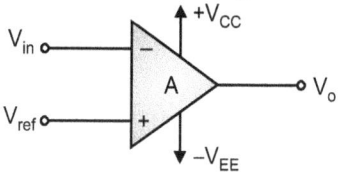

Fig. 3.10 : Basic comparator

- The output is produced either high or low output voltage depending upon which input is greater. The comparator has two output levels high or low. It is not linear with input voltage. The two voltages are compared with each other and output V_o is either $+V_{sat}$ or $-V_{sat}$ as A_{OL} is very large.

- Depending upon the application of the input to which terminal, the comparators are divided into two categories :
  1. Inverting comparator,
  2. Non-inverting comparator.

3.8.1.1 Basic inverting comparator

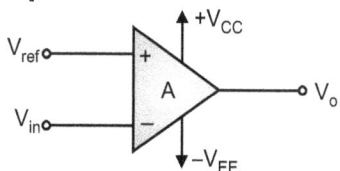

Fig. 3.11(a) : Inverting Comparator

- Fig. 3.11 (a) shows the inverting comparator in which the reference voltage V_{ref} is applied to the non-inverting input terminal of the op-amp and signal voltage V_{in} is applied to the inverting terminal of the op-amp. The V_{ref} can be set using a battery and potential divider.
- When V_{in} is less than V_{ref}, the output voltage V_o is at $+V_{sat}$ ($\approx +V_{CC}$) because of the output at the inverting input (−) is less than that at the non-inverting input.
- When V_{in} is greater than V_{ref}, the non-inverting (+) input becomes negative w.r.t. inverting input and V_o goes to $-V_{sat}$. The V_{ref} can be set positive and negative infinite values by using potential divider circuit.

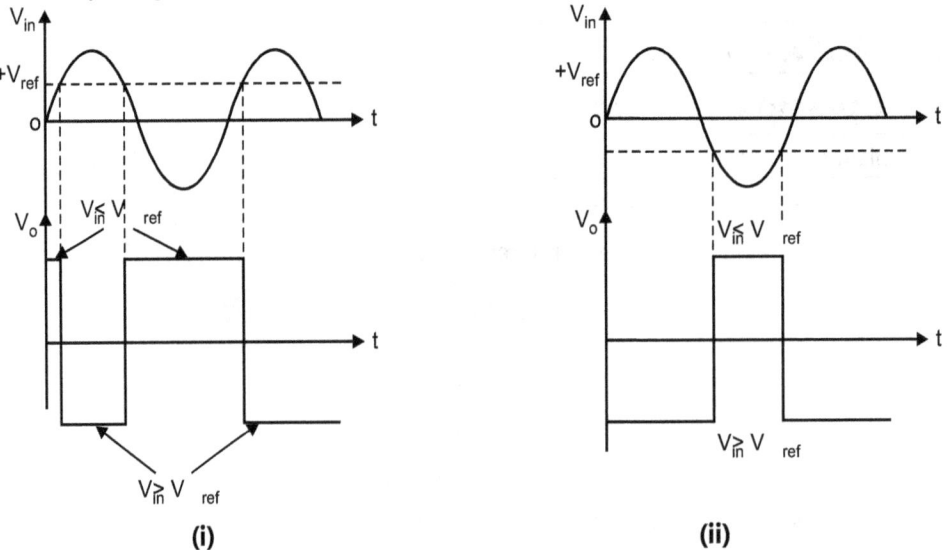

Fig. 3.11 (b) : Input and output waveforms when V_{ref} is (i) positive and (ii) negative

3.8.1.2 Non-inverting comparator

In a non-inverting comparator, a fixed reference voltage V_{ref} of 1 V is applied to the (−V) input and the other time-varying signal voltage V_{in} is applied to the (+) input.

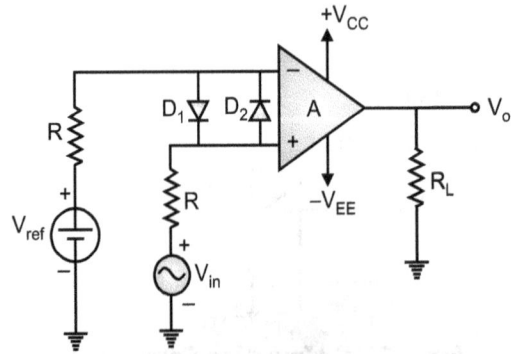

Fig. 3.12 : Practical non-inverting comparator

When V_{in} is less than V_{ref}, the output voltage V_o is at $-V_{sat}$ ($\approx -V_{EE}$) because the voltage at the (−) input is higher than that at the (+) input. On the other hand, when V_{in} is greater than V_{ref}, the (+) input becomes positive w.r.t. the (−) input, the V_o goes to $+V_{sat}$ ($\approx +V_{CC}$). The V_o changes from one saturation level to another whenever $V_{in} \approx V_{ref}$.

The comparator is a type of analog-to-digital converter. At any given time, the V_o waveform shows whether V_{in} is greater or less than V_{ref}. The comparator sometimes is also called as voltage level detector because for a desired value of V_{ref}, the voltage level of the input V_{in} can be detected.

In Fig. 3.12, diodes D_1 and D_2 are used to protect the op-amp from damage due to excessive input voltage V_{in}. The resistor R in series with V_{in} is used to limit the current through D_1 and D_2.

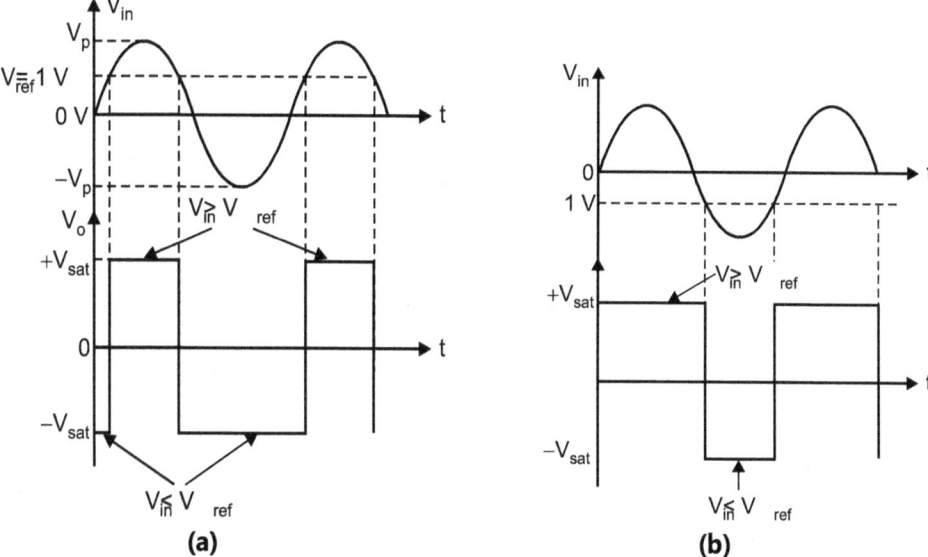

Fig. 3.13 : Input and output waveforms when V_{ref} is (a) positive and (b) negative

Fig. 3.13 shows the input and output waveforms for positive and negative reference voltage. If the reference voltage V_{ref} is negative w.r.t. ground, with a sinusoidal signal applied to the (+) input, the output waveforms will be as shown in Fig. 3.13 (b). When $V_{in} > V_{ref}$, V_o is $+V_{sat}$. On the other hand, when the $V_{in} < V_{ref}$, V_o is at $-V_{sat}$. Obviously, the amplitude of V_{in} must be large enough to pass through V_{ref} if the switching action is to take place.

3.8.1.3 Limitations of Op-amp as a comparator

- To obtain more accuracy of the comparator, a high CMRR, high gain and negligible input offset current and input offset voltage is required for the op-amp.
- To obtain the better response time, the switching of the op-amp must be fast between two saturation levels and it should also respond quickly to any change of input conditions.

3.8.1.4 Applications of comparators
- Voltage level detector.
- Zero crossing detector.
- Window detector.
- Pulse generator.
- Duty cycle controller.

3.8.1.5 Comparator characteristics
The important characteristics of the comparator are :
- Speed of operation
- Accuracy
- Compatibility.

1. Speed of operation :

The output of the comparator must switch rapidly between saturation levels and also respond instantly to any changes of input conditions. This implies that the bandwidth of the op-amp comparator must be rather wide; in fact, the wider the bandwidth, the higher is the speed of operation. The speed of operation of the comparator is improved with positive feedback (hysteresis).

2. Accuracy :

The accuracy of the comparator depends on its voltage gain, common-mode rejection ratio, input offsets and thermal drifts. High voltage gain requires a smaller difference voltage (hysteresis voltage) to cause the comparator's output voltage to switch between saturation levels.

On the other hand, a high CMRR helps to reject the common-mode input voltages, such as noise at the input terminals. Finally, to minimize the offset problems, the input offset current and input offset voltage must be negligible, also the changes in these offsets due to temperature variations, should be very slight.

3. Compatibility of output :

Since, the comparator is a form of analog-to-digital converter, its output must swing between the two logic levels suitable for a certain logic family such as Transistor-Transistor Logic (TTL).

3.8.1.6 Comparator IC

µA 311 Comparator :

µA 311 is a precision comparator designed for low level signal detection and high level output drive capability. It can operate from ± 15 V op-amp supplies down to single + 5 V supply used for IC logic. In addition, it's output can drive RTL, DTL, TTL and MOS logic as well as lamps or relays. Outputs can also be wire ORed. The input slew rate can be increased by increasing the input stage current

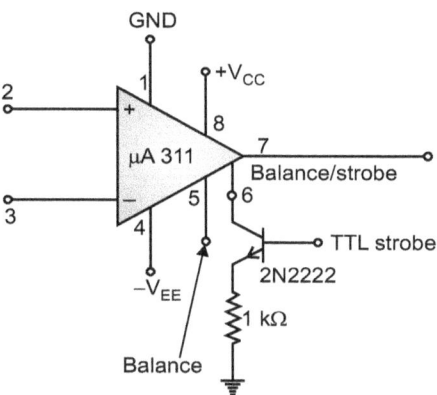

Fig. 3.14 : µA 311 comparator connection diagram

The µA 311 has input offset voltage balancing and TTL strobe capability. The strobe capability allows the comparator's output to either respond to input signals or be independent of input signals. The response time is typically 200 ns for 100 mV input step with 5 mV overdrive.

The µAF 311 is a FET input comparator that has two input currents (I_{io} and I_B) more than 1000 times lower than the µA 311. Except for this difference, the µAF 311 has the same characteristics and features as the µA 311.

3.8.2 Schmitt Trigger

3.8.2.1 Inverting schmitt trigger

Q. Explain with neat diagram Schmitt Trigger as an application of op-amp. [Dec. 10, 8 M]
Q. Explain application of op-amp as Schmitt Trigger. [May 11, 8 M]

Fig. 3.15 (a) shows the inverting comparator with positive feedback. The circuit has the ability to convert an irregular-shaped waveform to a square wave or pulse. The circuit is known as Schmitt trigger or Squaring circuit.

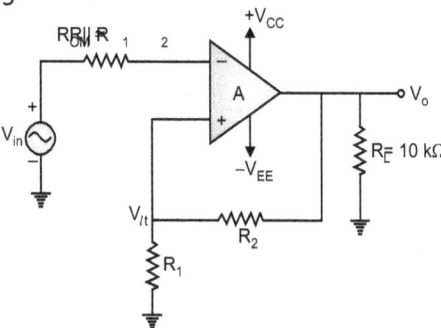

Fig. 3.15 (a) : Inverting comparator as a Schmitt trigger

The input voltage V_{in} triggers or changes the state of the output V_o every time it exceeds certain voltage levels called the upper threshold voltage V_{ut} and lower threshold voltage V_{lt} as shown in Fig. 3.15 (b) (waveforms).

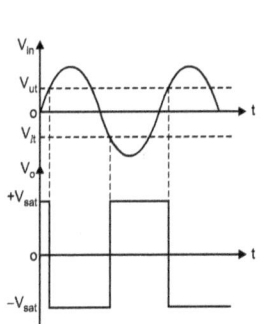
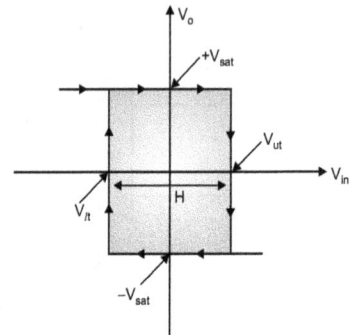

Fig. 3.15 (b) : Input and output waveforms of Schmitt trigger

Fig. 3.15 (c) : V_o versus V_{in} plot of the hysteresis voltage

$$H = V_{ut} - V_{lt}$$

These threshold voltages are obtained by using the voltage divider $R_1 - R_2$ where the voltage across R_1 is fed back to the (+) input. The voltage across R_1 is a variable reference threshold voltage that depends on the value and polarity of the output voltage V_o.

When $V_o = +V_{sat}$, the voltage across R_1 is called the upper threshold voltage V_{ut}. The input voltage V_{in} must be slightly more positive than V_{ut} in order to cause the output V_o to switch from $+V_{sat}$ to $-V_{sat}$. As long as $V_{in} < V_{ut}$, V_o is at $+V_{sat}$. Using the voltage divider rule,

$$V_{ut} = \frac{R_1}{R_1 + R_2}(+V_{sat})$$

On the other hand, when $V_o = -V_{sat}$, the voltage across R_1 is referred to as the lower threshold voltage V_{lt}. V_{in} must be slightly more negative than V_{lt} in order to switch from $-V_{sat}$ to $+V_{sat}$.

$$V_{lt} = \frac{R_1}{R_1 + R_2}(-V_{sat})$$

Thus, if the threshold voltages V_{ut} and V_{lt} are made larger than the input noise voltages, the positive feedback will eliminate the false output transitions. Also, the positive feedback, because of its regenerative action, will make V_o switch faster between $+V_{sat}$ and $-V_{sat}$.

Fig. 3.15 (b) shows the output of the Schmitt trigger is a square wave when input is a sine wave.

The comparator with positive feedback is said to exhibit hysteresis, a dead band condition means, when the input of the comparator exceeds V_{ut}, its output switches from $+V_{sat}$ to $-V_{sat}$, and reverts back to its original stage, $+V_{sat}$, when input goes below V_{lt}. The hysteresis voltage is equal to the difference between V_{ut} and V_{lt}.

$$V_H = V_{ut} - V_{lt}$$
$$= \frac{R_1}{R_1 + R_2}[+V_{sat} - (-V_{sat})]$$

3.8.2.2 Non-inverting schmitt trigger

When the input is applied to non-inverting terminal with positive feedback then the circuit is called as non-inverting Schmitt trigger. Fig. 3.16 shows the circuit diagram of the non-inverting Schmitt trigger.

Fig. 3.16 (a) non-inverting Schmitt trigger.

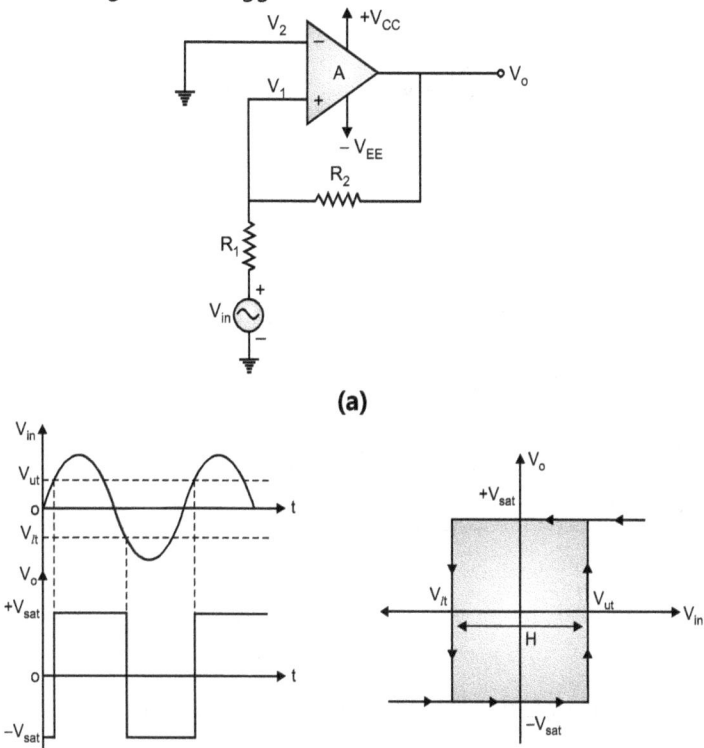

(b) Input and output waveforms of non-inverting Schmitt trigger

(c) V_o versus V_{in} plot the hysteresis voltage

Fig. 3.16

When the input voltage V_{in} is more negative, the output voltage will be $-V_{sat}$ because the input is applied to non-inverting terminal of the op-amp. To change the state increase V_{in} such that $V_1 = 0$. This point when the output changes its state from $-V_{sat}$ to $+V_{sat}$ is called upper threshold level and the value of V_{in} such that $V_1 = 0$ forces the op-amp to change its output from $+V_{sat}$ to $-V_{sat}$ is called lower threshold level.

The value of V_1 can be obtained by applying superposition rule as :

$$V_1 = \frac{R_1}{R_1 + R_2} V_o + \frac{R_2}{R_1 + R_2} \times V_{in}$$

To obtain V_{ut} and V_{lt} point V_1 should be 0 V.

$$\therefore \quad 0 = \frac{R_1}{R_1 + R_2} V_o + \frac{R_2}{R_1 + R_2} V_{in}$$

$$\frac{-R_1}{R_1 + R_2} V_o = \frac{R_2}{R_1 + R_2} V_{in}$$

$$\therefore \quad V_{in} = \frac{-R_1}{R_2} V_o$$

$$\therefore \quad V_{ut} = \frac{-R_1}{R_2}(-V_{sat}) = \frac{R_1}{R_2} V_{sat}$$

$$\therefore \quad V_{lt} = \frac{-R_1}{R_2}(+V_{sat})$$

$$= \frac{-R_1}{R_2} V_{sat}$$

The hysteresis voltage or hysteresis width (H) is given by

$$H = V_{ut} - V_{lt} = \frac{R_1}{R_2} V_{sat} + \frac{R_1}{R_2} V_{sat} = \frac{2R_1}{R_2} V_{sat}$$

3.8.3 Comparison of Schmitt Trigger and Comparator :

Comparator	Schmitt trigger
1. It does not use feedback.	1. It uses feedback.
2. The op-amp is used in open loop configuration.	2. The op-amp is used in closed loop configuration.
3. False triggering is possible due to noise.	3. False triggering due to noise is not possible.
4. A single reference voltage is present i.e. V_{ref} to trigger.	4. The two different triggering voltages are present i.e. V_{ut} and V_{lt}.

3.8.4 Zero Crossing Detector

Q. Explain the application of op-amp as ZCD. [Dec. 11, 5 M]
Q. Explain op-amp use used as ZCD and it practical applications. [May 12, 8 M]
Q. Explain op-amp as zero crossing detector. [Dec. 12, 4 M]

The basic comparator can be used as a zero crossing detector provided with $V_{ref} = 0$ V. Fig. 3.17 (a) shows the inverting comparator used as a zero crossing detector. Fig. 3.17 (b) also shows the output voltage V_o waveform when and in what direction an input signal V_{in} crosses the zero volts. That is the output V_o is driven into negative saturation when the input signal V_{in} passes through zero in the positive direction.

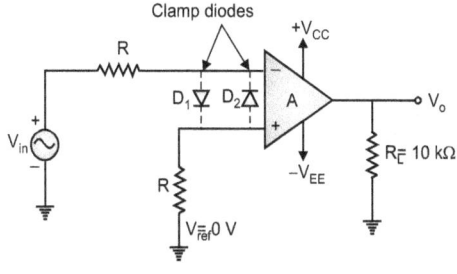
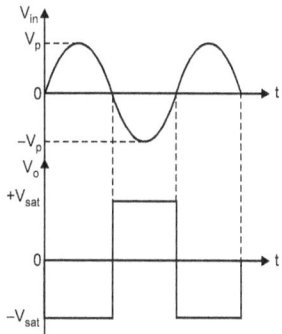

Fig. 3.17 (a) : Zero crossing detector

Fig. 3.17 (b) : Typical input and output waveforms

- In some applications, the input V_{in} may be a slowly changing waveform, that is, a low-frequency signal. Therefore, it will take V_{in} more time to cross 0 V; therefore V_o may not switch quickly from one saturation voltage to the other.

- On the other hand, because of the noise at the op-amp's input terminals, the output V_o may fluctuate between two saturation voltages $+V_{sat}$ and $-V_{sat}$, detecting zero reference crossings for noise voltages as well as V_{in}.

- Both of these problems can be solved with the use of regenerative or positive feedback that causes the output V_o to change faster and eliminate any false output transitions due to noise signals at the input.

3.8.5 Current to Voltage Converter

Current Scaling

The op-amps considered previously are suitable for scaling input signal voltages. In many applications there is a need to scale the output from current sources such as light sensitive diodes. Light sensitive diodes provide a reverse leakage current proportional to the light intensity at their PN junction.

A current-to-voltage converter is also called as transresistance amplifier. It converts an input current I_{in} into the output voltage V_o such that

$$V_o = A\, I_{in}$$

where A is the gain of the circuit in volts/ampere. Fig. 3.18 shows the current to voltage converter, which is the special case of the inverting amplifier.

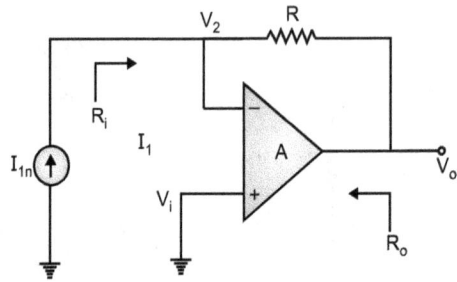

Fig. 3.18 : Basic I to V converter

Assume that op-amp is ideal

∴ $V_1 = V_2$

Apply KCL at node V_2

$$I_{in} + \frac{V_o - V_2}{R} = 0$$

Since $V_2 = 0$

$$I_{in} = \frac{-V_o}{R}$$

$$\boxed{V_o = -R\, I_{in}}$$

Here the gain is – R and is negative. The magnitude of the gain is also called as the sensitivity of the converter since it gives the amount of output voltage change for a given input current change. The gain can be varied by replacing R by a potentiometer when the feedback element is not pure resistive then the circuit is called as transimpedance amplifier.

There are two parameters that must be considered while designing current to voltage converter. They are

(a) The possibility of closed-loop in instability.

(b) The reduction of drift errors that determines conversion accuracy.

1. Closed-loop stability :

The closed loop stability is assured by externally connected capacitor C_f in parallel with scaling resistor R. The importance of offset is dependent upon the size of the current to be measured and the processing accuracy required. Fig. 3.19 shows an op-amp current-to-voltage converter.

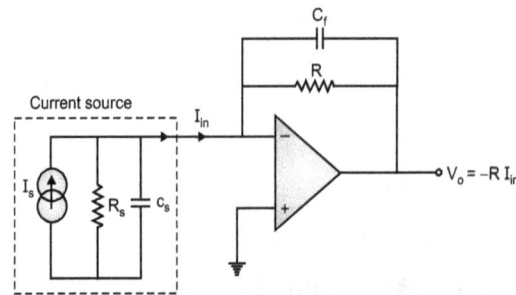

Fig. 3.19 : Current to voltage converter for stability analysis

Stability is determined by the source capacitance source capacitance causes a phase lag in the feedback signal at the higher frequencies, which can lead to insufficient phase margin.

2. Conversion Accuracy :

In many practical applications of the current-to-voltage converter, R_s will be greater than the value of scaling resistor R. If the impedance of the source current is lower than R, then noise gain will increase and loop gain decreases. Therefore accuracy decreases and there will be increase in drift error due to op-amp input offset voltage temperature dependence.

The total input offset voltage is given by

$$V_{os} = V_{ios} + (R \| R_s) I_b^-$$

The equivalent input and error current is given by

$$I_{os} = \left[1 + \frac{R}{R_s}\right] \frac{V_{os}}{R}$$

$$= \frac{V_{ios}}{(R_s \| R)} + I_b^-$$

The input bias current is the main source of the error. Therefore, a low bias current op-amp must be chosen for accurate measurement of small current. Generally FET input op-amps are used for measurement of small currents.

3.8.5.1 High Sensitivity I-V converter

High sensitivity applications requires large resistances. The resistance of the surrounding medium comes in parallel with R which decreases the net feedback resistance and degrade the accuracy of the circuit. Therefore a T-network is used to achieve high sensitivity without requiring unrealistically large resistances. Fig. 3.20 shows the high sensitivity I-V converter.

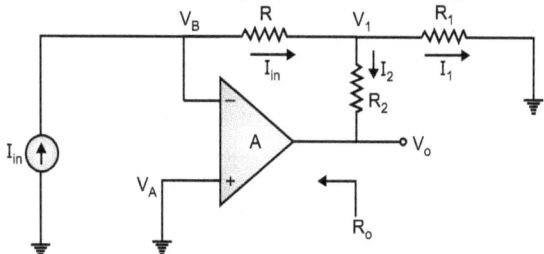

Fig. 3.20 : High sensitivity I-V converter

Apply KCL at node V_1

$$V_{in} - I_1 - I_2 = 0$$

$$I_{in} = I_1 + I_2$$

But

$$I_{in} = \frac{V_B - V_1}{R} = \frac{0 - V_1}{R} = \frac{-V_1}{R}$$

$$I_1 = \frac{V_1}{R_1}, \quad I_2 = \frac{V_1 - V_o}{R_2}$$

$$\frac{-V_1}{R} = \frac{V_1}{R_1} + \frac{V_1 - V_o}{R_2}$$

$$\frac{V_1}{R} - \frac{V_1}{R_1} - \frac{V_1}{R_2} + \frac{V_o}{R_2} = 0$$

$$-V_1 \left[\frac{1}{R} + \frac{1}{R_1} + \frac{1}{R_2} \right] = \frac{-V_o}{R_2}$$

$$V_1 \left[\frac{1}{R} + \frac{1}{R_1} + \frac{1}{R_2} \right] = \frac{V_o}{R_2}$$

$$V_o = R_2 V_1 \left[\frac{1}{R} + \frac{1}{R_1} + \frac{1}{R_2} \right]$$

Substitute the value of V_1

$$V_o = -I_{in} R R_2 \left[\frac{1}{R} + \frac{1}{R_1} + \frac{1}{R_2} \right]$$

$$V_o = -K R I_{in}$$

where,
$$K = 1 + \frac{R_2}{R} + \frac{R_2}{R_1}$$

The sensitivity of the original I to V converter has been increased by a factor K.

3.8.5.2 Application of I-V converter

One of the most frequent I-V converter application is sensing the current from photodetectors.

Photodetectors are transducers that produce electrical current in response to incident light or other forms of radiation, such as X-rays. I-V converter is used to covert this current to a voltage as well as eliminating possible loading both at the input and at the output.

Commonly used photodetector is the silicon photodiode. The device can be used either with a reverse bias voltage, in the photoconductive mode or zero bias, in the photovoltaic mode.

The photoconductive mode offers high speed therefore it is used for the detection of high-speed light pulses and to high-frequency light beam modulation applications.

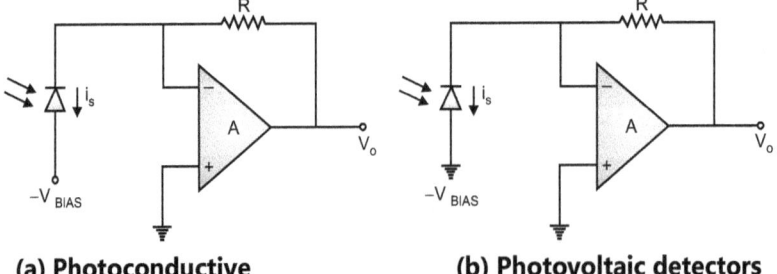

(a) Photoconductive   (b) Photovoltaic detectors

Fig. 3.21

The photovoltaic mode offers lower noise and is suited to measurement and instrumentation applications. Therefore, it is used as a light meter by calibrating its output directly in units of light intensity.

3.8.6 Voltage to Current Converter with Floating Load

Fig. 3.22 shows a voltage to current converter in which load resistor R_L is floating (i.e. not connected to ground).

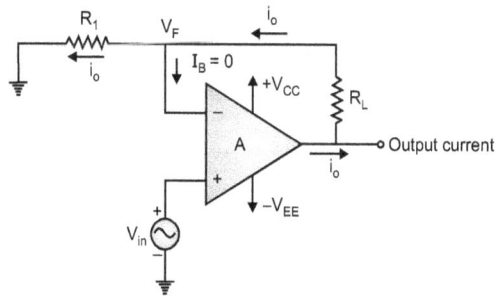

Fig. 3.22 : Voltage to current converter with floating load

Input voltage is applied to non-inverting input terminal and the inverting input is drived by the feedback voltage across R_1. This type of circuit is also called a current series negative feedback amplifier because the feedback voltage across R_1 depends on the output current i_o and it is in series with the input difference voltage V_{id}.

Applying Kirchhoff's voltage equation for the input loop,

$$V_{in} = V_{id} + V_f \quad \text{... (3.1)}$$

But $V_{id} \approx 0$ V. Since, A is very large, therefore,

$$V_{in} = V_f$$

$$V_{in} = R_1 i_o \quad \text{... (3.2)}$$

or

$$i_o = \frac{V_{in}}{R_1} \quad \text{... (3.3)}$$

Thus, it is shown that an input voltage V_{in} is converted into an output current of V_{in}/R_1.

3.8.6.1 Voltage to current converter with grounded load

Q. Explain grounded type load voltage to current converter.	[Dec. 10, 8 M]
Q. Explain voltage to current converter for grounded type load.	[May 12, 8 M]

Fig. 3.23 shows another version of the voltage to current converter. In this, one terminal of the load is grounded and load current is controlled by an input voltage.

Apply Kirchhoff's current law at node V_1.

$$I_1 + I_2 = I_L \quad \text{... (3.4)}$$

$$\frac{V_{in} - V_1}{R} + \frac{V_o - V_1}{R} = I_L$$

$$V_{in} + V_o - 2V_1 = I_L R$$

Therefore,
$$V_1 = \frac{V_{in} + V_o - I_L R}{2} \quad \ldots (3.5)$$

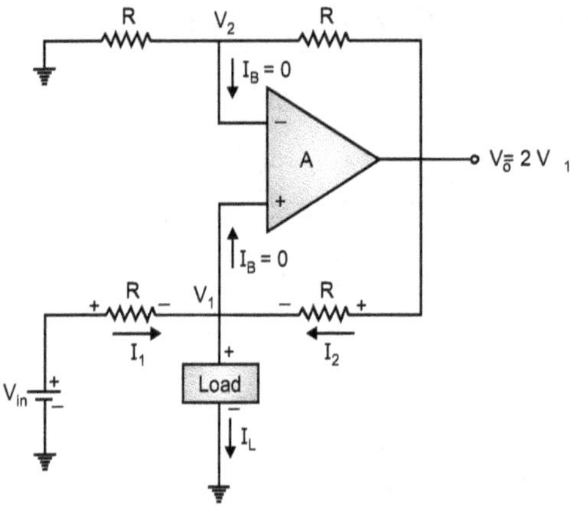

Fig. 3.23 : Voltage to current converter with grounded load

As the op-amp is connected in the non-inverting mode, the gain of the circuit is $1 + R/R = 2$. Then, the output voltage is

$$V_o = 2V_1 \quad \ldots (3.6)$$
$$V_o = V_{in} + V_o - I_L R$$
$$V_{in} - I_L R = 0$$

That is
$$V_{in} = I_L R$$

∴
$$I_L = \frac{V_{in}}{R} \quad \ldots (3.7)$$

It shows that the load current depends on the input voltage V_{in} and resistor R.

The voltage to current converter with grounded load may be used in testing devices such as zener and LEDs. The circuit will perform satisfactorily when the load size ≤ R value.

Applications of voltage to current converters :
- Low voltage DC and AC voltmeters.
- Diode match finders.
- Light emitting diodes (LEDs) and zener diode testers.

3.9 VOLTAGE REGULATORS

A voltage regulator is a circuit that provides a constant voltage even if there is a change in input voltage, or change in load current or change in temperature.

IC voltage regulators are versatile and relatively inexpensive. These ICs are available with various features such as :

- Programmable output,
- Current / Voltage boosting,
- Internal short-circuit current limiting,
- Thermal shutdown,
- Floating operation for high voltage applications.

3.9.1 Types of Voltage Regulators

- Fixed output voltage regulators,
- Adjustable output voltage regulators,
- Switching regulators,
- Special regulators.

Except the switching regulators, all other types are called linear regulators.

The impedance of a linear regulator's active element may be continuously varied to supply a desired current to the load.

In switching regulator a switch is turned ON and OFF at a rate such that the regulator delivers the desired average current in periodic pulses to the load.

Switching regulator is more efficient than the linear regulators because it dissipates negligible power in either the ON or OFF state.

3.9.2 Advantages of Voltage Regulators

- Simple to use.
- Reliable.
- Low in cost.
- Availability in a variety of voltage and current ratings.

3.9.3 Applications of Voltage Regulators

- Used for on-card regulation.
- Used for laboratory type power supplies.
- Switching regulators are used in pulse width modulation.
- Switching regulators are used in push-pull bridges and series type switch mode supplies.

3.10 BLOCK DIAGRAM OF 3 PIN IC REGULATOR

Three pin IC regulator has three terminals namely input, output and ground.

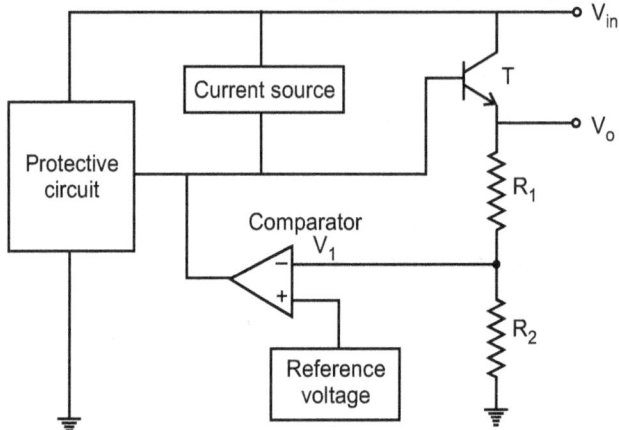

Fig. 3.24 : Block diagram of a 3 terminal regulator

- The reference voltage is generated internally into the IC. Due to zener diode which is inside the IC gives the reference voltage. The voltage V_1 is the fraction of the output voltage given by

$$V_1 = \left(\frac{R_2}{R_1 + R_2}\right) V_0$$

- This V_1 voltage is compared by comparator with the internally generated reference voltage. This comparator is also called as an error amplifier. The output of comparator controls the series pass transistor (T) and protection circuit.
- The main function of protective circuit is to protect the IC from any damage. The protective circuit controls the base current of series pass transistor.
- The protective circuit consists of current limit circuit, thermal shutdown circuit and safe area protection circuit. The thermal shutdown circuit prevents IC from any heating. The series pass transistor corrects the output voltage to the desired value of voltage. While designing a series pass regulator, the control element i.e. series pass transistor should be selected properly. The current source gives proper current to the base of a series pass transistor when required.

3.10.1 IC 78XX Positive Voltage Regulators

- The 78XX series is a three terminal positive voltage regulator with seven voltage options as 5, 6, 8, 12, 15, 18, 24V. These ICs are designed with adequate heat sinking which can deliver output currents in excess of 1 A. These ICs do not require external components. Internal thermal overload protection and internal short circuit current limiting is provided.
- IC 78XX is the positive voltage regulator. It is a three terminal IC namely, input, ground and output. The pin configuration of IC 78XX is shown in Fig. 3.25.

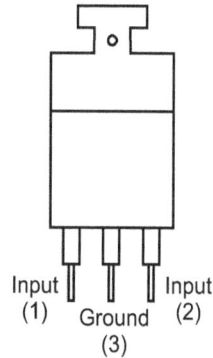

Fig. 3.25 : Pin configuration of IC 78XX

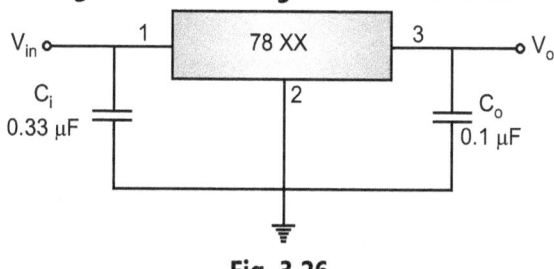

Fig. 3.26

- The difference between input and output voltages ($V_{in} - V_o$), called **dropout voltage**, must be typically 2.0 V even during the low point on the input ripple voltage.
- The capacitor C_i is used when the regulator is located an appreciable distance from a power supply filter. C_o is used to improve the transient response of the regulator.

3.10.1.1 Special Features

- It allows output current upto 1 A.
- It has internal thermal overload protection.
- It does not require external component.
- It also has output transistor safe area protection.
- For current limit, it has internal short circuit.

IC 7805, IC 7806, IC 7808, IC 7810, IC 7812 give the regulated positive voltages +5 V, +6 V, +8 V, +10 V and +12 V respectively. This shows that two digits after 78 prefix indicate the regulated output voltage. IC 78XX series is available in an aluminum package or plastic package which will allow load current upto 1 A. The adequate heat sink is provided. The internal shutdown circuit prevents the IC from overheating. It does not require external component. IC 78XX series is very cheap and easy to use.

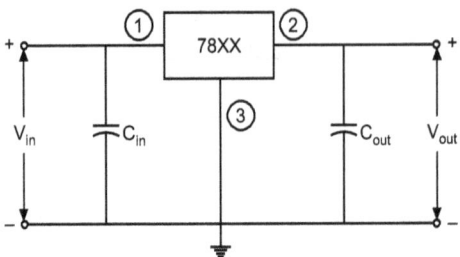

Fig. 3.27 : IC 78XX series positive voltage regulator

An unregulated input voltage V_{in} is applied to terminal (1) and we get regulated output voltage from terminal (2). This IC 78XX gives regulated output voltage even when the input voltage can vary. The input capacitor C_{in} and output capacitor C_{out} connected to ground are useful to maintain the output d.c. voltage. These capacitors are also useful to filter any high frequency voltage variation. The series of IC 78XX provides fixed positive voltage from 5 V to 24 V.

3.10.2 IC 79XX Negative Voltage Regulator Series :

- The 79XX series of fixed output negative voltage regulators are complements to the 7800 series devices. There are also available in the same seven options as the 78XX series. In addition, two extra voltage options, – 2 V and –5.2 V are also available in the negative 79XX series.
- IC 79XX is the negative voltage regulator. It is also three terminal IC namely, input, output and ground. The pin configuration of IC 79XX is shown in Fig. 3.28.

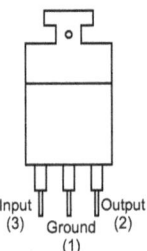

Fig. 3.28 : Pin configuration of IC 79XX

3.10.2.1 Special Features

- It does not require any external component for voltage regulator circuit.
- For current limit, it has internal short circuit.
- It has internal thermal overload protection.
- It allows output current upto 1 A.
- It also has output transistor safe area protection.

IC 7905, IC 7906, IC 7908, IC 7910 and IC 7912 give the regulated negative voltages −5 V, −6 V, −8 V, −10 V and −12 V respectively. Also IC 79XX series available in an aluminium package or plastic package allow load current upto 1 A. The adequate heat sink is provided. The internal shutdown circuit prevents the IC from overheating. IC 79XX is smaller in size and easy to use.

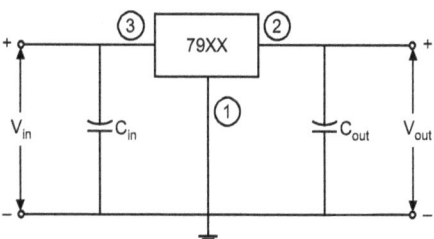

Fig. 3.29 : IC 79XX series negative voltage regulator

- An unregulated input voltage V_{in} is applied to terminal (3) and we get regulated output voltage at terminal (2). The input and output capacitors i.e. C_{in} and C_{out} are useful to maintain the regulated d.c. voltage. Any high frequency voltage is filtered out by capacitors. The series of IC 79XX provides fixed negative voltage from −5 V to −24 V.

- Finally, a current source circuit using a voltage regulator can be designed for a desired value of load current I_L. Here V_{in} depends upon the size of R_L and also the dropout voltage of the regulator.

3.11 PERFORMANCE PARAMETERS OF VOLTAGE REGULATORS

- Line regulation.
- Load regulation.
- Temperature stability.
- Ripple rejection.
- Line regulation is defined as the change in output voltage for a change in the input voltage and usually expressed in millivolts or as a percentage of output voltage V_o.
- Load regulation is the change in output voltage for a change in load current and is also expressed in millivolts or a percentage of V_o.
- Temperature stability or average temperature coefficient of output voltage (TCV$_o$) is the change in output voltage per unit change in temperature and is expressed in millivolts/°C or parts per million (ppm)/°C.
- Ripple rejection is the measure of a regulator's ability to reject ripple voltages. It is usually expressed in decibels.

The smaller the value of load regulation, line regulation and temperature stability, the better will be the regulator.

3.12 ADJUSTABLE VOLTAGE REGULATORS

Adjustable voltage regulators gives the answers to the excessive inventory and production costs because a single device satisfies many voltage requirements from 1.2 V upto 37 V.

Advantages of Adjustable Voltage Regulators over Fixed Voltage Regulators
- Improved system performance by having better line and load regulation.
- Improved overload protection allows greater output current over operating temperature range.
- Improved system reliability with each device being subjected to 100% thermal limit burn-in.

The LM317 is the most commonly used general purpose adjustable voltage regulator.

3.12.1 LM 317 Regulator

Q. Using LM317 explain variable voltage regulator with neat diagram.	[Dec. 10, 4 M]
Q. Explain the function of LM 317 as a voltage regulator.	[May 12, 8 M]
Q. Explain LM 317 as an adjustable voltage regulator.	[Dec. 12, 9M]

- LM317 series is a adjustable three terminal positive voltage regulators. The different grades are available in the series with output of 1.2 to 37 V and output current from 0.1 A to 1.5 A. The three terminals are V_{IN}, V_{OUT} and ADJUSTMENT (ADJ). Fig. 3.30 shows the diagram for the LM317 regulator.

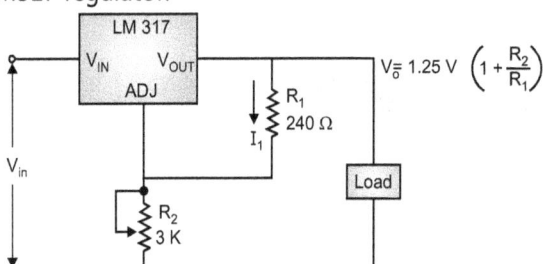

$$V_{\bar{o}} = 1.25\ V\ \left(1 + \frac{R_2}{R_1}\right)$$

Fig. 3.30 : Typical connection diagram for LM317 regulator

- When configured as shown in Fig. 3.30, the LM317 develops a nominal 1.25 V, referred to as the reference voltage V_{REF} between the output and adjustment terminal. This reference voltage is generated across resistor R_1 and since the voltage is constant, the current I_1 is also constant for a given value of R_1. Because resistor R_1 sets current I_1, it is called current set or program resistor.
- In addition to the current I_1, the current I_{ADJ} from the adjustment terminal also flows through the output set resistor R_2.
- The LM317 is designed such that I_{ADJ} is very small and constant with line and load changes. The maximum value of adjustment pin current I_{ADJ} is 100 μA.

From Fig. 3.30, the output voltage V_O is

$$V_O = R_1 I_1 + R_2 (I_1 + I_{ADJ})$$

where,

$$I_1 = \frac{V_{REF}}{R_1}$$

R_1 = Current (I_1) set resistor
R_2 = Output (V_O) set resistor
I_{ADJ} = Adjustment pin current

Substituting the value of I_1 and rearranging, we get

$$V_O = V_{ref}\left(1 + \frac{R_2}{R_1}\right) + I_{ADJ} R_2$$

where, V_{REF} = 1.25 V

Since I_{ADJ} is very small and constant, the voltage drop across R_2 due to I_{ADJ} is also very small and can be neglected.

$$V_O = 1.25\left(1 + \frac{R_2}{R_1}\right)$$

3.12.1.1 Practical circuit diagram of LM317 voltage regulator

Q. Using LM 317 explain variable voltage regulator with neat diagram.	[Dec. 10, 4 M]
Q. Explain the function of LM 317 as a voltage regulator.	[May 12, 8 M]
Q. Explain LM 317 as an adjustable voltage regulator.	[Dec. 12, 3 M]

Normally no capacitors are needed unless the LM317 is situated far from the power supply filter capacitors.

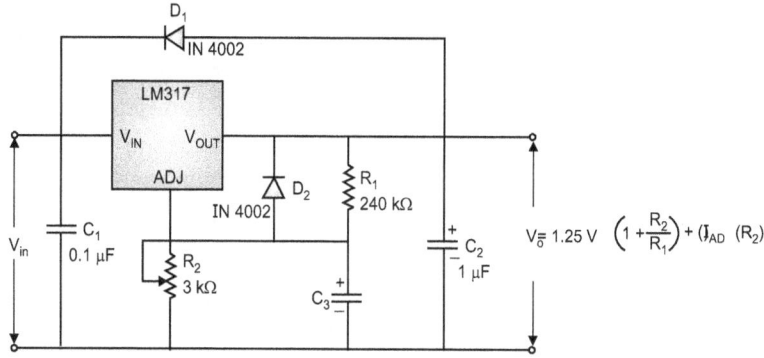

Fig. 3.31 : Practical LM317 regulator with capacitors and protective diodes

A 0.1 µF disc or 1 µF tantalum capacitor is suitable for input bypassing. Also an output capacitor C_2 can be added to improve transient response. Output capacitors in the range of 1 to 1000 µF of aluminium or tantalum electrolytic are commonly used to provide improved impedance and rejection of transients. The adjustment terminal can be bypassed with C_3 to obtain very high ripple rejection ratios, with a 10 µF bypass capacitor C_3, 80 dB ripple rejection is obtainable at any output level. Protection diodes are used to prevent the capacitors from discharging through low current points into the regulator. Protection diodes are included for use with outputs greater than 25 V and high values of output capacitance.

The important specifications of LM 317/LM 337 are given below:

Power dissipation (based on the package)	– 0.6 W to 20 W
Adjustable output voltage	– 1.2 V to 37 V
Line regulations	– 0.1 % / V (Typ)
Load regulation	– 0.1 % (Typ)
Standard 3-lead transistor packages	– TO_3, TO-39, TO-200 TO-202 and TO-92
Ripple rejection	– 80 dB

3.12.2 IC µA 723 Voltage Regulator

The µA 723 is a precision integrated-circuit voltage regulator.

3.12.2.1 Features of IC µA723

- 150-mA load current without external power transistor.
- Adjustable current limiting capability.
- Input voltages up to 40 V.
- Output adjustable from 2 V to 37 V.
- High ripple rejection.
- Excellent input and load regulation.
- Excellent temperature stability.

The µA 723 is a precision integrated circuit voltage regulator. The circuit consists of a temperature-compensated reference-voltage amplifier, an error amplifier, a 150-mA output transistor and an adjustable-output current limiter. The µA 723 is designed for use in positive or negative power supplies as a series, shunt, switching or floating regulator. For output currents exceeding 150 mA, additional pass elements can be connected.

3.12.2.2 Functional Block Diagram

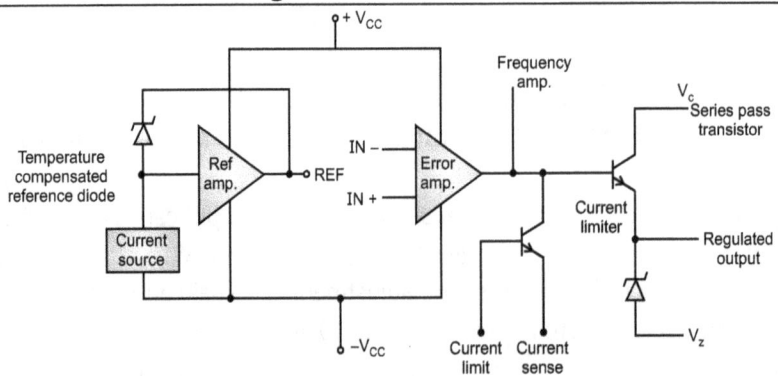

Fig. 3.32 : Functional block diagram

Fig. 3.32 shows the block diagram of IC µA 723. It is divided into four parts.
- Temperature compensated voltage reference source.
- Op-amp used as an error amplifier.
- A series pass transistor capable of 150 mA output current.
- Transistor to limit the output current.

The reference element consists of temperature compensated zener diode, constant current source and reference amplifiers. Zener diode is forced by the constant current source to operate at a fixed voltage. The output voltage is compared with the reference voltage of 7 V. V_{ref} is connected to the non-inverting input of the error amplifier.

The error amplifier is a high gain differential amplifier. The error amplifier controls the series pass transistor Q_1, which acts as a variable resistor. The series pass transistor is a small power transistor having about 800 mw dissipation.

Transistor Q_2 acts as a current limiter for short circuit condition. The frequency compensation terminal controls the frequency response of the error amplifier. The required roll-off is obtained by connecting a small capacitor of 100 pF between frequency compensation and inverting input terminals.

Fig. 3.33 below shows the pin diagram of IC µA 723.

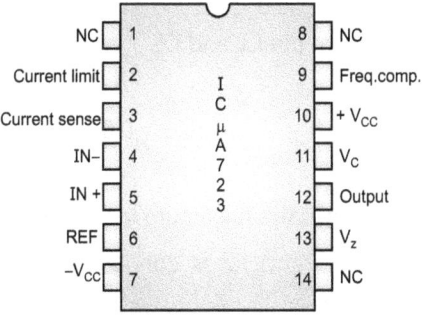

Fig. 3.33 : D or N package

3.12.2.3 Specification of IC µA 723

Table 3.3 shows the electrical specifications of IC 723.
Absolute maximum ratings over operating free-air temperature range.

Table 3.3

Peak voltage from V_{CC} + to V_{CC} (tw ≤ 50 ms)	50 V
Continuous voltage from V_{CC}^+ to V_{CC}^-	40 V
Input to output voltage differential	40 V
Differentials input voltage to error amplifier	± 5 V
Voltage between non-inverting input and V_{CC}^-	8 V
Current from V_z	25 mA
Current from V_{ref}	15 mA

Table 3.4 shows the recommended operating conditions.

Table 3.4

	Minimum	Maximum	Unit
Input voltage, V_i	9.5	40	V
Output voltage, V_o	2	37	V
Input-to-output voltage differential ($V_c - V_o$)	3	38	V
Output current, I_o	–	150	mA
Operating free-air temperature range TA	0	70	°C

3.12.2.4 Applications of IC µA 723

Different types of regulator circuits can be designed using IC 723.

3.12.2.5 Basic low voltage regulator

Fig. 3.34 shows the basic low voltage regulator whose output voltage can be obtained between 2 V to 7 V.

The resistor R_{sc} is connected between pin CL and CS.

The value of R_{sc} can be obtained as

$$R_{sc} = \frac{V_{sense}}{I_{limit}} = \frac{0.6}{I_{limit}}$$

I_{limit} can be selected as 1.2 to 1.5 times the maximum load current.

A potential divider made up of R1 and R2 is connected between v_{ref} and non-inverting terminals.

$$V_{non-inverting} = V_{ref} \times \frac{R_2}{R_1 + R_2}$$

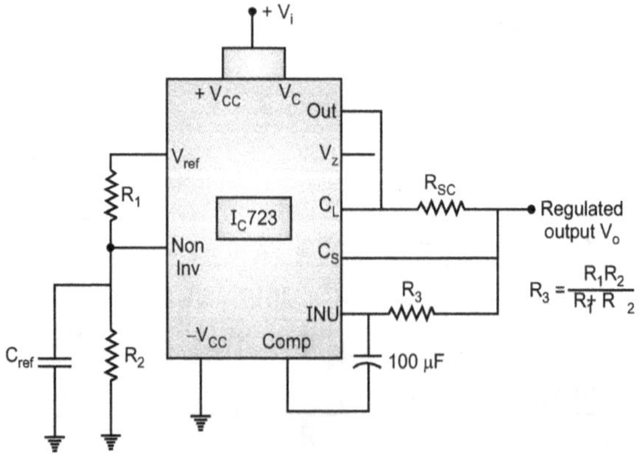

Fig. 3.34 : Basic low voltage regulator

Series pass transistor works as a emitter follower.

$$V_o = V_{ref} \times \frac{R_2}{R_1 + R_2}$$

$$R_3 = R_1 \parallel R_2$$

$$= \frac{R_1 R_2}{R_1 + R_2}$$

Maximum load current can be 150 mA.

3.12.2.6 Basic high voltage regulator (V_o = 7 V to 37 V)

Fig. 3.35 shows basic positive high voltage regulator. The output varies from 7 V to 37 V.

The gain $A = 1 + \dfrac{R_1}{R_2}$

The output voltage is calculated as

$$V_o = V_{ref}\left(1 + \frac{R_1}{R_2}\right)$$

$$= V_{ref}\left(\frac{R_1 + R_2}{R_2}\right)$$

$$R_{sc} = \frac{0.6}{I_{limit}}$$

$$= \frac{V_{sense}}{I_{sc}}$$

$$R_3 = R_1 \parallel R_2$$

$$= \frac{R_1 R_2}{R_1 + R_2}$$

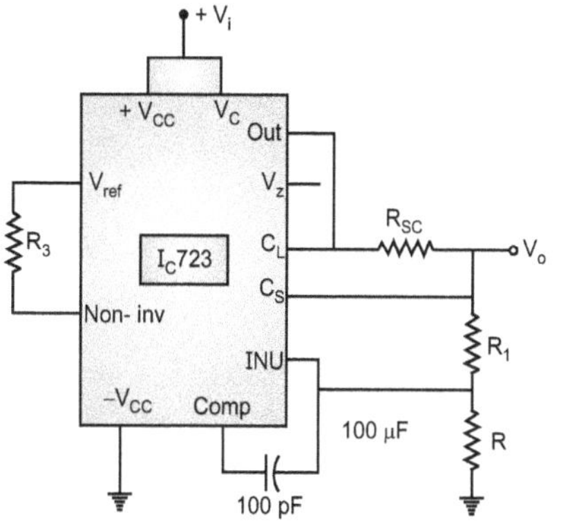

Fig. 3.35 : Basic high voltage regulator

3.12.2.7 Negative voltage regulator

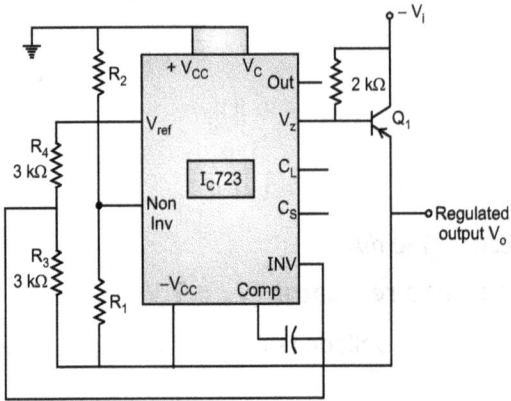

Fig. 3.36 : Negative voltage regulator

- Fig. 3.36 shows the IC µA 723 to obtain negative voltage regulator. An external PNP transistor, Q_1 is connected. Resistance can be used from 1 kΩ to 10 kΩ.

$$R_3 = R_4$$

$$V_{out} = \left[\frac{V_{ref}}{2} + \frac{R_1 + R_2}{R_1} \right]$$

- If magnitude of $-V_i$ is less than 9 V, connect V_{cc}^+ and V_c to a positive supply such that V_{cc}^+ to V_{cc}^- is greater than 9 V, for proper functioning of the IC.

Unit - IV

WAVE FORM GENERATION USING OP-AMP

4.1 SINE WAVE GENERATORS

- A sine wave generator or oscillator may be defined as a circuit which converts d.c. energy into a.c. energy at very high frequency.
- An amplifier produces an output signal whose waveform is similar to the input signal but its power level is generally high. This additional power to the output is supplied by the external d.c. source. Hence, an amplifier is essentially an energy converter i.e., it takes energy from the external d.c. source and converts it into energy at signal frequency.
- While oscillator does not require an external signal either to start or maintain energy conversion process. It produces an output signal as long as the d.c. power source is connected.

Types of oscillators :
Electronic oscillators are broadly divided into two groups, which are
(1) Sinusoidal oscillators.
(2) Non-sinusoidal oscillators.

Sinusoidal Oscillator
- An electronic device that generates sinusoidal oscillations of desired frequency is known as sinusoidal oscillator. The output of this oscillator is sine wave.

Non-sinusoidal Oscillator
- The oscillators which generate waveforms other than sine waveform are called non-sinusoidal oscillators. Non-sinusoidal waveforms include square wave, rectangular wave, sawtooth wave and pulse-shaped waves.

4.1.1 Barkhausen Criterion for Oscillations

- An amplifier with proper positive feedback can act as an oscillator i.e. it can generate oscillations without any external signal source.

For amplifier with positive feedback, the voltage gain is given by

$$A_f = \frac{V_o'}{V_{in}} \qquad \ldots(4.1)$$

Or

$$A_f = \frac{A}{1 - \beta A}$$

where, A = open-loop gain
βA = feedback factor
and A_f = closed-loop gain

To start oscillations a quick trigger signal is given to the circuit. Once the oscillations have started, no external signal source is needed. Since no external signal source is needed, the gain of the amplifier becomes infinite. This is possible only when $1 - \beta A = 0$ or $\beta A = 1$. This relation is called **Barkhausen criterion**.

4.2 RC PHASE-SHIFT OSCILLATOR USING IC 741

> Q. Explain sine wave generator using op-amp. Draw output waveforms. **[Dec. 10, 8 M]**
> Q. Draw the diagram and waveform of op-amp as sine wave generator. **[May 11, 6 M]**
> Q. Draw neat circuit diagram and explain op-amp as a sine wave generator.
> **[Dec. 12, 9 M]**

- IC 741 is an operational amplifier. The circuit diagram for phase-shift oscillator is shown in Fig. 4.18.
- It consists of conventional operational amplifier and RC phase-shift network. The phase-shift network consists of three sections each of RC and acts as a feedback circuit.
- It provides feedback voltage from the output back to the input of the amplifier. At some particular frequency f_o, the phase shift in each RC section is 60° so that the total phase shift produced by the RC network is 180°.
- This frequency is called frequency of oscillation and is given by

$$f_o = \frac{1}{2\pi \sqrt{6}\, RC} \qquad \ldots (4.2)$$

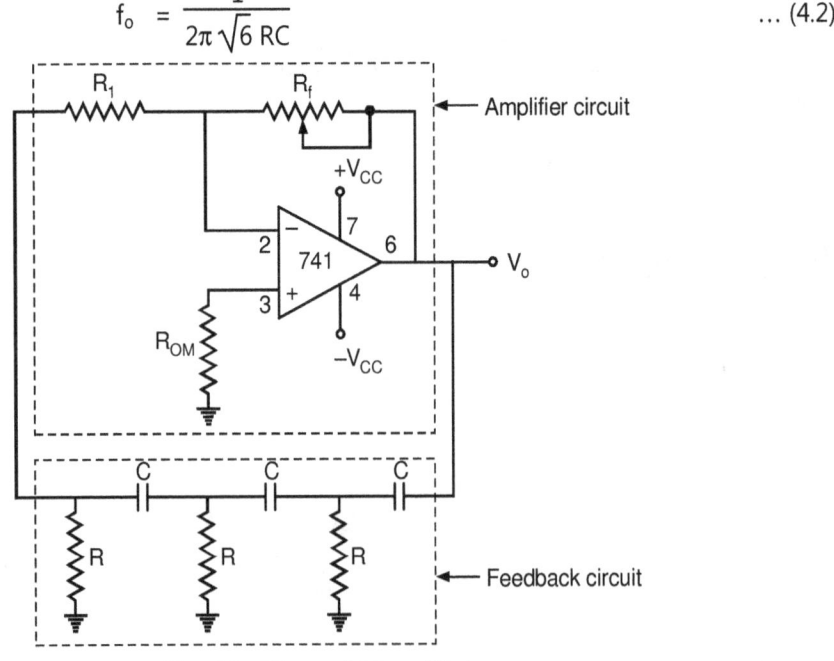

Fig. 4.1 : Phase-shift oscillator

- When the circuit is switched ON, it produces oscillations of frequency determined by equation (4.23). The output V_o of the op-amp is fed back to RC feedback network. The RC network produces 180° phase shift and a voltage V_i appears at its output.
- This voltage V_i is applied to the op-amp. The op-amp is used in the inverting mode, therefore, any signal that appears at the inverting terminal is shifted by 180° at the output. Thus, the phase shift around the entire loop is 360°.

4.2.1 Wein Bridge Oscillator using IC 741

- The Wein bridge oscillator is a standard oscillator circuit for all frequencies in the range of 10 Hz to about 1 MHz. Because of its simplicity and stability, it is most frequently used in audio oscillator.
- Fig. 4.2 shows the Wein bridge oscillator in which the Wein bridge circuit is connected between amplifier input terminal and the output terminal.
- The bridge circuit consists of a series R_1C_1 network in one arm and a parallel R_2C_2 network in the adjoining arm. The remaining two arms consist of resistors R_3 and R_F as shown in Fig. 4.2.

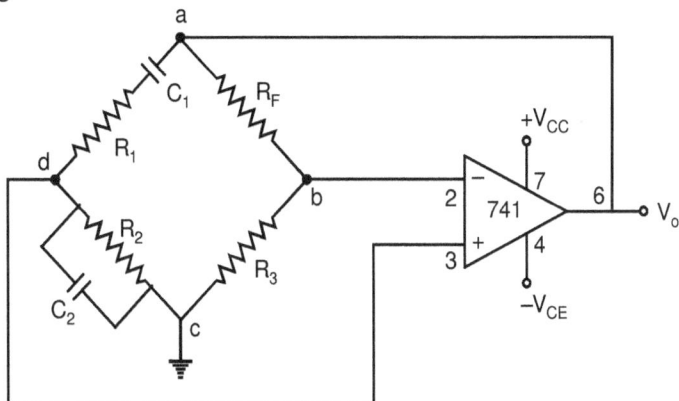

Fig. 4.2 : Wein bridge oscillator with IC 741

- The op-amp output is connected as the bridge input at points a and c. The bridge circuit output at points b and d is the input to the op-amp.
- The phase angle criterion for oscillation is that the total phase shift around the circuit must be zero (0°). This condition occurs only when the bridge is balanced i.e. at **resonance**.

The condition for balanced bridge is

$$\frac{R_F}{R_3} = \frac{R_1}{R_2} + \frac{C_2}{C_1}$$

and the resonant frequency is

$$f_o = \frac{1}{2\pi \sqrt{R_1C_1\,R_2C_2}} \quad \ldots (4.3)$$

If $R_1 = R_2 = R$ and $C_1 = C_2 = C$, the resultant oscillator frequency is

$$f_o = \frac{1}{2\pi RC} \qquad \ldots (4.4)$$

and $\dfrac{R_F}{R_3} = 2$ or $R_F = 2R$

The gain required for sustained oscillation is

$$A_f = 1 + \frac{R_F}{R_3} \text{ or } A_f = 3 \qquad \ldots (4.5)$$

Thus, to maintain oscillations, the closed-loop gain of the amplifier must be 3.

4.3 A SQUARE WAVE GENERATOR (ASTABLE)

Q. How can op-amp be used as generator ? Draw the necessary waveforms of the operation. [Dec. 11, 8 M]

- Square wave outputs are generated when the op-amp is forced to operate in the saturated region. That is, the output has to swing repetitively between positive saturation $+V_{sat}$ ($\cong +V_{CC}$) and negative saturation $-V_{sat}$ ($\cong -V_{EE}$), resulting in the square wave output.
- The square wave generator is also called as a free running or astable multivibrator. The output of the op-amp in this circuit will be in positive or negative saturation, depending on whether the differential voltage V_{id} is positive or negative respectively.

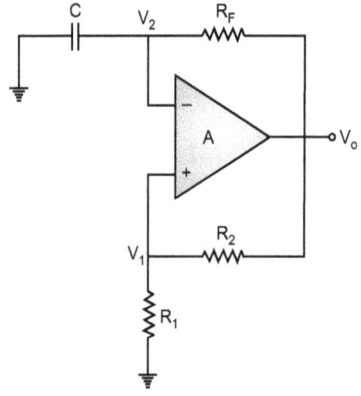

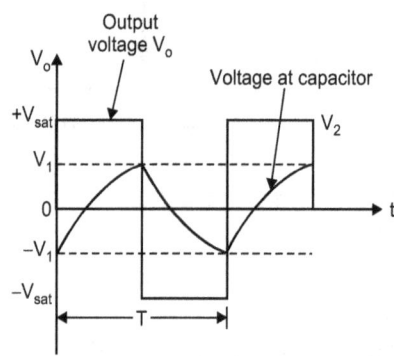

(a) Square wave generator   (b) Waveforms of output voltage

Fig. 4.3

- Assume that voltage across capacitor C is zero voltage when the DC supply voltages $+V_{CC}$ and $-V_{EE}$ are applied. This means that the voltage at the input inverting terminal is initially zero. At the same time the voltage V_1 at the non-inverting terminal is a very small finite value due to output offset voltage V_{OOT} and the values of resistors R_1 and R_2.

- Thus, the differential voltage V_{id} is equal to V_1. The voltage V_1 drives the op-amp into saturation. The capacitor C starts charging towards $+V_{sat}$ through resistor R.
- When the voltage V_2 across capacitor C is slightly more positive than V_1, the output of op-amp is forced to switch to a negative saturation $-V_{sat}$. The voltage V_1 across R_1 is also negative.

$$V_1 = \frac{R_1}{R_1 + R_2}(-V_{sat})$$

- Thus, the net differential voltage $V_{id} = V_1 - V_2$ is negative, which holds the op-amp in negative saturation. The output remains in negative saturation until the capacitor C discharges and then recharges to a negative voltage slightly higher than $-V_1$.
- As soon as the capacitor's voltage V_2 becomes more negative than $-V_1$, the net differential voltage V_{id} becomes positive and hence drives the op-amp back to positive saturation.

$$V_1 = \frac{R_1}{R_1 + R_2}(+V_{sat})$$

The time period T of the waveform is given by

$$T = 2RC \ln\left(\frac{2R_1 + R_2}{R_2}\right)$$

or

$$f_o = \frac{1}{2RC \ln\left[(2R_1 + R_2)/R_2\right]} \quad \ldots (4.6)$$

4.4 TRIANGULAR WAVE GENERATOR USING OP-AMP

Q. Explain application of op-amp as triangular wave generator. Also draw output waveform. **[May 11, 9 M]**

Q. How can op-amp be used as generator ? Draw the necessary waveforms of the operation. **[Dec. 11, 8 M]**

Q. Explain how triangular waveform can be generated using op-amp? Also draw waveform. **[May 12, 8 M]**

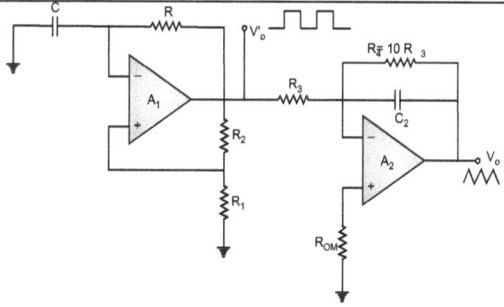

Fig. 4.4 (a) : Triangular wave generator using op-amp

- A triangular wave generator can be formed by simply connecting an integrator to a square wave generator as the output of the integrator is triangular if its input is a square wave.
- For fixed values of R_1, R_2 and C_1 the frequency of the square wave as well as the triangular wave depends on the resistance R. As R is increased or decreased, the frequency of the triangular wave will decrease or increase respectively.
- Since, the amplitude of the square wave is constant ($\pm V_{sat}$); the amplitude of the triangular wave decreases with an increase in its frequency and vice versa.

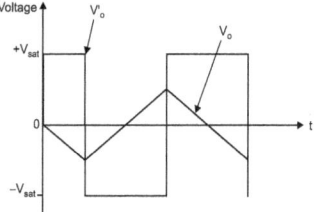

Fig. 4.4 (b) : Waveforms

- The frequency of oscillation is given by

$$f_o = \frac{R_3}{4R_1C_1R_2} \qquad \ldots(4.7)$$

4.5 PEAK DETECTOR

- A conventional ac voltmeter cannot be used to measure non-sinusoidal waveforms because it is designed to measure the rms value of the pure sine wave.
- The solution to this problem is to measure the peak value of the non-sinusoidal waveforms.
- Fig. 4.7 (a) shows a peak detector that measures the positive peak values of the square wave input.

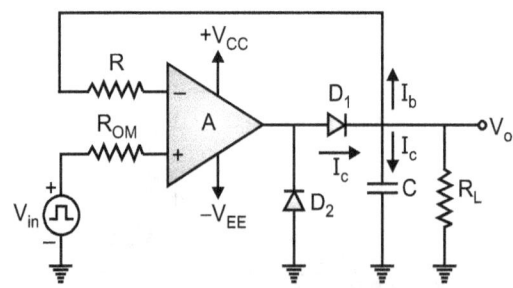

Fig. 4.5 (a) : Peak detector circuit

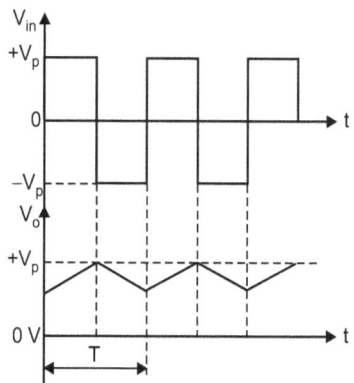

Fig. 4.5 (b) : Input and output waveforms

- During the positive half cycle of V_{in}, the output of the op-amp drives D_1 ON, charging capacitor C to the positive peak value V_p of the input voltage V_{in}. Thus, when D_1 is forward biased, the op-amp operates as a voltage follower.
- On the other hand, during the negative half cycle of V_{in}, diode D_1 is reverse biased and voltage across C is retained. The only discharge path for C is through R_L since the input bias current I_B is negligible for proper operation of the circuit, the charging time constant (CR_d) and discharging time constant (CR_L) must satisfy the following conditions :

$$CR_d \leq \frac{T}{10} \qquad \ldots (4.8)$$

where, R_d = Resistance of the forward diode, 100 Ω typically

T = Time period of the input waveform

and $CR_L \geq 10\,T$

where R_L is the load resistor.

- If R_F is very small then to satisfy the condition above, use a buffer between capacitor C and load resistor R_L. The resistor R is used to protect the op-amp against the excessive discharge currents, especially when the power supply is switched OFF.
- The resistor R_{OM} = R minimizes the offset problems caused by input currents. In addition, diode D_2 conducts during the negative half cycle of V_{in} and hence prevents the op-amp from going into negative saturation. The negative peaks of input signal V_{in} can be detected simply by reversing diodes D_1 and D_2.

4.6 INSTRUMENTATION AMPLIFIERS

Q. What is the role of op-amp as an instrumentation amplifier ?	[Dec. 11, 2 M]
Q. What is instrumentation amplifier ?	[Dec. 11, 2 M]
Q. Write a short note on op-amp as instrumentation amplifier.	[Dec. 12, 8 M]

- The measurement and control of physical quantities are very important in many industrial and consumer applications.

- Examples are :
  1. Measurement of temperature and humidity inside a dairy or meat plant to maintain the product quality.
  2. Precise temperature control of a plastic furnace is needed to produce a particular type of plastic.
- Generally, transducers are used to convert one form of energy into another form. An instrumentation amplifier is used to measure the output signal produced by a transducer and to control the physical signal producing it. Fig. 4.6 shows the simplified block diagram of such a system.

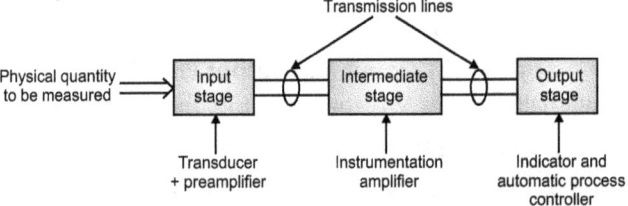

Fig. 4.6 : Block diagram of an instrumentation amplifier

- The input stage is composed of a preamplifier and some sort of transducer, depending on the physical quantity to be measured.
- The output stage may be devices such as meters, oscilloscopes, charts or magnetic recorders. The connecting lines between the blocks represents transmission lines, used when the transducer is at remote test site monitoring hazardous conditions. For example, high temperatures of liquid levels of flammable chemicals.
- The length of the transmission line depends upon the physical quantities to be monitored and an system requirements.
- The input to the instrumentation amplifier is the output of the transducer. Some transducers produce outputs with sufficient strength to use it directly, but many do not permit to use it directly. To amplify the low level output of the transducer, instrumentation amplifier is used.
- So, Instrumentation amplifier is used to amplify the low level output of the transducer.

4.6.1.1 Requirements of Instrumentation Amplifier

> **Q.** What are the basic requirements of good instrumentation amplifier ? **[May 12, 4 M]**

- Low level signal amplification where low noise, low thermal and time drifts.
- High input resistance.
- Accurate closed loop gain.
- Low power consumption.
- High common-mode rejection ratio.
- High slew rate.
- There are many instrumentation amplifiers such as µA 725, ICL 7605 and LH 0036.
- The requirements for instrumentation op-amp is more rigid than those for general purpose applications. Most of the instrumentation amplifiers use a transducer in a bridge circuit.

4.6.1 Instrumentation Amplifier using Transducer Bridge

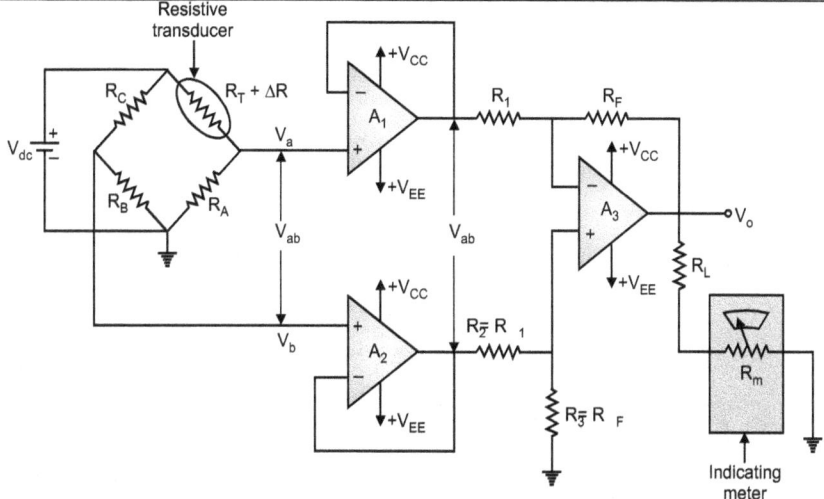

Fig. 4.7 : Differential instrumentation amplifier using a transducer bridge

Fig. 4.7 shows the simplified differential instrumentation amplifier using a transducer bridge.

- A resistive transducer whose resistance changes as a function of some physical energy is connected in one arm of the bridge with a small circle around it and is denoted by ($R_T \pm \Delta R$), where R_T is the resistance of the transducer and ΔR is the change in resistance R_T. The bridge is excited by DC.

- The bridge balance condition is

$$V_b = V_a$$

or

$$\frac{R_B (V_{dc})}{R_B + R_C} = \frac{R_A (V_{dc})}{R_A + R_T}$$

That is

$$\frac{R_C}{R_B} = \frac{R_T}{R_A}$$

- Generally, resistors R_A, R_B and R_C are selected so that they are equal in value to the transducer resistance R_T at some reference condition.

- The bridge is balanced at some reference condition. As the physical quantity to be measured changes, the resistance of the transducer also changes which causes the bridge to unbalance ($V_a \neq V_b$).

- Let the change in resistance of the transducer be ΔR. Since, R_B and R_C are fixed, the voltage V_b will be constant. Voltage V_a varies as a function of the change in transducer resistance.

- Therefore, according to voltage divider rule,

$$V_a = \frac{R_A (V_{dc})}{R_A + (R_T + \Delta R)}$$

$$V_b = \frac{R_B (V_{dc})}{R_B + R_C}$$

The voltage V_{ab} across the output terminals of the bridge is

$$V_{ab} = V_b - V_a = \frac{R_A V_{dc}}{R_A + R_T + \Delta R} - \frac{R_B V_{dc}}{R_B + R_C}$$

However, if $R_A = R_B = R_T = R$, then

$$V_{ab} = \frac{R V_{dc}}{2R} - \frac{R V_{dc}}{2R + \Delta R}$$

$$= \frac{(2R^2 + R \Delta R - 2R^2) V_{dc}}{2R (2R + \Delta R)} = \frac{R \Delta R V_{dc}}{2R (2R + \Delta R)}$$

$$= \frac{\Delta R V_{dc}}{2 (2R + \Delta R)}$$

- The output voltage V_{ab} is then applied to the differential instrumentation amplifier composed of three op-amps. The voltage follower is used to avoid the loading effect of the bridge circuit. The gain of the basic differential amplifier is $(- R_F/R_1)$, therefore, the output V_o of the circuit is

$$V_o = V_{ab} (- R_F/R_1)$$

$$= \frac{(\Delta R) V_{dc}}{2 (2R + \Delta R)} \times \frac{R_F}{R_1}$$

- Generally, the change in resistance of the transducer ΔR is very small. Therefore, we can approximate $(2R + \Delta R) \cong 2R$.

$$\therefore \quad V_o = \frac{R_F}{R_1} \cdot \frac{\Delta R}{4R} V_{dc} \qquad \ldots(4.9)$$

- It indicates that the V_o is directly proportional to the change in resistance ΔR of the transducer.

4.6.2 Instrumentation Amplifier Using Three Op-amps

Q. Explain the 3 op-amp instrumentation amplifier.	[Dec. 10, 4 M]
Q. Draw an explain three op-amp instrumentation amplifier.	[May 12, 4 M]

- The op-amps A_1 and A_2 are the non-inverting amplifiers forming the input stage of the instrumentation amplifier. The op-amp A_3 is the normal difference amplifier forming an output stage of the amplifier.

$$V_o = \frac{R_2}{R_1} (V_{o_2} - V_{o_1})$$

- From the realistic assumptions potential of node B is also at V_1 and hence potential of G is also at V_1. The potential of node C is at V_2 and hence potential of H is also at V_2.

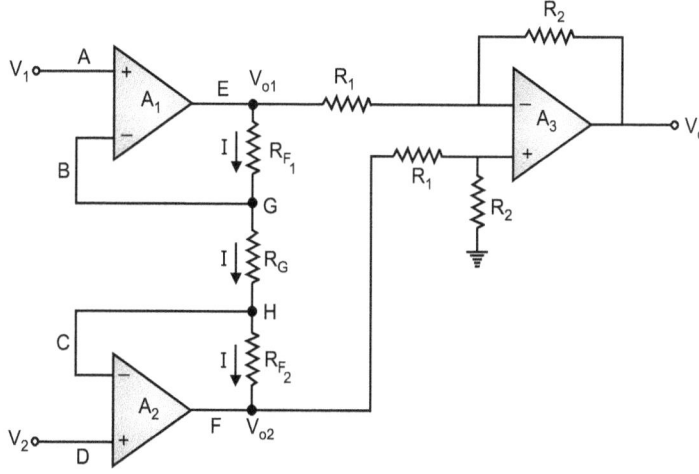

Fig. 4.8 : Instrumentation amplifier using three op-amps

- As the input currents for op-amps are zero, current I remains same through R_{F_1}, R_G and R_{F_2}.
- Apply Ohm's law between node E and F, the current I will be

$$I = \frac{V_{o_1} - V_{o_2}}{R_{F_1} + R_G + R_{F_2}}$$

$$R_{F_1} = R_{F_2} = R_F$$

$$I = \frac{V_{o_1} - V_{o_2}}{2R_F + R_G}$$

- Now from the observation of nodes G and H,

$$I = \frac{V_G - V_H}{R_G} = \frac{V_1 - V_2}{R_G}$$

$$\frac{V_{o_1} - V_{o_2}}{2R_F + R_G} = \frac{V_1 - V_2}{R_G}$$

$$\left(\frac{R_G}{2R_F + R_G}\right) V_{o_1} - V_{o_2} = V_1 - V_2$$

$$V_{o_1} - V_{o_2} = \frac{2R_F + R_G}{R_G}(V_1 - V_2)$$

$$V_{o_2} - V_{o_1} = \frac{2R_F + R_G}{R_G}(V_2 - V_1)$$

$$V_o = (V_{o_2} - V_{o_1}) A$$

$$= \frac{R_2}{R_1}\left(\frac{2R_F + R_G}{R_G}\right)(V_2 - V_1)$$

$$V_o = \frac{R_2}{R_1}\left(1 + \frac{2R_F}{R_G}\right)(V_2 - V_1)$$

4.7 PRECISION RECTIFIERS

Q. Explain op-amp as precision rectifier. [Dec. 12, 4 M]

- In conventional rectifier circuit,

$$V_o = V_{in} - V_D (ON) \text{ V} \quad \text{for } V_i \geq V_D (ON)$$
$$V_o = 0 \text{ V} \quad \text{for } V_i < V_D (ON)$$

- To keep V_o equal to $V_i > 0$ V, an op-amp is used along with diodes called as precision rectifiers. Thus, this circuit can rectify voltages when $V_i < 0.7$ V.
- There are two types of precision rectifiers :
    1. Precision half wave rectifier
    2. Precision full wave rectifier

4.7.1 Precision Half Wave Rectifier

- These are of two types :
    (i) Positive half wave rectifier,
    (ii) Negative half wave rectifier.

4.7.1.1 Positive half wave rectifier

- Here the cut-in-voltage is divided by the open loop gain of the op-amp so that cut-in-voltage is virtually eliminated.

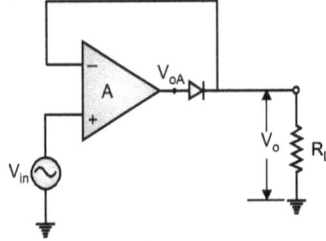

Fig. 4.9 (a)

- When the input voltage $V_i > V_\lambda/A_{OL}$, then V_{OA}, the output of the op-amp exceeds V_λ and the diode D conducts.
- Thus, the circuit acts as a voltage follower for input $V_i > V_\lambda/A_{OL}$.

- When V_i is negative or less than V_λ/A_{OL}, the diode D is OFF and no current flows to the R_L load.

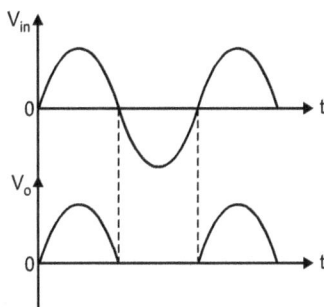

Fig. 4.9 (b) : Waveforms

4.7.1.2 Negative half wave rectifier

- Fig. 4.9 (a) shows a negative small-signal half wave rectifier. In this, during the positive half cycle of input voltage V_{in}, D_1 is reverse biased, therefore, $V_o = 0$ V. On the other hand, during the negative half cycle, D_1 is forward biased, hence V_o follows V_{in}.

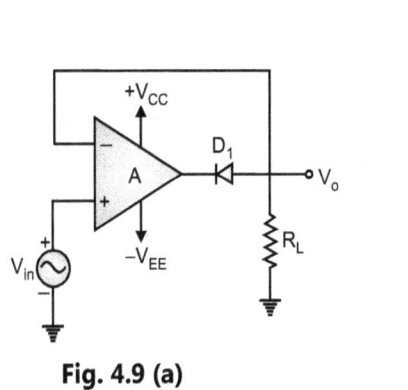

Fig. 4.9 (a)   **Fig. 4.9 (b)**

- Yet another negative half wave rectifier is shown in Fig. 4.9 (a). In this circuit, two diodes are used so that the output V_o' of the op-amp does not saturate. This minimizes the response time and increases the operating frequency range of the op-amp.
- Here the op-amp is used in the inverting mode and the output is measured at the anode of diode D_1 w.r.t. ground. Also, the output resistance is non-uniform since it depends on the state of diode D_1. In other words, the output impedance is low when D_1 is ON and high when D_1 is OFF.
- During the positive half cycle of V_{in}, output V_o' is negative, which forward biases diode D_1 and closes the feedback loop through R_F. Since, $R_1 = R_F$, $V_o = V_{in}$.

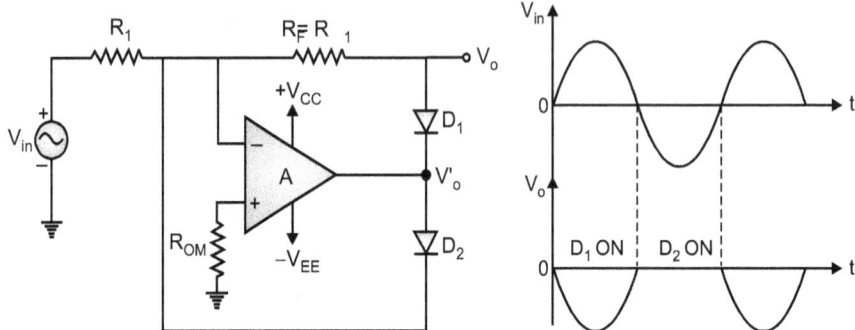

Fig. 4.10 (a) : Negative half wave rectifier   Fig. 4.10 (b) : Input and output waveforms

- During the negative half cycle of V_{in}, output V'_o is positive; hence diode D_2 is forward biased. In fact, it is this diode that prevents the op-amp from going into positive saturation. Since, diode D_1 is OFF, output $V_o = 0$ V.

4.7.2 Full Wave Precision Rectifiers

- Here the circuit accepts an AC input and inverts either positive or negative half and delivers both inverted and non-inverted halves at the output. Fig. 4.54 shows the precision full wave rectifier.
- When $V_i > 0$, diode D_1 is forward biased i.e. D_1 is ON and D_2 is reverse biased i.e. D_2 is OFF. Both the op-amps A_1 and A_2 acts as inverter.

$$V_o = \left(-\frac{R}{R}\right) \cdot \left(-\frac{R}{R}\right) = V_i$$

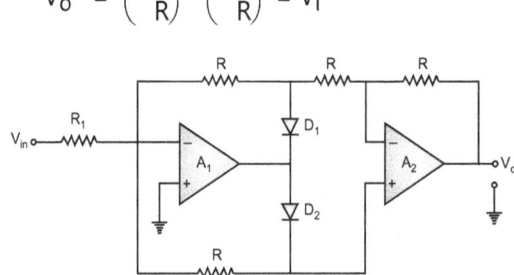

Fig. 4.11 : Precision full wave rectifiers

- When $V_i < 0$, the output voltage of A_1 swings to positive making diode D_2 forward biased and D_1 reverse biased. It can be shown that $V_o = -V_i$.

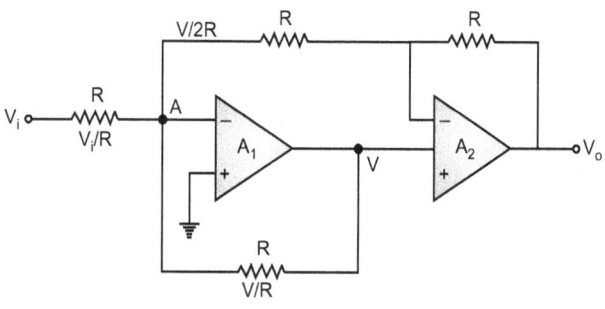

Fig. 4.12

Apply KCL at node A,

$$\frac{V_i}{R} + \frac{V}{2R} + \frac{V}{R} = 0$$

$$\frac{V_i}{R} + \frac{V + 2V}{2R} = 0$$

$$\frac{V_i}{R} + \frac{3V}{2R} = 0$$

$$\frac{V_i}{R} = -\frac{3}{2}\frac{V}{R}$$

$$V = -\frac{2}{3}V_i$$

$$V_o = \left(1 + \frac{R_F}{R_1}\right) V_i$$

$$= \left(1 + \frac{R}{2R}\right)\left(-\frac{2}{3}V_i\right)$$

$$= \left(\frac{3R}{2R}\right) \times -\frac{2}{3} V_i$$

∴ $V_o = -V_i$

The input and output waveforms are as shown in Fig. 4.56 (b).

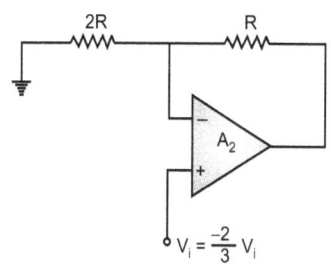

$V_i = -\frac{2}{3}V_i$

Fig. 4.13 (a)

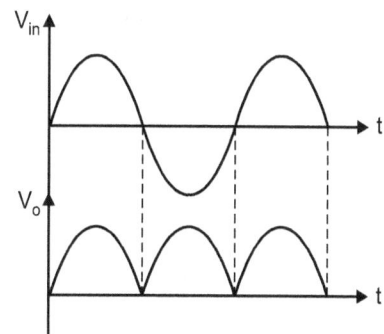

Fig. 4.13 (b)

4.8 TIMER IC 555

- Signetics corporation introduced this device as the SE/NE 555 in the early 1970. The 555 is a monolithic timing circuit that can produce accurate and highly stable time delays. The device is available as 8-pin metal can, an 8-pin mini DIP, or a 14-pin DIP.

Fig. 4.14 shows block diagram and connection diagram of IC SE/NE 555 timer.

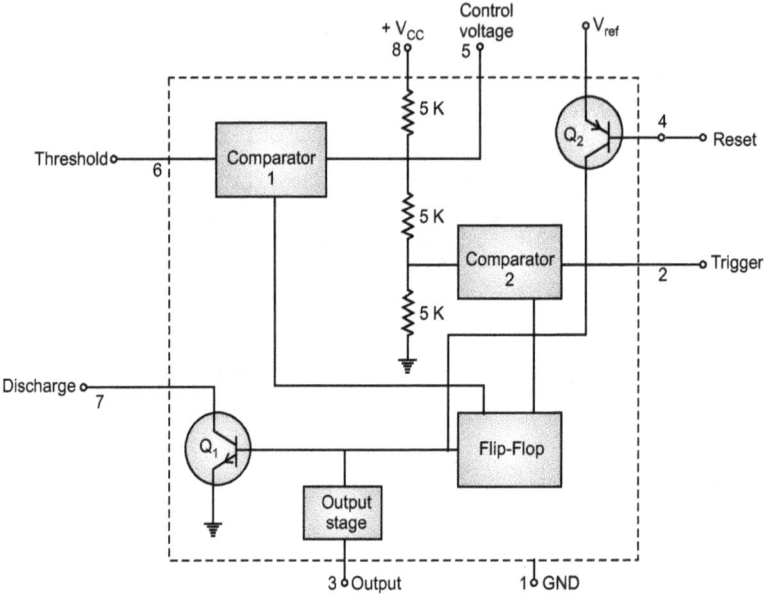

Fig. 4.14

Features of IC 555 :

- It is a 8-pin metal can, an 8-pin mini DIP or a 14-pin DIP IC.
- It's operating temperature range is 0° to +70°C.
- It operates on +5 to +18 V supply voltage.
- It has an adjustable duty cycle.
- It generates timings from microseconds to hours.
- It has a high current output.
- It can source or sink 200 mA.
- The output can drive TTL.
- It provides the temperature stability 50 parts per million (ppm) per degree celsius change in temperature or 0.005% / °C.
- It is reliable easy to use and low cost.

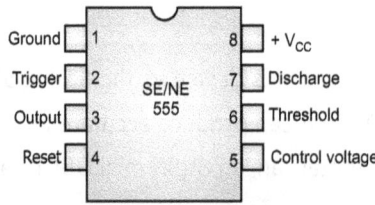

Fig. 4.15 : 555 timer (a) Connection diagram (b) Pin diagram

4.8.1 Pin Description

1. **Pin No. 1 Ground :** All the voltages are measured with respect to ground.
2. **Pin No. 2 Trigger :** The output of the timer depends on the amplitude of the external trigger pulse applied to this pin. If the voltage at this pin is greater than 2/3 V_{CC} then the output is low.
   When a –ve going pulse of amplitude greater than 1/3 V_{CC} is applied at this pin, then the comparator 2 output goes low, which in turn 'switches the output of the timer high'. The output remains high as long as the trigger terminal is held at a low voltage.
3. **Pin No. 3 Output :** The load at the output can be connected in two ways between pin 3 and ground or between pin 3 and + V_{CC} supply voltage.
   When the output is low, the load current flows through the load connected between pin 3 and +V_{CC} into the output terminal and is called the sink current is called as normally on load and when load is connected between pin 3 and ground. It is called as normally off load.

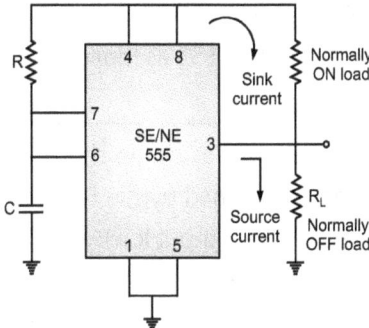

Fig. 4.16 : Normally off load

When the output is high, the current through the load connected between pin 3 and +V_{CC} is zero. Therefore, output terminal supplies current to the normally off load. This current is called as source current. The maximum value of source and sink current is 200 mA.

4. **Pin No. 4 : Reset :** The timer can be reset by applying a negative pulse to this pin. When the reset function is not in use, it is connected to +V_{CC} to avoid false triggering.
5. **Pin No. 5 : Control Voltage :** To change the threshold voltage or trigger voltage, an external voltage is applied to this terminal. The pulse width of the output waveform can be varied by giving some voltage on this pin or by connecting a potentiometer between this pin and ground. When this pin is not in use, it is connected to the ground through a 0.01 µf capacitor to avoid noise pick-ups.
6. **Pin No. 6 : Threshold :** This pin monitors the voltage across the external capacitor. When the voltage at this pin is ≥ threshold voltage 2/3 V_{CC}, the output of the comparator 1 goes high, to switch the output of the timer low.
7. **Pin No. 7 : Discharge :** This pin is internally connected to the collector of transistor Q_1. When output is high, Q_1 is off and acts as an open circuit to the external capacitor C connected across it.

When the output is low, Q_1 is saturated and acts a short circuit. Shorting out the external capacitor C to the ground.

8. **Pin No. 8 : +V_{CC} :** The supply voltage of + 5 V to + 18 V is applied to this pin with respect to ground.

4.9 MULTIVIBRATORS

There are three types of multivibrators :
- Astable multivibrator.
- Monostable multivibrator.
- Bistable multivibrator.

4.9.1 IC 555 as a Monostable Multivibrator

> **Q.** Draw and explain monostable multivibrator. [Dec. 10, 4 M]
> **Q.** Draw the diagram and waveform of IC555 as monostable multivibrator.
> [May 11, 6 M, Dec. 12, 9 M]

- Monostable multivibrator is also called as single-shot multivibrator. It generates a pulse of fixed duration which can be determined by the RC network connected externally to IC 555 timer. It has only one stable state (output low).
- When an external pulse is applied, the output is forced to go high. The time period for which the output remains high is determined by the external RC circuit. At the end, the output automatically goes back to its original stage.

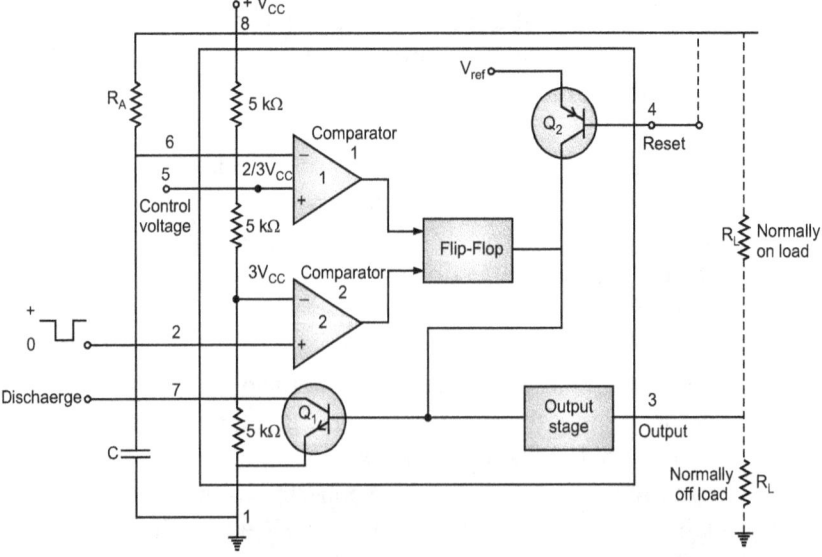

Fig. 4.17(a) : Monostable multivibrator using IC 555 timer

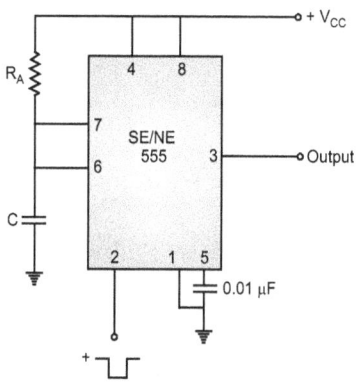

Fig. 4.17 (b) : Monostable multivibrator using IC 555 timer

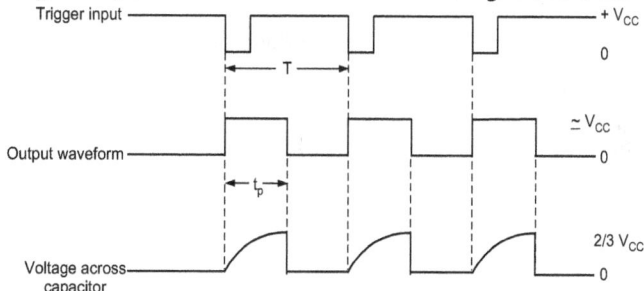

Fig. 4.17(c) : Input and output waveforms

Operation :

- When the output is low, the circuit is in stable state, transistor Q_1 is ON and capacitor C is shorted to ground.

- When the negative trigger pulse is applied at pin No. 2, transistor Q_1 becomes OFF. Now the capacitor C starts charging towards V_{CC} through R_A. When the voltage across the capacitor equals 2/3 V_{CC}, comparator 1 output changes from low to high which drives the output to its low state through the flip-flop.

- At the same time the output of the flip-flop turns transistor Q_1 ON and hence capacitor C starts discharging. The output of the monostable remains low until a trigger pulse is applied again. Thus, the cycle repeats.

- Fig. 4.26 (c) shows the input and output waveform. The width of the trigger pulse must be smaller than the expected pulse width of the output waveform. Also, the trigger pulse must be a negative going input signal with an amplitude larger than 1/3 V_{CC}.

4.9.1.1 Derivation of the Pulse Width

The instantaneous voltage across the capacitor is given by

$$V_C(t) = V_{max}(1 - e^{-t_p/T})$$

$$V_C(t) = 2/3\, V_{CC}$$

$$V_{max} = V_{CC}\ 2/3\ V_{CC} = V_{CC}(1 - e^{-t_p/RC})$$

$$\left(\frac{2}{3} - 1\right) = e^{-t_p/RC}$$

$$\frac{-t_p}{RC} = -1.0986$$

$$t_p = 1.0986\ RC$$

$$t_p = 1.1\ RC \qquad \qquad ...(4.12)$$

- In practice, a decoupling capacitor (10 µf) is connected between +V$_{CC}$ and ground to eliminate unwanted voltage spikes in the output waveform. Sometimes, a waveshaping circuit consisting of R, C$_2$ and diode D is connected between pin no. 2 and V$_{CC}$ to prevent any possibility of mistriggering of the monostable multivibrator on positive pulse edges.

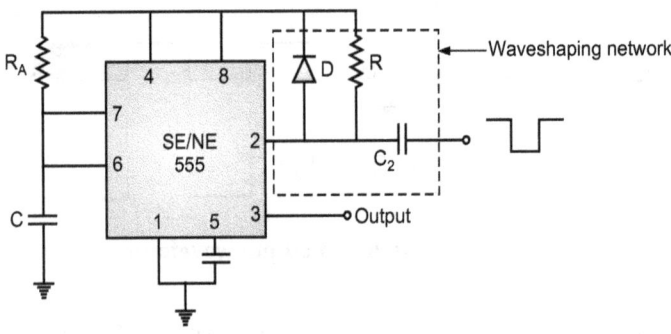

Fig. 4.18 : Monstable multivibrator with waveshaping network

4.9.1.2 Monostable Multivibrator Applications

Q. State the applications of monostable multivibrator. [Dec. 10, 4 M]

(a) Frequency Divider : Monostable multivibrator can be used as a frequency divider by adjusting the length of the timing cycle t_p w.r.t. the time period T of the trigger input signal applied to pin no. 2.

- To use the monstable multivibrator as a divide-by-2 circuit, the timing interval t_p must be slightly larger than the time period T of the trigger input signal.
- Similarly to design divide-by-3 circuit, t_p must be slightly larger than twice the period of the input trigger signal and so on.
- The frequency divider application is possible because the monostable multivibrator cannot be triggered during the timing cycle.

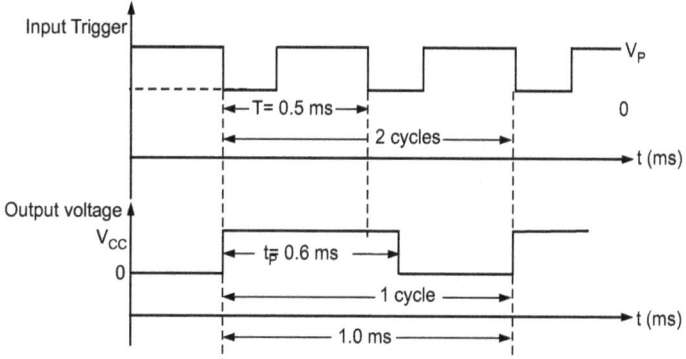

Fig. 4.19 : Input and output waveforms of monostable multivibrator as a divide-by-2 network

(b) Pulse Stretcher : This application makes the use of fact that output pulse width of the monostable multivibrator is of longer duration than the negative pulse width of the input trigger.

- The output pulse width of the monostable multivibrator can be viewed as a stretched version of the narrow input pulse, hence it is called as pulse stretcher.
- The pulse stretcher can be used to drive LED display. Fig. 4.20 shows the monostable multivibrator used as a pulse stretcher with an LED indicator at the output.
- The LED will be ON during timing interval $t_p = 1.1\ R_A\ C$ which can be varied by changing the value of R_A and /or C.

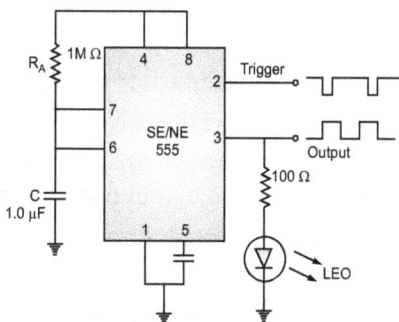

Fig. 4.20: Monostable multivibrator as a pulse stretcher

4.9.2 IC 555 as an Astable Multivibrator

Q. Draw the diagram and waveform of IC 555 as astable multivibrator.   [May 11, 6 M]
Q. Draw and explain IC 555 as an astable multivibrator with neat connection diagram.
   [Dec. 11, 4 M, May 12, 5 M]

- Astable multivibrator is also called as free running oscillator. The circuit does not require any external trigger to change the state of the output.

- Therefore, it is called as free running oscillator. The time period is determined by two resistors and a capacitor which are external to 555 timer Fig. 4.21 shows the IC 555 used as a Astable Multivibrator.

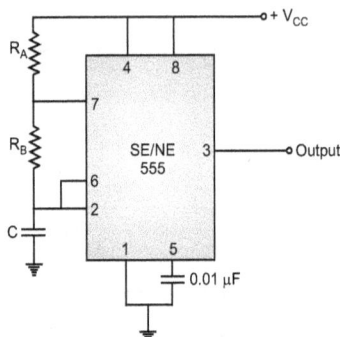

Fig. 4.21 (a) : Circuit diagram

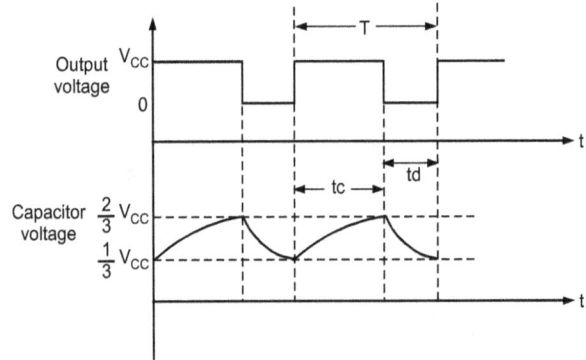

Fig. 4.21(b) : Output and capacitor voltage waveforms

- **Circuit Operation :** Assume that initially output is high, and capacitor C starts charging towards V_{CC} through R_A and R_B. When the voltage across the capacitor becomes 2/3 V_{CC} comparator 1 triggers the flip flop and the output becomes low.
- Now, the capacitor starts discharging through R_B and transistor Q_1, when voltage across C becomes 1/3 V_{CC}, comparator 2's output triggers the flip-flop and the output goes high. Thus, the cycle repeats. The output voltage and capacitor voltage waveforms are shown in Fig. 4.21 (b).
- The time period during which the capacitor charges from 1/3 V_{CC} to 2/3 V_{CC} is equal to the time the output is high and is given by

$$t_c = 0.69 (R_A + R_B) C \qquad ...(4.13)$$

where R_A and R_B is in ohms and C is in farads.
- The time during which the capacitor discharges from 2/3 V_{CC} to 1/3 V_{CC} is given by

$$t_d = 0.69 R_B \cdot C$$

The total time period

$$T = t_c + t_d$$

$$T = 0.69 (R_A + 2 R_B) C$$

Thus, the frequency of oscillation is given as

$$f_o = \frac{1}{T} = \frac{1.45}{(R_A + 2R_B)C}$$

The % duty cycle is calculated as

$$\% \text{ Duty cycle} = \frac{t_c}{T} \times 100 = \frac{R_A + R_B}{R_A + 2R_B} \times 100 \qquad ...(4.14)$$

When R_A is much smaller than R_B the duty cycle approaches to 50% and the output waveform becomes square wave.

4.9.2.1 Applications of Astable Generator

Q. State the applications of astable multivibar. [May 12, 5 M]

1. As a square wave generator : In astable timer circuit it is not possible to achieve 50% duty cycle. Some modifications are done to obtain the square wave as shown in Fig. 4.31.

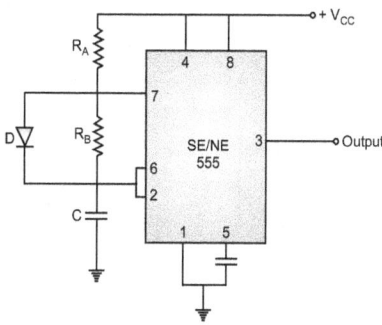

Fig. 4.22 : Square wave generator

Here capacitor C charges through R_A and diode D and discharges through R_B.

2. FSK Generator : Binary codes 1's and 0's can be transmitted by shifting a carrier frequency. Fixed frequency represents one and other represents zero. Such type of transmission is called frequency shift keying (FSK). IC 555 can be used to generate FSK. Fig. 4.32 shows the circuit for FSK generation.

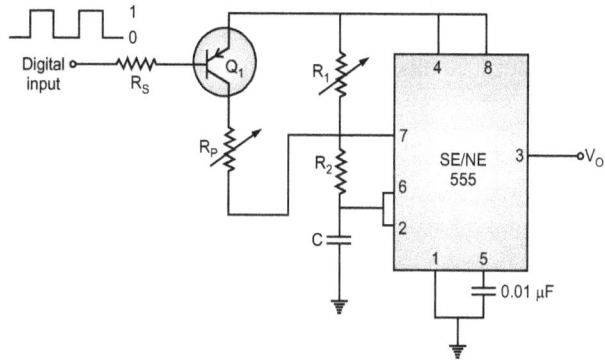

Fig. 4.23 : FSK generator

When digital input is High (or logic 1), transistor Q_1 is OFF and IC 555 works as a normal astable timer. The frequency of the output waveform can be given as

$$f_o = \frac{1.45}{(R_1 + 2R_2)C} \quad \ldots(4.15)$$

When input is Low (logic 0), transistor Q_1 is ON and connects the resistance R_P in parallel with R_1. The frequency of output waveform is given by

$$f_o = \frac{1.45}{[(R_1 \| R_P) + 2R_2]C}$$

4.9.3 Bistable Multivibrator

- A multivibrator circuit that has both the states are stable. It goes from one stable state to another when triggered. It is nothing but flip-flop.

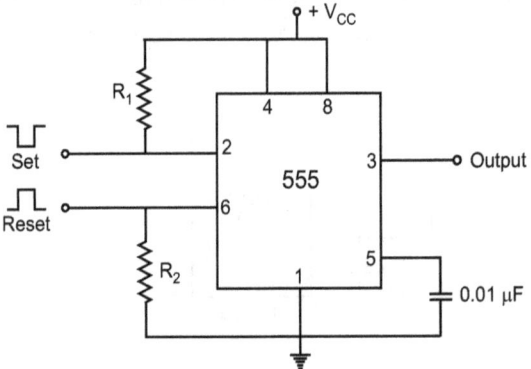

Fig. 4.24 : Circuit diagram of bistable multivibrator

4.10 ACTIVE FILTERS

- A filter is a circuit that is designed to pass a specified band of frequencies while attenuating all the signal outside the band. It is also called as a frequency selective device.

Advantages of Active Filters :

- Small size and weight because all components are available in integrated form.
- Low cost.
- Op-amp gain can be easily controlled in closed loop mode. Therefore, active filter input signal is not attenuated.
- Tuning of the active filters is easy due to flexibility in gain and frequency adjustments.
- Loading effect of the source or load is avoided.
- Since inductors are not used, modern active filters are more economical.
- Active filters can be realized under number of class of functions such as butterworth, Thomson, Chebyshev, Cauver, etc.

- Improved frequency response compared to passive filters.
- Design procedure is simple.

Disadvantages or Limitations of Active Filters :

- Bandwidth is restricted upto 500 kHz, whereas the passive filters can be used upto 500 MHz.
- Active elements are much sensitive to the temperature changes or environmental changes than passive components.
- It requires power supply for its operation. The passive filters do not require the DC supply.

Types of Filters :

The active filters are classified into four categories :

- Low-pass filters
- High-pass filters
- Band-pass filters
- Band-reject filters.

Time domain and frequency domain analysis of active filters.

(a) Time domain representation (b)

Fig. 4.25

$$H(S) = \frac{V_o(S)}{V_{in}(S)}$$

$$H(j\omega) = \frac{V_o(j\omega)}{V_{in}(j\omega)}$$

$$H(j\omega) = |H(j\omega)| \angle H(j\omega)$$

Thus, the magnitude of the transfer function $|H(j\omega)|$ is called the gain of the filter.

The filter in which denominator polynomial of its transfer function is a Butterworth polynomial is called a Butterworth filter.

4.10.1 First Order Low pass Butterworth Filter

> Q. Explain with neat connection diagram of low passfilter.[May 12, 10 M, Dec. 12 , 9 M]
> Q. Draw and explain first order low pass filter using op-amp.[May 11, 9M, Dec. 12, 9 M]

Fig. 4.26 shows a first order low-pass butterworth filter that uses an RC network for filtering. Op-amp is used in the non-inverting configuration, hence there is no load on the RC network. Resistors R_1 and R_F determine the gain of the filter.

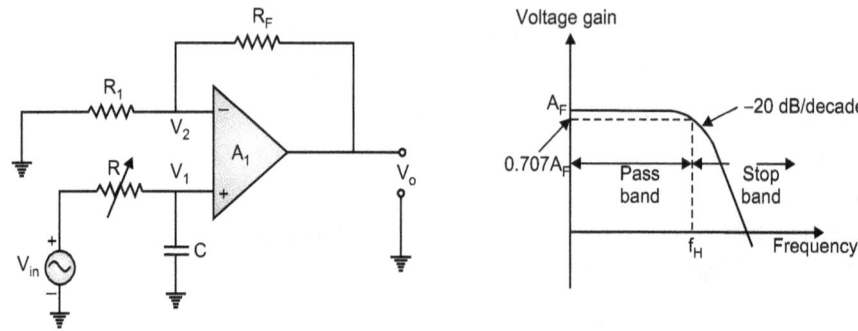

(a) Circuit diagram   **(b) Frequency response**
Fig. 4.26 : First order low-pass butterworth filter

According to the voltage divider rule, the voltage at the non-inverting terminal (across capacitor C) is

$$X_C = \frac{1}{2\pi fC} = -jX_C$$

$$V_1 = \frac{-jX_C}{R - jX_C} \cdot V_{in} \qquad \text{... (4.17)}$$

where, $j = \sqrt{-1}$ and $-jX_C = \frac{1}{j2\pi fC}$

$$V_1 = \frac{-j\left(\frac{1}{2\pi fC}\right)}{R - j\left(\frac{1}{2\pi fC}\right)} \cdot V_{in} = \frac{\frac{-j}{2\pi fC}}{\frac{2\pi f_R R_C - j}{2\pi fC}} \cdot V_{in}$$

$$= \frac{-j}{2\pi fC} \times \frac{2\pi fC}{2\pi f RC - j} \cdot V_{in}$$

$$= \frac{-j}{2\pi f RC - j} \cdot V_{in}$$

$$-j = \frac{1}{j} \; ; -\frac{1}{j} = j$$

$$V_1 = \frac{V_{in}}{1 + j \, 2\pi f \, RC}$$

and output voltage, $V_o = \left(1 + \frac{R_F}{R_1}\right) V_1$

$$V_o = \left(1 + \frac{R_F}{R_1}\right) \cdot \frac{V_{in}}{1 + j \, 2\pi f \, RC}$$

$$\frac{V_o}{V_{in}} = \frac{A_F}{1 + j \, (f/f_H)} \qquad \text{... (4.18)}$$

where, $\dfrac{V_o}{V_{in}}$ = Gain of the filter as a function of frequency

$$A_F = 1 + \dfrac{R_F}{R_1} = \text{Passband gain of the filter}$$

$$f = \text{Frequency of the input signal}$$

$$f_H = \dfrac{1}{2\pi RC} = \text{High cut off frequency of the filter}$$

The gain magnitude and phase angle equations are obtained by converting equation (4.17) into its polar form as follows :

$$\left|\dfrac{V_o}{V_{in}}\right| = \dfrac{A_F}{\sqrt{1 + (f/f_H)^2}} \qquad \text{... (4.19)}$$

$$\phi = -\tan^{-1}\left(\dfrac{f}{f_H}\right)$$

The operation of the low pass filter can be varied from the gain-magnitude equation.

(1) At very low frequencies, i.e. $f < f_H$,

$$\left|\dfrac{V_o}{V_{in}}\right| \cong V_F \qquad \text{... (4.20)}$$

(2) At $f = f_H$, $\left|\dfrac{V_o}{V_{in}}\right| = \dfrac{A_F}{\sqrt{2}} = 0.707\, A_F$ ... (4.21)

(3) At $f > f_H$, $\left|\dfrac{V_o}{V_{in}}\right| < A_F$ ... (4.22)

Example 4.1
Design a low pass filter at a cut-off frequency of 15.9 kHz with a passband gain 1.5.

Solution :

$$f_H = 15.9\ \text{kHz}$$

Choose $C = 0.001\ \mu F$

$$f_H = \dfrac{1}{2\pi RC}$$

$$15.9 \times 10^3 = \dfrac{1}{2 \times \pi \times R \times 0.001 \times 10^{-6}}$$

$$R = 10\ k\Omega$$

For frequency scaling use 20 K pot.

$$A_F = 1.5$$

$$\therefore \quad 1.5 = 1 + \frac{R_F}{R_1}$$

$$\therefore \quad \frac{R_F}{R_1} = 1.5 - 1 = 0.5$$

$$\therefore \quad R_F = 0.5\, R_1 \quad \text{where } R_1 = 10\, k\Omega$$

$$\therefore \quad R_F = 0.5 \times 10\, k\Omega = 5\, k\Omega$$

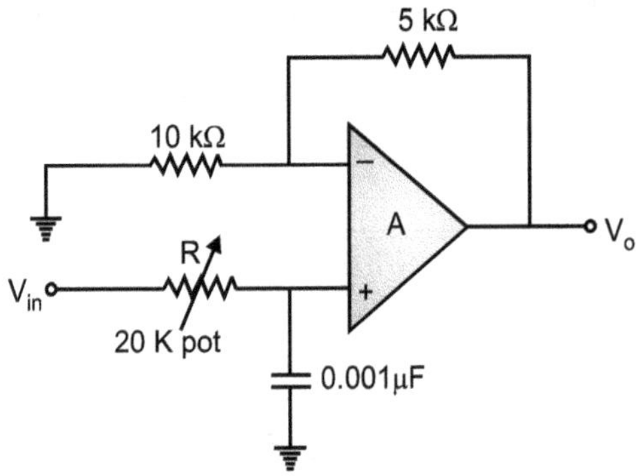

Fig. 4.27

Filter Design :

A low pass filter can be designed by implementing the following steps :

- Choose a higher cut-off frequency value f_H.
- Select a value of C less than or equal to 1 µF. Mylar or tantalum capacitors are recommended for better performance.
- Calculate the value of R using

$$R = \frac{1}{2\pi f_H C}$$

- Finally select values of R_1 and R_F dependent on the desired passband gain A_F using

$$A_F = 1 + \frac{R_F}{R_1}$$

4.10.2 First Order High Pass Butterworth Filter

Q. Draw and explain the connection diagram for first order high pass filter. [Dec. 11, 8M]

First order high pass filter is formed from a first order low pass type by interchanging components R and C. Fig. 4.28 shows a first order high pass Butterworth filter with a low cut-off frequency of f_L. All frequencies higher than f_L are passband frequencies.

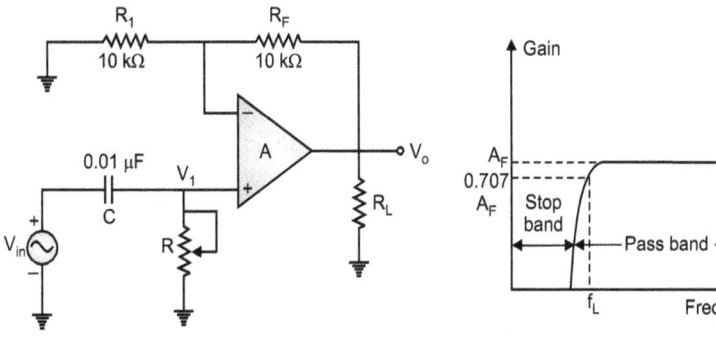

(a) First order high pass Butterworth filter   **(b)** Its frequency response

Fig. 4.28

By the voltage divider rule,

$$V_1 = V_{in} \cdot \frac{R}{R - jX_C}$$

$$= V_{in} \cdot \left[\frac{R}{-jX_C\left(1 + \frac{R}{-jX_C}\right)}\right]$$

$$-\frac{1}{j} = j$$

$$\frac{1}{-jX_C} = \frac{j}{X_C} = \frac{j}{\left(\frac{1}{2\pi fC}\right)} = j2\pi fC$$

∴ $$V_1 = V_{in}\left[\frac{R/-jX_C}{1 + \frac{R}{-jX_C}}\right]$$

$$= V_{in}\left[\frac{j2\pi fRC}{1 + j2\pi fRC}\right]$$

This can be represented as

$$V_1 = V_{in}\left[\frac{j(f/f_L)}{1 + j(f/f_L)}\right]$$

where, $$f_L = \frac{1}{2\pi RC}$$

The output voltage is

$$V_o = \left(1 + \frac{R_F}{R_1}\right)V_1$$

$$= \left(1 + \frac{R_F}{R_1}\right)V_{in}\left[\frac{j(f/f_L)}{1 + j(f/f_L)}\right]$$

Unit 4 | 4.29

$$\frac{V_o}{V_{in}} = A_F \left[\frac{j(f/f_L)}{1 + j(f/f_L)} \right] \qquad \ldots (4.23)$$

where,
$$A_F = 1 + \frac{R_F}{R_1} = \text{Passband gain of the filter}$$

$$f = \text{Frequency of the input signal (Hz)}$$

$$f_L = \frac{1}{2\pi RC} = \text{Low cut-off frequency (Hz)}$$

Hence, the magnitude of the voltage gain is

$$\left| \frac{V_o}{V_{in}} \right| = \frac{A_F (f/f_L)}{\sqrt{1 + (f/f_L)^2}} \qquad \ldots (4.24)$$

(1) So at low frequencies, $f < f_L$

$$\left| \frac{V_o}{V_{in}} \right| < A_F$$

(2) At $f = f_L$,
$$\left| \frac{V_o}{V_{in}} \right| = 0.707 \, A_F \qquad \ldots (4.25)$$

(3) At $f > f_L$,
$$\left| \frac{V_o}{V_{in}} \right| \cong A_F \qquad \ldots (4.26)$$

At high frequencies, 1 can be neglected as compared to (f/f_L) from denominator.

Example 4.2 :

Design a high-pass filter with a cut-off frequency of 10 kHz with a passband gain of 1.5. Also plot the frequency response for the designed filter.

Solution :

Given : $\qquad f_L = 10 \text{ kHz}$

Choose C less than 1 µF

$\qquad C = 0.02 \, \mu F$

Calculate R. $\qquad f_L = \dfrac{1}{2\pi RC}$

$\therefore \quad 10 \times 10^3 = \dfrac{1}{2\pi R \times 0.02 \times 10^{-6}}$

$\therefore \qquad\qquad R = 795.77 \, \Omega$

For frequency scaling use a pot of 1 kΩ.

$$A_F = 1.5$$

$$1 + \frac{R_F}{R_1} = 1.5$$

∴ $\quad \dfrac{R_F}{R_1} = 0.5$

∴ $\quad R_F = 0.5\, R_1$

Select $\quad R_1 = 10\text{ k}\Omega$

∴ $\quad R_F = 5\text{ k}\Omega$

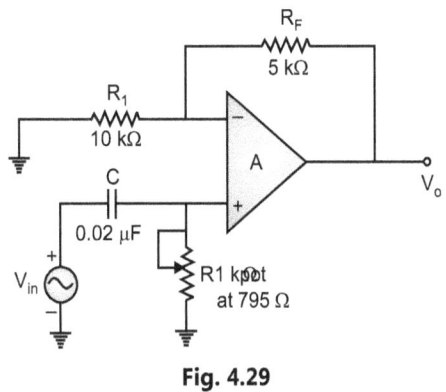

Fig. 4.29

4.10.3 Band-Pass Filters

A band-pass filter has a passband between two cut-off frequencies f_H and f_L such that $f_H > f_L$. Any input frequency outside this passband is attenuated. Basically, there are two types of band-pass filters : (1) Wide band-pass filter, (2) Narrow band-pass filters.

Filters are divided as wide band-pass if its figure of merit or quality factor Q < 10. When Q > 10, then the filter is called as narrow band-pass filter. Q is the measure of selectivity, more the value of Q, the more selective is the filter or narrower is its bandwidth (BW).

$$Q = \frac{f_C}{BW} = \frac{f_C}{f_H - f_L} \qquad \ldots(4.27)$$

For wide band-pass filter the centre frequency f_C can be defined as

$$f_C = \sqrt{f_H f_L}$$

where, $\quad f_H$ = High cut-off frequency (Hz)

$\quad f_L$ = Low cut-off frequency of the wide band filter (Hz)

4.10.3.1 Wide Band-Pass Filter

A wide band-pass filter can be formed by simply cascading high-pass and low-pass sections and is generally the choice for simplicity of design and performance.

To obtain a ± 20 dB/decade band-pass, first order high pass and first order low pass sections are cascaded. Fig. 4.30 shows the ± 20 dB/decade wide band-pass filter which is composed of first order high-pass and first order low-pass filters. To obtain a band-pass response f_H must be larger than f_L.

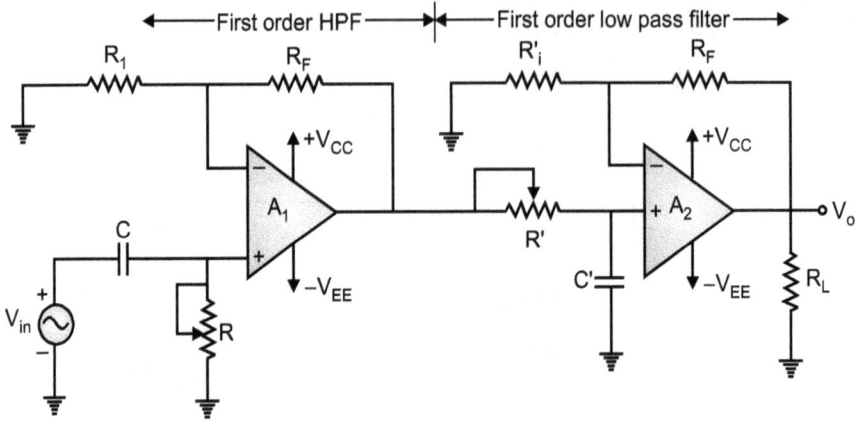

(a) ± 20 dB/decade wide band-pass filter

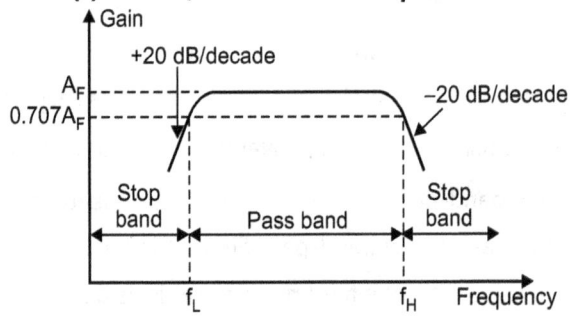

(b) Its frequency response

Fig. 3.10

$$\left|\frac{V_o}{V_{in}}\right| = \frac{A_F}{\sqrt{1 + (f/f_H)^2}} \quad \text{for low pass}$$

$$\left|\frac{V_o}{V_{in}}\right| = \frac{A_F (f/f_L)}{\sqrt{1 + (f/f_L)^2}} \quad \text{for high pass}$$

As the two circuits are in cascade, the overall gain of wide band-pass filter is the product of the two gains.

$$\left|\frac{V_o}{V_{in}}\right| = \frac{A_{F_T} (f/f_L)}{\sqrt{[1 + (f/f_L)^2][1 + (f/f_H)^2]}} \quad \text{... (4.28)}$$

where, $A_{F_T} = A_1 A_2$

Example 4.3 :

Design a wide band-pass filter with f_L = 200 Hz, f_H = 1 kHz, and a pass band gain of 4.

(a) Draw the frequency response plot of this filter.
(b) Calculate the value of Q for the filter.

Solution :

(1) Design the low pass filter.

$$f_H = 1 \text{ kHz}$$

Let
$$C = 0.01 \text{ μF}$$

$$f_H = \frac{1}{2\pi R'C'}$$

$$R' = \frac{1}{2\pi \times 1 \times 10^3 \times 0.01 \times 10^{-6}} = 15.9 \text{ kΩ}$$

(2) Design the high pass filter.

$$f_L = 200 \text{ Hz}$$
$$C = 0.05 \text{ μF}$$

$$R = \frac{1}{2\pi f_L C} = \frac{1}{2\pi \times (200) \times 5 \times 10^{-8}}$$

$$= 15.9 \text{ kΩ}$$

$$A_{F_T} = A_1 A_2$$

$$A_1 A_2 = 2$$

$$A_1 = A_2 = 1 + \frac{R_F}{R_1} = 2$$

∴ $$\frac{R_F}{R_1} = 1$$

Select $R_F = R_1 = 10 \text{ kΩ}$

$$f_C = \sqrt{f_H f_L} = \sqrt{1 \times 10^3 \times 200} = 447.2 \text{ Hz}$$

$$BW = f_H - f_L = 1000 - 200 = 800 \text{ Hz}$$

$$Q = \frac{f_C}{BW} = \frac{447.2}{1000 - 200} = 0.56$$

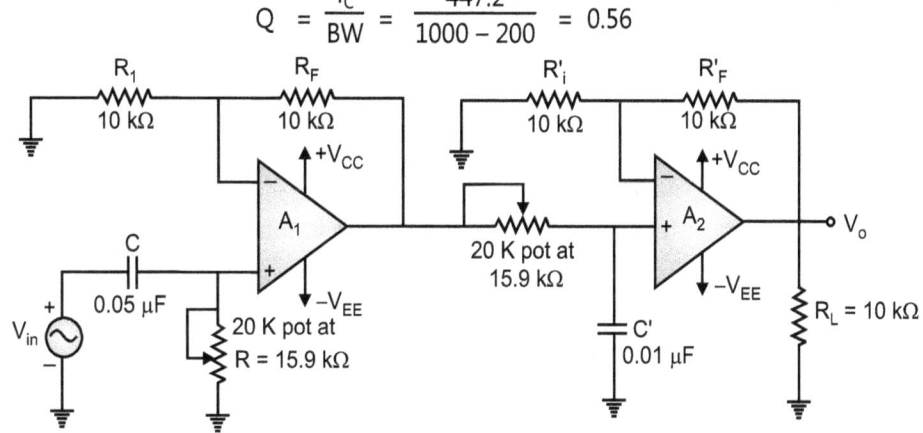

Fig. 4.31

4.10.3.2 Narrow Band-Pass Filter

This filter is unique as it has two feedback paths. Hence, it is called as multiple-feedback filter.

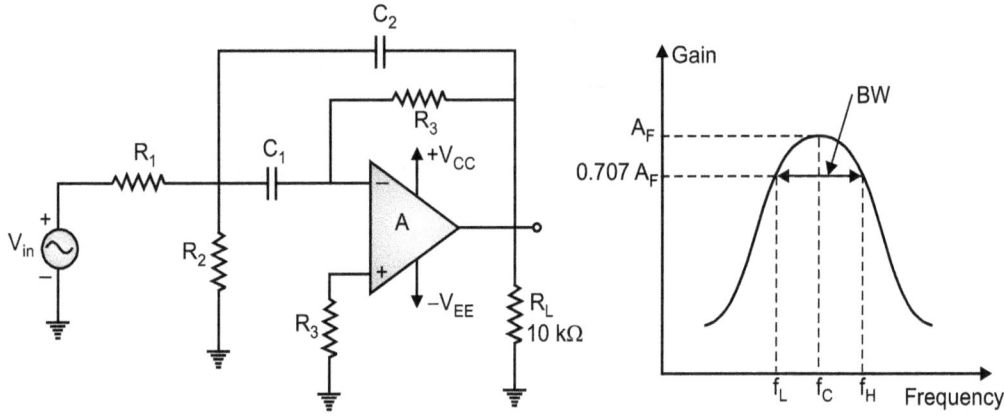

(a) Multiple feedback narrow band-pass filter   (b) Its frequency response

Fig. 4.32

Generally, the narrow band-pass filter is designed for specific values of centre frequency f_C and Q or f_C and bandwidth. The circuit components are determined from the following relationships.

Choose
$$C_1 = C_2 = C$$

$$R_1 = \frac{Q}{2\pi f_C C A_F}$$

$$R_2 = \frac{Q}{2\pi f_C C (2Q^2 - A_F)}$$

$$R_3 = \frac{Q}{\pi f_C C}$$

where A_F is the gain at f_C given by

$$A_F = \frac{R_3}{2R_1} \qquad \qquad \text{... (4.29)}$$

The gain A_F, must satisfy the condition
$$A_F < 2Q^2$$

The advantage of multiple feedback filter is that its centre frequency f_C can be changed to a new frequency f_C' without changing gain or bandwidth.

$$R_2' = R_2 \left(\frac{f_C}{f_C'}\right)^2 \qquad \qquad \text{... (4.30)}$$

◊ ◊ ◊

Unit - V

BIPOLAR JUNCTION TRANSISTOR AMPLIFIER

5.1 INTRODUCTION

- Amplification is a process of magnifying the input signal without changing it's shape. The circuit which amplifies a small input signal is called an amplifier.
- In a stereo, radio or T.V., the input signal is very small. After several stages of voltage gain, however the signal becomes large and uses entire d.c. load line.
- Small signal transistors have power rating of less than 1 W whereas power transistors have power rating of more than 1 W. Hence, small signal transistors are used at front end of system whereas power amplifier is used at near end of system (because signal power and current are high).

5.2 CLASSIFICATION OF AMPLIFIER

There are different ways to classify amplifiers. We can classify them
(a) By their class of operation
(b) By their interstage coupling or
(c) By their frequency range.

(a) Classification based on their class of operation

1. Class-A operation : In this type, the transistor operates in active region at all times. This means that collector current flows for 360° of a.c. cycle, as shown in Fig. 5.1 (a). In class-A amplifier, Q point is somewhere near the middle of the load line. In this way, the signal can swing over the maximum possible range without saturating or cutting off the transistor, which would distort the signal.

2. Class-B operation : It means the collector current flows for only half cycle (or 180°) as shown in Fig. 5.1 (b). In this case, the designer has to locate the Q point at cut-off. Then, only the positive half of a.c. base voltage can produce base current. This reduces the wasted heat of power transistor.

3. Class-C operation : It means that collector current flows for less than 180° of the a.c. cycle as shown in Fig. 5.1 (c). With such class operation, only part of positive half cycle of a.c. base voltage produces collector current. As a result, we get brief pulses of collector current as shown in Fig. 5.1 (c).

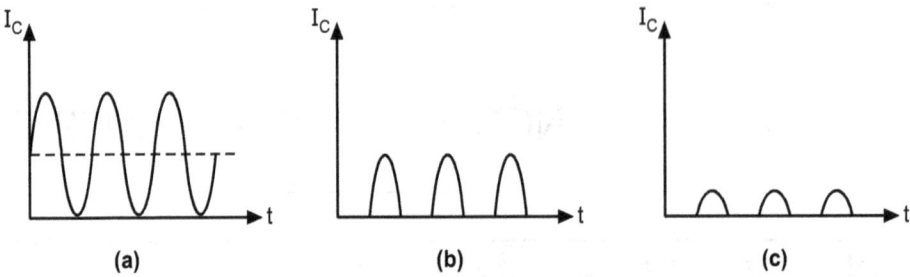

Fig. 5.1 : Various modes of operation

(b) Classification based on the type of coupling :
- Fig. 5.2 (a) shows the capacitive coupling. The coupling capacitor transmits the amplified a.c. voltage to next stage.
- Fig. 5.2 (b) shows the transformer coupling. In transformer coupling, the a.c. voltage is coupled through a transformer to next stage.
- Transformer coupling and capacitive coupling are both examples of a.c. coupling which block the d.c. voltage.
- Direct coupling is different than these two. In such coupling collector of first transistor is directly connected to base of second transistor. Because of such coupling both the d.c. and a.c. voltages are coupled. As there is no lower frequency limit, a direct coupled amplifier is also called as d.c. amplifier.

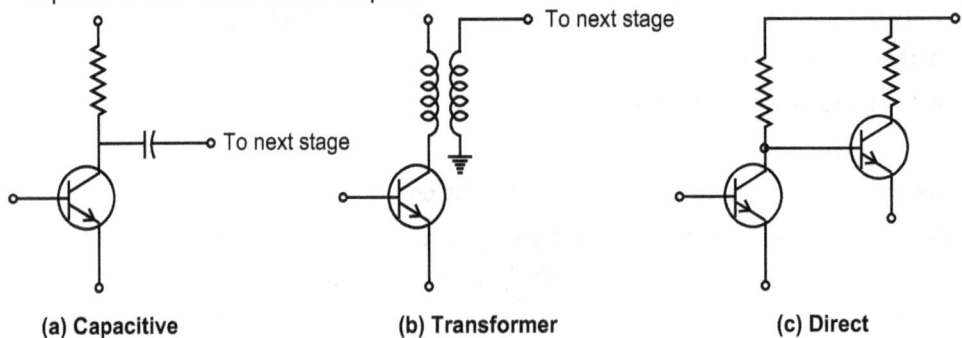

Fig. 5.2 : Types of coupling

(c) Classification based on the input ranges of frequency :
- Amplifiers can be described by stating their frequency ranges. For example, audio amplifier operates in audible range (20 Hz – 20,000 Hz) and radio frequency (R.F.) amplifier frequencies above 20 kHz.
- The R.F. amplifiers in AM radios amplify frequencies between 535 and 1605 kHz while the R.F. amplifiers in FM radio amplify frequencies between 88 and 108 MHz.

Amplifiers are also classified in following ways :

1. Narrow band amplifier : It works over a small frequency range like 450 Hz to 460 kHz. Narrow band amplifiers are usually tuned R.F. amplifiers which means that their a.c. load is a high Q resonant tank tuned to radio station or TV channel.

2. Wide band amplifier : It operates over a large frequency range like 0 to 1 MHz. Wide band amplifiers are usually untuned, hence their a.c. load is resistive.

Fig. 5.3 (a) is an example of a tuned R.F. amplifier. It has LC tank which is resonant at some frequency. If tank circuit has high Q, the bandwidth is narrow. The output is capacitively coupled to next stage.

Fig. 5.3 (b) is an example of a tuned R.F. amplifier. In such amplifier, the narrow band output signal is transformer coupled to the next stage.

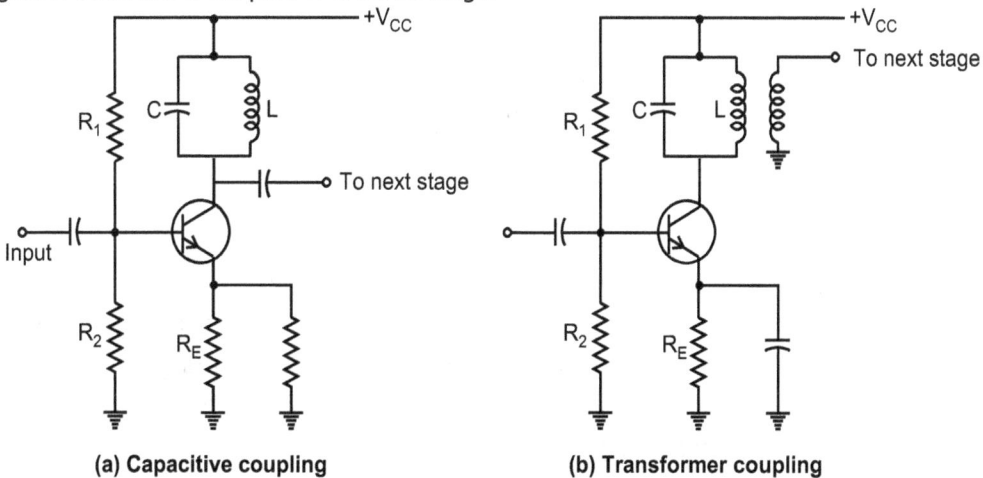

(a) Capacitive coupling   (b) Transformer coupling

Fig. 5.3 : Tuned R.F. amplifier

5.3 LOAD LINE ANALYSIS

Q. Explain AC-DC load line analysis using CE configuration.   [Dec. 10, 8 M]

Definition of dc biasing :

- We know that a transistor is to be operated in any one of the three regions of operations that is cutoff, active region and saturation. So, we need external dc power supplies. This is known as dc biasing of a transistor.

5.3.1 DC Load Line

Q. Explain DC load line analysis of CE configuration amplifier.   [Dec. 12, 8 M]

For dc analysis of consider the common emitter configuration as shown in Fig. 5.4 (a) and the output circuit of Fig. 5.4 (b).

1. Consider the collector circuit of the CE configuration (Fig. 5.4(b)). If we apply KVL to this circuit then,

$$V_{CC} - V_{CE} - I_C R_C = 0$$

2. Rearranging this equation we get,

$$I_C = \left[-\frac{1}{R_C}\right] V_{CE} + \frac{V_{CC}}{R_C}$$

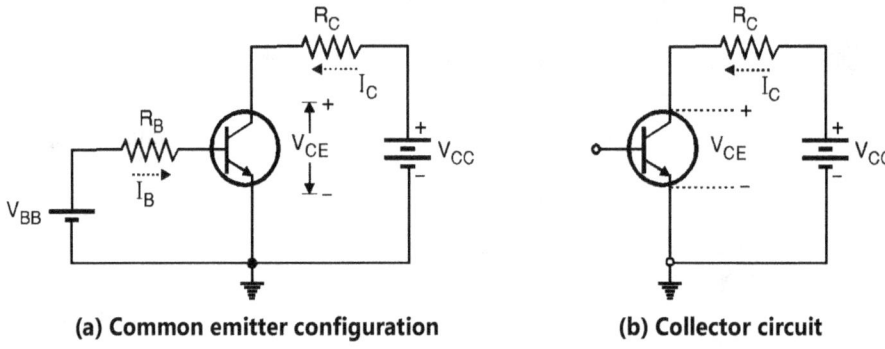

(a) Common emitter configuration (b) Collector circuit

Fig. 5.4

3. Comparing this equation with the general equation of a straight line.

i.e. $\quad y = mx + C$

we get, $\quad y = I_C \qquad x = V_{CE}$

$\qquad m = -1/R_C \qquad C = V_{CC}/R_C$

Thus, we can say that the equation is of a straight line and it is known as the **dc load line**.

4. If we substitute $V_{CE} = 0$ in above equation, we get $I_C = V_{CC}/R_C$ which is $I_{C(max)}$ or point "A" in Fig. 5.5 and substituting $I_C = 0$ we get $V_{CE} = V_{CC}$, which represents point "B" in Fig. 5.5. The dc load line is drawn on the output characteristics as shown in Fig. 5.5.

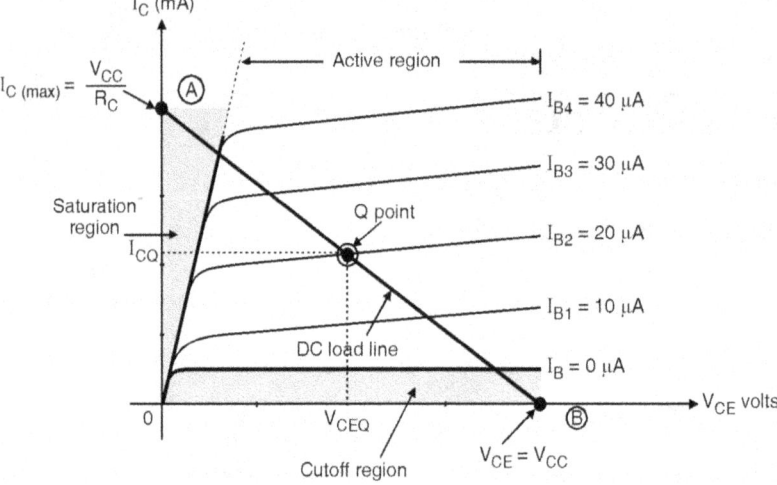

Fig. 5.5: DC load line showing the Q point on output characteristics of the transistor

5.3.2 The Quiescent Point (Q point)

- The Q point is nothing but the "operating point" or "bias point". The word quiescent means quiet, still or inactive.
- It represents the dc current through a transistor (I_{CQ}) and the voltage across it (V_{CEQ}), when no ac signal is applied or we can say that it represents the dc biasing condition.

- The dc load line is a set of infinite number of such operating points and the user or designer can choose any point on the dc load line as the operating point.
- The position of operating point on the load line depends on which purpose the transistor is being used and the shape of amplifier output signal depends on the position of Q point.

5.3.3 AC Load Line

Q. Explain AC-DC load line analysis using common emitter configuration. [Dec. 10, 8 M]

- Fig. 5.6 shows a part of the amplifier circuit. The dc load resistance is R_C and the AC load resistance is ($R_C \| R_L$).
- If a load line is drawn such that the slope is $-1/(R_C \| R_L)$ then it is called as an AC load line and it is used when the transistor is operating as an amplifier. Thus AC operating conditions are represented by the AC load line.

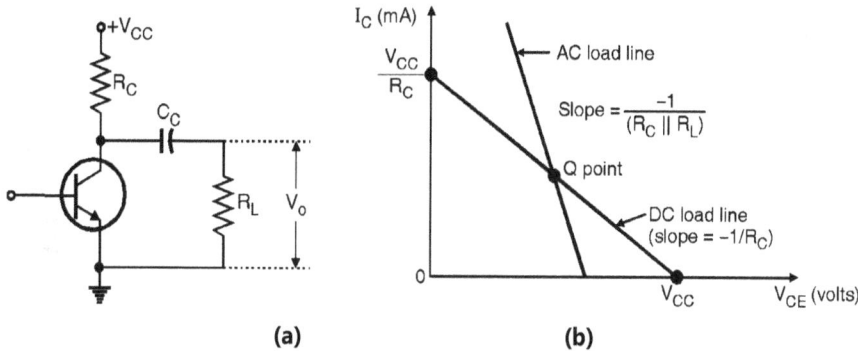

(a)   (b)

Fig. 5.6 : Amplifier circuit drawn partially   Fig. 5.7 : AC and DC load lines

- The parallel combination ($R_C \| R_L$) is always less than R_C. Hence, the slope of AC load line is higher than that of the DC load line as shown in Fig. 5.7.

5.3.4 Factors Affecting the Stability of Q Point

- Ideally the Q point is expected to be "**stable**" i.e. should not shift up or down on the load line.
- But practically it is not so. In fact the Q point is quite unstable and keeps changing its position on the dc load line.

5.4 POWER AMPLIFIERS

Classification based on the position of Q point.

The classification has been done on the basis of position of the Q point or operating point on the load line. The type of amplifier and the position of Q point are listed in Table 5.1.

Table 5.1 : Types of power amplifiers

Sr. No.	Type of power amplifier	Position of Q point
1.	Class A	At the centre of load line.
2.	Class B	In the cut-off region.
3.	Class AB	Just above the cut-off region.
4.	Class C	Below the cut-off region.

5.5 CLASS-A POWER AMPLIFIER

Voltage divider bias amplifier as shown in Fig. 5.7 is a class-A amplifier as long as the output signal is not clipped.

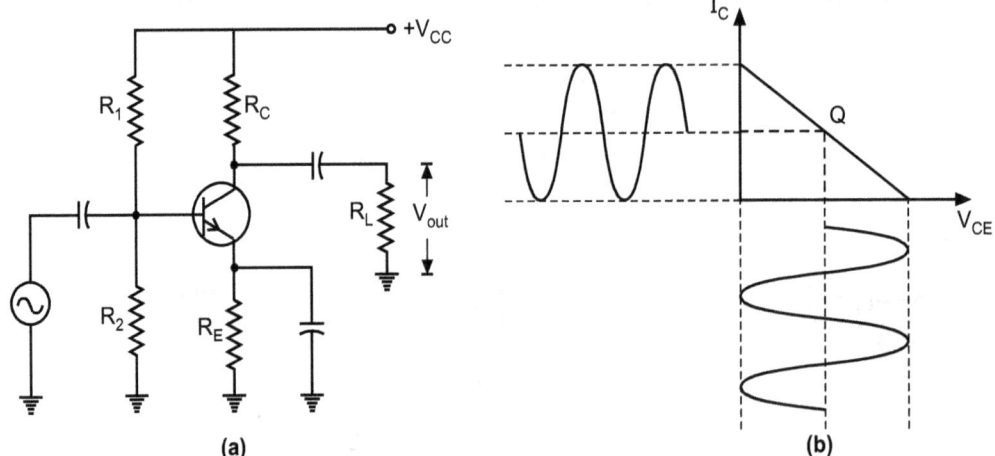

(a) (b)

Fig. 5.7 : Class-A amplifier

- An amplifier is referred to as a class-A amplifier if transistor used for amplification conducts for full cycle duration of the input a.c. signal. In class-A operation, the Q point is adjusted exactly at the centre of load line as shown in Fig. 5.7 (b). Due to this the output signal is obtained for full cycle of a.c. input.
- As we apply the a.c. signal to the base of transistor, the base current changes sinusoidally below and above the quiescent base current I_{BQ}. In response of changes in I_B, the collector current changes sinusoidally above and below it's quiescent current value I_{CQ}. The collector current and base current are in phase with each other. Due to changes in I_C, the voltage V_{CE} will also fluctuate sinusoidally.
- Note that V_{CE} and I_C are 180° out of phase.
- In class-A operation the transistor remains in the active region for all values of input signal and never enters in saturation or cut-off region. The transistor conducts for complete cycle of a.c. input.

Advantages of class-A amplifier :
1. Simple construction.
2. Distortionless output voltage.

Disadvantages of class-A amplifier :
1. As transistor continuously operates in active region, the voltage V_{CE} across it and current I_C passing through the transistor are both simultaneously high. Therefore, large power will be dissipated in the transitor in the form of heat.
2. Due to large power dissipation, efficiency is very low (25% or 50%).

Power gain : Power gain is a ratio of a.c. output power to a.c. input power.

i.e.
$$G = \frac{P_{out}}{P_{in}}$$

Output power : We measure the output voltage of Fig. 5.4 (a). In r.m.s. volt, the output power is given by

$$P_{out} = \frac{V_{rms}^2}{R_L}$$

We measure output voltage as peak to peak volts with an oscilloscope.

$$V_{pp} = 2\sqrt{2}\, V_{rms}$$

$$P_{out} = \frac{V_{out}^2}{8R_L}$$

- The maximum output occurs when amplifier is producing the maximum peak to peak output voltage as shown in Fig. 5.7 (b). In this case, V_{pp} equals the maximum peak to peak output voltage. The maximum output power is

$$P_{out\,(max)} = \frac{MPP^2}{8R_L}$$

Transistor power dissipation :
When no signal drives the amplifier, the quiescent power dissipation is

$$P_{DQ} = V_{CEQ}\, I_{CQ}$$

i.e. the quiescent power dissipation equals the d.c. voltage times the d.c. current.

- When a signal is present, the power dissipation of transistor decreases. This is because the transistor converts some of the quiescent power to signal power. For this reason, the quiescent power dissipation is the worst case. Hence, power rating of class-A amplifier must be greater than P_{DQ}, otherwise the transistor will be destroyed.

Current drain : The d.c. voltage source has to supply a d.c. current I_{dc} to the amplifier. This d.c. current has two components, the biasing current through voltage divider and the collector current through transistor. The d.c. current is called the current drain of the stage. If you are using multistage transistor, you have to add the individual current drain to get the total current drain.

Efficiency : The d.c. power supplied to an amplifier by d.c. source is

$$P_{dc} = V_{cc} I_{dc}$$

Efficiency equals the a.c. output power divided by d.c. input power

$$\eta = \frac{P_{out}}{P_{in}} \times 100$$

- Efficiency gives us a way to compare two designs because it indicates how well an amplifier converts the d.c. input power to a.c. power. This is important in battery operated equipment because high efficiency means that batteries last longer.
- The maximum efficiency of a class-A amplifier with a d.c. collector resistance and a separate load resistance is 25%. In some application such low efficiency is acceptable. For example, the small signal stages near the front of a system usually work fine with low efficiency, because d.c. input power is small.

5.6 CLASS-B PUSH PULL AMPLIFIER

| Q. Explain push-pull amplifier with neat circuit diagram. | [May 11, Dec. 11, 8 M] |
| Q. Explain with neat circuit diagram working of push-pull amplifier. | [Dec. 12, 8 M] |

- A power amplifier is referred to as a class-B amplifier if output signal is obtained only for one half cycle period of input a.c. signal. The transistor conducts only in half cycle of input and collector current therefore flows for 180°.
- For this the Q point is adjusted to be at cut-off on X-axis and thus in absence of a.c. input signal the transistor remains in off state.

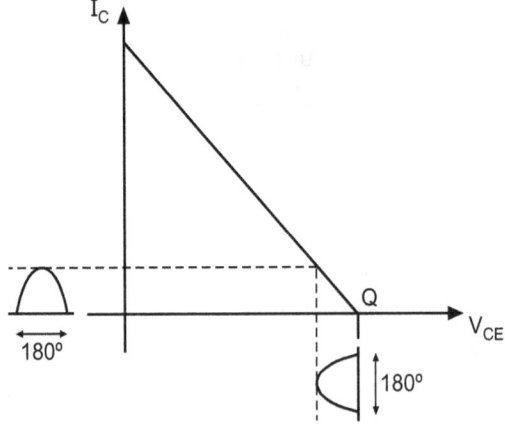

Fig. 5.8

Push-Pull Circuit :

Fig. 5.9 shows a push-pull amplifier. When transistor operates as class B, it clips off half a cycle. To avoid the resulting distortion, we can use two transistors in push-pull arrangement. Push pull means that one transistor conducts for half a cycle while the other is off and vice a versa.

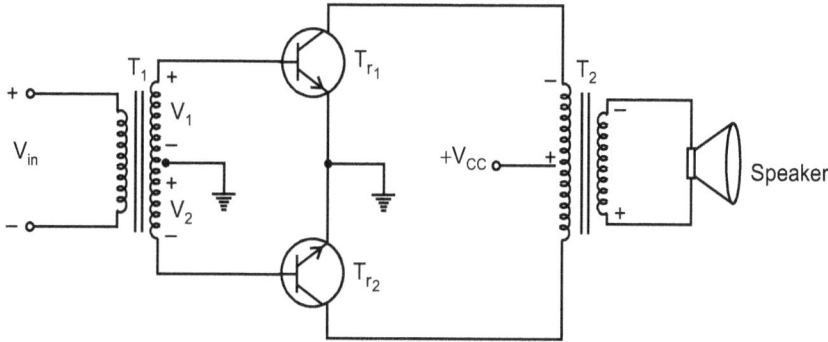

Fig. 5.9 : Class-B push-pull amplifier

Working :
- On the positive half cycle of input voltage, secondary windings of transformer T_1 has voltages V_1 and V_2 as described in Fig. 5.8. Therefore, the upper transistor (T_{r1}) conducts and lower transistor (T_{r2}) remains in cut-off state. The collector current through T_{r1} flows through upper half of the output primary windings. This produces an amplified and inverted voltage which is transformer coupled to the load speaker.
- On the next half cycle of input voltage, the polarity reverses. Now, the lower transistor turns on and upper transistor turns off. The lower transistor amplifies the signal and alternate half cycle appears across the load speaker.
- As each transistor, amplifies one half of input cycle, the loud speaker receives a complete cycle of amplified signal.

Advantages :
- Since there is no bias in Fig. 5.9, each transistor is at cut-off whenever there is no input signal. It is an advantage because there is no current drain when the signal is zero.
- **Improved efficiency :** The maximum efficiency of class-B push-pull amplifier is 78.5%. So a class-B push-pull power amplifier is more commonly used for an output state than a class-A power amplifier.
- Zero power dissipation under quiescent condition.
- Impedance matching with load is possible.

Disadvantages :
- Audio transformers are bulky and expensive.
- Crossover distortion is present in output waveform.

5.7 TYPES OF COUPLING (QUANTITATIVE ANALYSIS)

- We have already introduced the classification of amplifier according to coupling methods. i.e. direct coupled amplifier, RC coupled amplifier, LC coupled amplifier and transformer coupled amplifier. Now, we study the effect on performance parameter of an amplifier due to different coupling methods used.

5.7.1 Direct Coupled Amplifier

Consider two stage direct-coupled amplifier using transistor as shown in the Fig. 5.10 below.

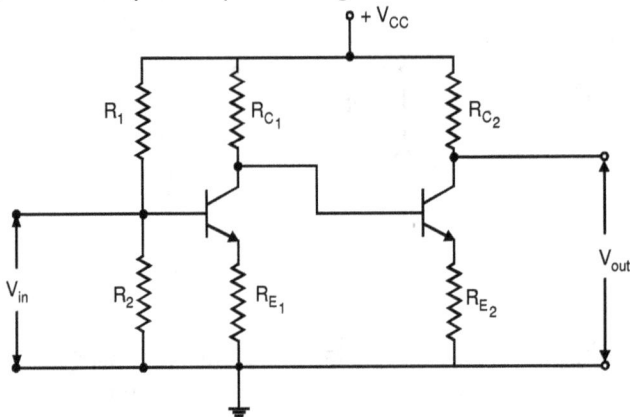

Fig. 5.10 : Two stage direct coupled amplifier

- In this circuit, coupling and bypass capacitors are not used. Therefore, both d.c. as well as a.c. signals are coupled to the next stage. As far as d.c. signal is concerned, collector voltage of first stage is connected to the base of next stage, one has to consider biasing circuit carefully for second stage.

Advantage

- The advantage of the direct coupling can be understood if we remember reactance of a capacitor which is frequency dependent. At lower frequencies upto 10 Hz, the capacitive reactance is very high. Hence, if they are used in coupling and bypass position, they provide a large impedance which will not serve their purpose in the circuit, otherwise one has to use a very high value of capacitance upto 1000 µF in the circuit which is not suitable for circuit operation. Thus, direct coupling is suitable at lower frequency operating amplifiers. For example, thermocouple output connected to the amplifier must be directly coupled. This is because the production of thermoemf with respect to temperature is very low frequency operation. Hence, for the proper calibration of temperature measurement, direct coupled amplifier is suitable.

Disadvantage

- Since the two stages are directly coupled, change in V_{BE} and β due to temperature causes drift to the output. This is because output of the first stage is directly coupled to the next stage. Hence, the drift voltage causes unwanted changes at the output. This problem of drift can be minimized by using two stage direct coupled amplifier using FET.

5.7.2 Transformer Coupled Amplifier

> **Q.** Explain transformer coupled multistage amplifier with neat circuit diagram. Also state its advantages and disadvantages. **[May 12, 8 M]**

Consider transformer coupled amplifier as shown in the Fig. 5.11.

- Here we see that the two stages of amplifier are coupled by transformer. A coupling transformer is used to feed the output of one stage to the input of the next stage via mutual induction.
- The collector load of first stage is replaced by primary of transformer, and the voltage across secondary provides input to the second stage. Thus, voltage developed across primary is transferred to the next stage by the secondary coil.

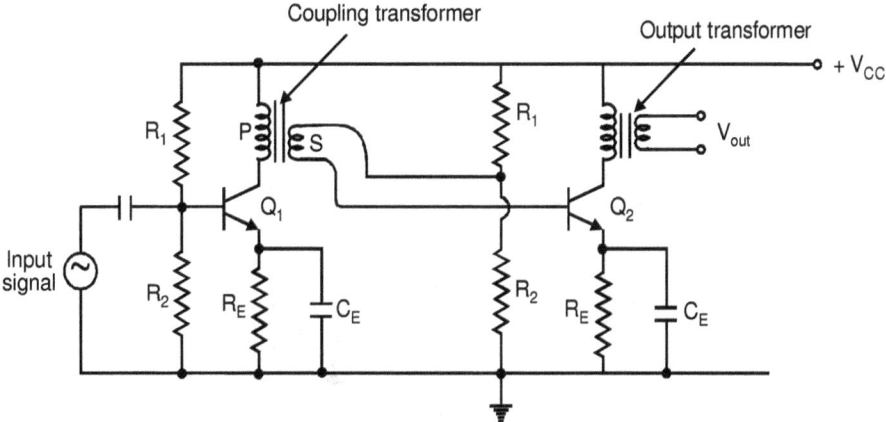

Fig. 5.11 : Transformer coupled amplifier

- In the transformer coupling, we get excellent impedance matching, causing maximum power transfer. The signal is not lost at collector or base, which provides higher gain. This type of coupling of amplifiers is used in power stage of the systems.
- The disadvantages of the transformer coupling are poor frequency response, distortion. Also these are bulky and expensive elements.
- The frequency response of transformer coupled amplifier is very poor, this is because of the reactance of the coil, and mode of capacitance between the turns of coil in primary and secondary coil.
- At low frequencies, the reactance of the windings begins to fall ($X_L = 2\pi f L$). Hence, gain is reduced, whereas the capacitance between turns of coil acts as bypass capacitor causing low output voltage and gain. Thus, transformer coupled amplifier introduces frequency distortion.

5.7.3 RC Coupled Amplifier

Q. Draw and explain RC coupled BJT amplifier.	[Dec. 11, 8 M]
Q. State advantages and applications of multistage amplifiers.	[Dec. 10, 3 M]

Consider two stage R-C coupled amplifier as shown in the Fig. 5.12.
- Here we see that a coupling capacitor C_C is used to connect the output of first stage amplifier to the base of the second stage amplifier as a input. This capacitor C_C is followed by a shunt resistor R_2, the biasing resistor of second stage, hence these amplifiers are called resistance-capacitor coupled or RC coupled amplifiers.

- The coupling capacitor C_C transmits a.c. signal to the next stage while blocks d.c. voltage. Hence, d.c. interference is avoided, which also stabilizes the operating point.
- The overall gain of the amplifier is increased. But the total gain is less than the product of the gains of individual stages. This is because, effective load resistance of first stage is reduced due to shunting effect of the input resistance of second stage.

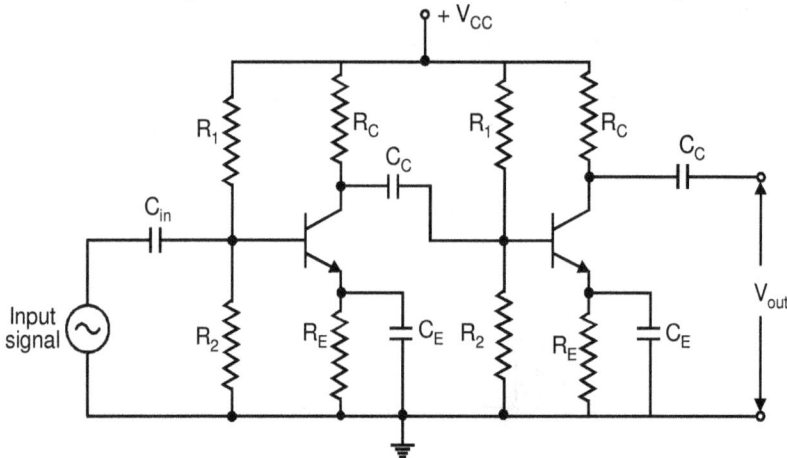

Fig. 5.12 : RC coupled amplifier

- The effect of coupling capacitor on frequency response is different for high, low and mid-frequency range.
- At the lower frequencies < 50 Hz, the reactance of C_C is very high, causing a very small signal to be passed to the next stage, hence gain of amplifier decreases. Whereas at the high frequencies > 20 kHz, the reactance of C_C is very small and it acts as short circuit causing loading effect to the second stage. Hence, the gain is reduced at a higher frequencies.
- But in the mid-frequency range from 50 Hz to 20 kHz, voltage gain of amplifier is constant. This is because, as frequency increases, reactance of C_C decreases, which causes to increase in gain. But at the same time, the first stage is loaded due to lower reactance causing lowering of gain.
- Thus, this results in a uniform gain at mid-frequency range. The RC coupling is most popular and cheaper method. It provides constant gain over audio frequency range. The RC coupled amplifiers are used in audio amplifiers, public address systems.
- There are certain disadvantages of RC coupling of amplifier. First one is lower voltage and power gain. The circuit becomes noisy at different environmental conditions, particularly in moist climate and also the impedance matching is very poor. Hence, RC coupling amplifiers are not used at the final stages of system. It is replaced by transformer coupling to achieve impedance matching as well as maximum power transfer to load.

5.7.4 Multistage RC Coupled CE Amplifier

- We have already discussed the RC coupled amplifier in the previous section. Now, we shall study effect of coupling capacitor and bypass capacitor on frequency response for multistage amplifier, and their application area in this section.

- When a number of amplifier stages are used in succession, it is called a multistage amplifier or cascaded amplifier. The output of first stage is connected to the input of the second stage through a coupling device and so on.

- Consider a three stage amplifier shown by block diagram in the Fig. 5.13. Each stage consists of one transistor and its associated circuitary for amplification and is coupled to the next stage through a coupling device like capacitor.

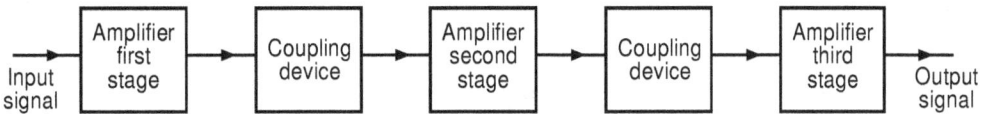

Fig. 5.13 : Block diagram of a multistage amplifier

- Here, we should note that the gain of a multistage amplifier is equal to the product of gains of individual stages.

  i.e. if A_1, A_2 and A_3 are the individual gains of three stage amplifier, then the total voltage gain A is given by,

  $$A = A_1 \times A_2 \times A_3.$$

- In practical cases, due to loading effect of next stages, A is less than $A_1 \times A_2 \times A_3$. Now to study the effect of coupling capacitor and bypass capacitor on frequency response, consider a RC coupled multistage amplifier as shown in the Fig. 5.14.

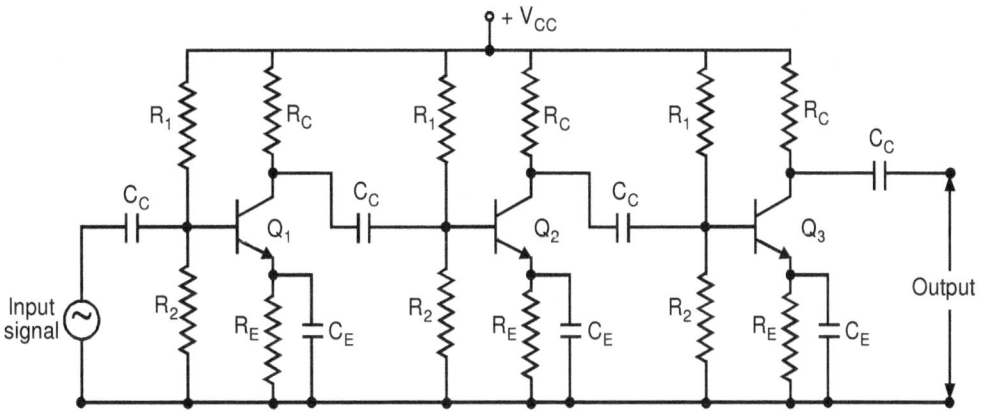

Fig. 5.14 : Multistage RC coupled amplifier

- The frequency response of a multistage RC coupled amplifier is as shown in Fig. 5.15.

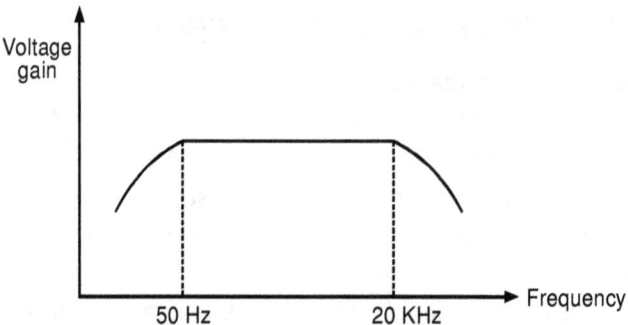

Fig. 5.15 : Frequency response

- Here, we see that gain drops off at low frequencies (less than 50 Hz) and at high frequencies (greater than 20 kHz); whereas it is constant in between 50 Hz to 20 kHz i.e. midrange frequency.
- Now, consider the effect of coupling capacitor C_C and bypass capacitor C_E on the frequency response at these frequency levels.

(a) Low frequency range (0 to 50 Hz) : At lower frequency, reactance of coupling capacitor C_C and bypass capacitor C_E are very high $\left(X_C = \dfrac{1}{2\pi fC}\right)$.

Hence, C_C cannot pass more signal to the next stage, whereas C_E cannot shunt the emitter resistance. Therefore, we see that there is fall of voltage gain at lower frequency range in multistage amplifier frequency response.

(b) High frequency range (greater than 20 kHz) : At higher frequency, reactance of coupling capacitor C_C and bypass capacitor C_E are very low and act like a short circuit.

Hence, C_C causes to load the next stage and reduces gain, whereas C_E shorts the R_E, which causes to reduce current gain. Hence, voltage gain falls at higher frequency range in the multistage amplifier frequency response.

(c) Mid frequency range (50 Hz to 20 kHz) : As the frequency increases from 50 Hz to 20 kHz, reactance of C_C and C_E go on decreasing.

As the reactance of C_C goes on decreasing, more voltage is fed to the next stage and voltage gain is increased; whereas C_E goes on shorting R_E which reduces the gain, hence as a overall effect uniform voltage gain is maintained due to coupling capacitor C_C at the mid frequency range.

Applications :
- Hence, RC coupled CE amplifiers are used in voltage amplifiers, audio amplifiers. In these applications, both the requirements of frequency bandwidth in audio frequency range and constant voltage gain in the audio frequency range are achieved. But because of poor impedance matching, RC coupled amplifiers are not used at the final stages, in order to deliver maximum power to the load.

5.7.5 Differential Amplifier

- Resistors, diodes and transistors are the practical components in typical ICs. Small capacitors of the order of 50 pF may also be used. IC designers cannot use coupling and bypass capacitor (used in discrete circuit).
- Instead of that, IC designers has to use direct coupling between stages and also need to eliminate emitter bypass capacitor without losing too much voltage gain.
- Differential amplifier is a circuit which can eliminate the need for an emitter bypass capacitor. Hence differential amplifier is used as the input stage of almost every IC op-amp.

Differential input and output :

- Fig. 5.16 shows differential amplifier. The circuit is two common emitter (CE) stages in parallel with common emitter resistors. Though it has two inputs V_1 and and V_2 and two collector voltages V_{C1} and V_{C2}, the whole circuit is considered to be as one stage. As there are no coupling or bypass capacitors, there is no longer cut-off frequency.

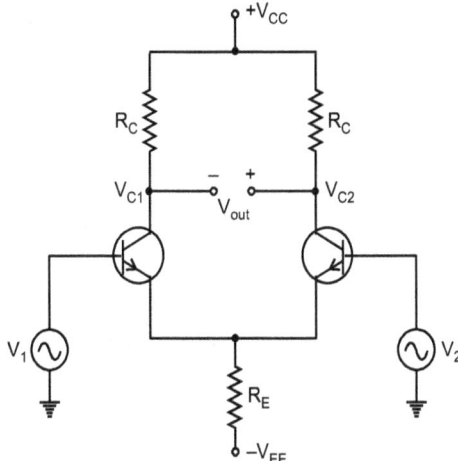

Fig. 5.16 : Differential input and differential output

- The a.c. output voltage is the voltage between the collectors with polarity shown in Fig. 5.16.

$$V_{out} = V_{C2} - V_{C1}$$

- This voltage is called *differential output* because it combines two a.c. collector voltages into one voltage that equals the difference of the collector voltages.
- In ideal situation the circuit has two identical transistors and equal collector resistors. With perfect symmetry $V_{out} = 0$ when two inputs are equal. When $V_1 > V_2$, output has polarity as shown in Fig. 5.16. When $V_2 > V_1$, the output voltage is inverted and has opposite polarity.

- The differential amplifier has two separate inputs. Input V_1 is called non-inverting input because V_{out} is in phase with V_1. The other output V_2 is called inverting input because V_{out} is 180° out of phase with V_2.
- When both inverting and non-inverting voltages are present, the total inputs are called *differential input* because output voltage equals the voltage gain times the difference of the two input voltages.

$$\therefore \quad V_{out} = A(V_1 - V_2)$$
$$\text{where,} \quad A = \text{voltage gain}$$

Single ended output :

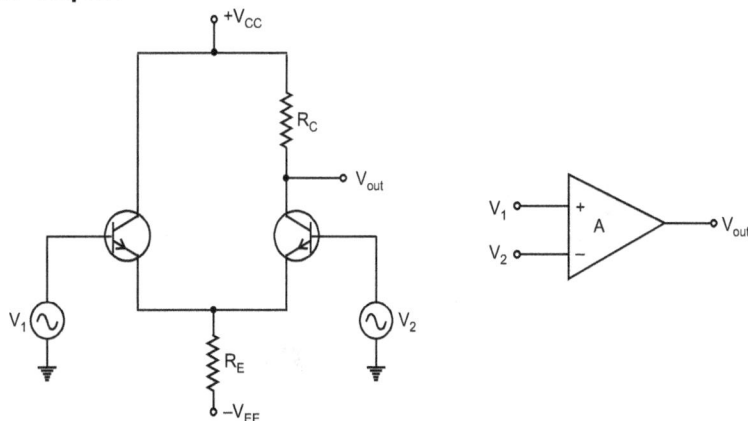

(a) Differential input and single ended output   (b) Block diagram symbol

Fig. 5.17

- The differential amplifier as shown in Fig. 5.17 requires a floating load because neither end of the load can be grounded. This is inconvenient in many cases since loads are often single ended; that is one end is grounded.
- Fig. 5.17(a) shows differential input and single ended output. It has many applications, since it can drive single end load like CE stages, emitter follower and other circuits. The a.c. output is given as

$$V_{out} = A(V_1 - V_2)$$

- With a single ended output, the voltage gain is half as much as differential output as output is coming from only one of the collectors.
- Fig. 5.17 (b) shows block diagram symbol for a differential amplifier with a differential input and a single ended output. The same symbol is used in operational amplifier. The positive sign represents the non-inverting input and minus sign represents the inverting input.

5.7.5.1 Non-inverting input configuration

- Sometimes only one of the input is active and the other is grounded as shown in Fig. 5.18(a). The configuration has a non-inverting input and a differential output.

Since
$$V_2 = 0$$
$$V_{out} = -AV_1$$

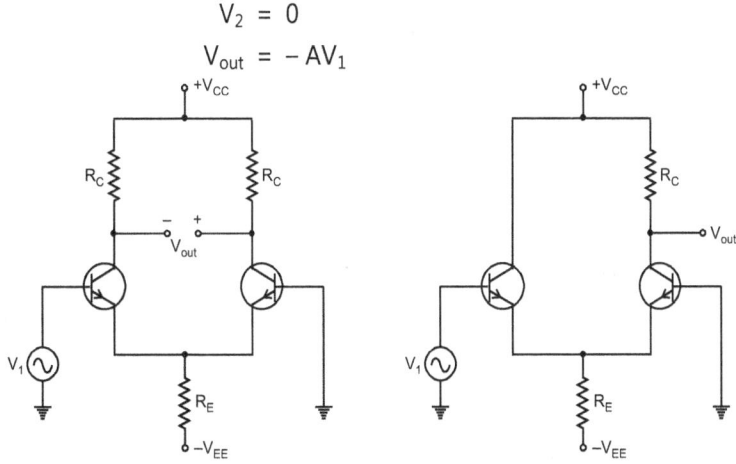

(a) Non-inverting input and differential output

(b) Non-inverting input and single ended output

Fig. 5.18

- Fig. 5.18 (b) shows another configuration for differential amplifier. This circuit has non-inverting input and single ended output. $V_{out} = -AV_1$ is still valid but voltage gain A will be half as much because the output is taken from only one side of differential amplifier.

5.7.5.2 Inverting input configuration

In some cases, V_2 is active input and V_1 is grounded as shown in Fig. 5.19 (a).

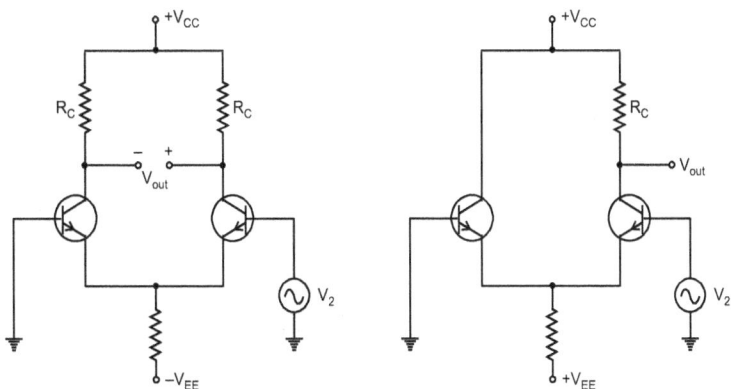

(a) Inverting input and differential output

(b) Inverting input and single ended output

Fig. 5.19

In this case,
$$V_{out} = -AV_2$$
Minus sign indicates the phase inversion.

Fig. 5.19(b) represents inverting input with single ended output. In this case also,
$$V_{out} = -Av_2.$$

5.8 FIELD-EFFECT TRANSISTORS

5.8.1 Introduction

- The transistors (BJTs) are current-controlled devices. They relied on two types of charge carriers : electrons and holes. The BJT has two types of disadvantages. Firstly, it has a low input impedance because of forward biased emitter-base junction. Secondly, it has considerable noise level. These drawbacks have been overcome to a great extent by a discovery of a new solid-state device called *field-effect transistor* abbreviated as FET. This device is unipolar because its operation depends on only one type of charge, either the free electrons or holes. In other words, an FET has majority charge carriers but not minority charge carriers.
- The FET is a three terminal unipolar solid state device in which the current is controlled by an electric field as in vacuum tubes. Here, current conduction takes place by only one type of charge carrier, i.e. either free electrons or holes.

5.8.2 Types of FETs

In a broad sense, following are the two main types of field-effect transistors (FETs).
1. Junction field-effect transistor (JFET).
2. Metal oxide-semiconductor field-effect transistor (MOSFET) or insulated gate field-effect transistor (IGFET).

Both of these types of FETs can be further sub-divided as shown in Table 5.2

Table 5.2 : Different types of field-effect transistor

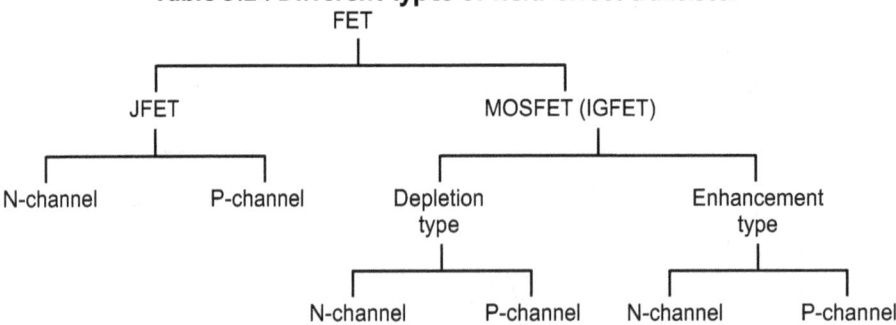

5.9 JUNCTION FIELD-EFFECT TRANSISTORS (JFETS)

- The JFET is a three terminal unipolar solid state device in which the current is controlled by the electric field. Here, the current conduction takes place by only one type of charge carrier, i.e. either free electrons or holes.
- The junction field-effect transistors (JFET) can be divided depending upon their structure into the following two categories : (1) N-channel JFET and (2) P-channel JFET.

- The basic constructional details of N-channel and P-channel JFETs are as shown in Fig. 5.20 (a) and (b) respectively.

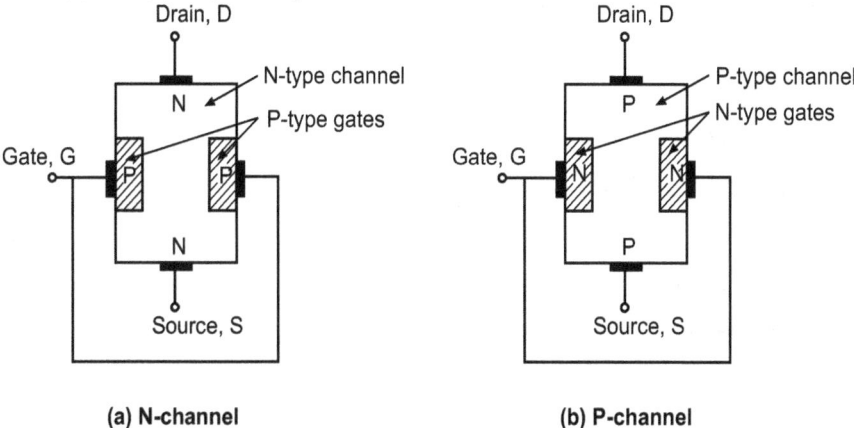

(a) N-channel   (b) P-channel

Fig. 5.20 : Construction of JFETs

5.10 CONSTRUCTION OF JFET

5.10.1 Construction of N-channel JFET

Q. Draw and explain construction of FET. [May 11, 2 M]

- The construction of an N-channel JFET is as shown in Fig. 5.20 (a). It consists of an N-type semiconductor, i.e. Silicon bar with two P-type heavily doped regions diffused on opposite sides of its middle part.
- The P-type regions form two PN junctions. *The space between the junctions, i.e. N-type regions is called a channel.* Both the P-type regions are connected internally and a single wire is taken out in the form of a terminal called the gate (G).
- The electrical connections (called ohmic contacts) are made to both ends of the N-type semiconductor and are taken out in the form of two terminals called *drain* (D) and *source* (S).
- The drain (D) is a terminal through which electrons leave the semiconductor bar and source (S) is a terminal through which electrons enter the semiconductor.

5.10.2 Construction of P-channel JFET

- A P-channel JFET is shown in Fig. 5.20 (b). Its construction is similar to that of N-channel JFET, except that it consists of a P-type silicon bar with two N-type heavily doped regions diffused on opposite sides of its middle part.
- The N-type regions form two P-N junctions. *The space between the junctions i.e. P-type junction is called a channel.* Both, the N-type regions are connected internally and a single wire is taken out in the form of a terminal called the *gate* (G).

- The electrical connections (called ohmic contacts) are made to both ends of the P-type semiconductor and are taken out in the form of two terminals called *drain* (D) and *source* (S).
- The drain (D) is a terminal through which electrons enter the semiconductor bar and source (S) is a terminal through which electrons leave the semiconductor.

5.10.3 Symbols of JFET

- Fig. 5.21(a) and (b) show the schematic symbol of N-channel and P-channel JFET respectively. In many low-frequency applications, the source and drain are interchangeable because we can use either end as the source and the other end as the drain.

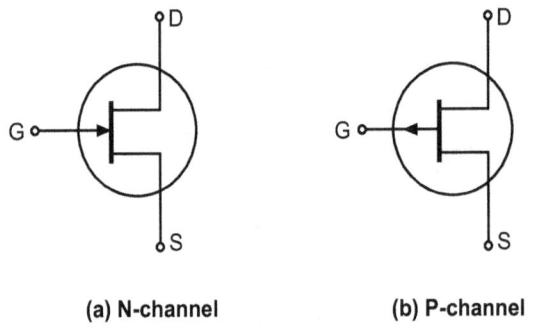

(a) N-channel   (b) P-channel

Fig. 5.21 : Symbols for JFETs

- The direction of arrowheads, in the symbols for JFETs, may be carefully noted. In an N-channel JFET, the arrowhead points towards the vertical line. The vertical line represents the N-channel in Fig. 5.21 (a).
- On the other hand, in a P-channel symbol, the arrowhead points away from the vertical line. Here the vertical line represents the P-channel as shown in Fig. 5.21 (b).

5.11 WORKING PRINCIPLE OF N-CHANNEL JFET

- Consider an N-channel JFET as shown in Fig. 5.22. Here P-type gate and N-type channel constitute P-N junctions. Since the P-region of an N-channel JFET is heavily doped, as compared to the N-channel, the depletion region extends into the P-region and deeper into the N-channel.
- When there is no applied voltage between the drain and source, the depletion region is symmetrical around the junction as shown in Fig. 5.22 (a).

- The conductivity of depletion region is zero because there are no mobile charge carriers in this region. The effective width of the N-channel reduces with the increased reverse bias voltage applied across the gate and source terminal of the JFET as shown in Fig. 5.22 (b).

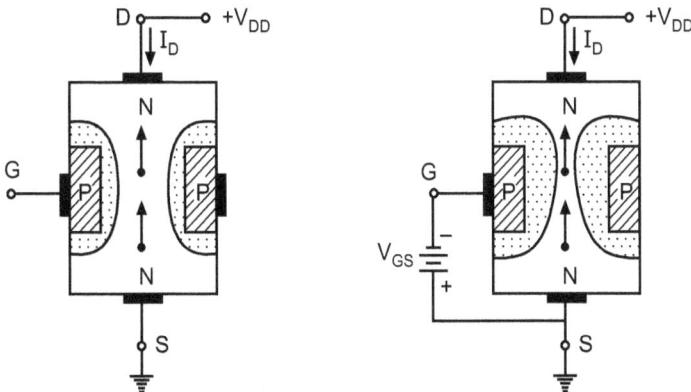

(a) Depletion region with no bias   (b) Depletion regions with reverse bias gate

Fig. 5.22 : Formation of Depletion region in N-channel JFET

- Consider an N-channel JFET as shown in Fig. 5.23 (a). When the voltage is applied between the drain and source with a battery V_{DS} and the gate is kept open, the electrons flow from source-to-drain through the narrow channel existing between the depletion regions. This constitutes the drain current I_D and its conventional direction is indicated from drain-to-source.

- The value of drain current is now maximum and this current is designated as I_{DSS}. When gate is directly connected to the source (i.e. no external bias), we say that $V_{GS} = 0$ [See Fig. 5.23 (a)]. The characteristic for $V_{GS} = 0$ is plotted in Fig. 5.23 (b).

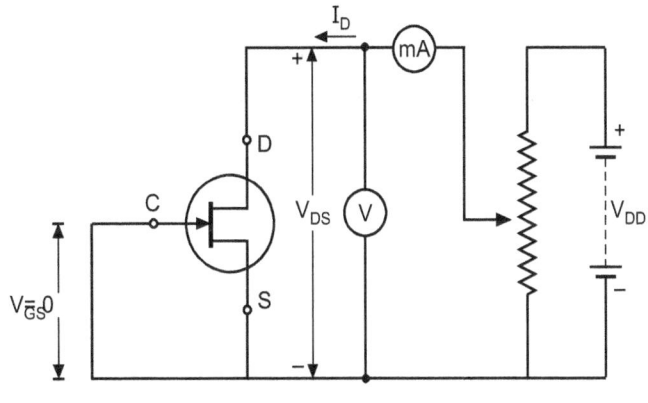

(a) N-channel JFET with zero gate voltage

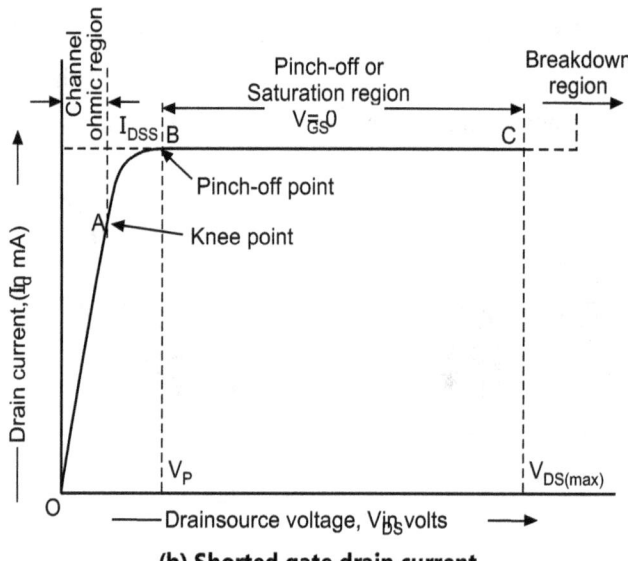

(b) Shorted gate drain current

Fig. 5.23 : Characteristics of N-channel JFET when $V_{GS} = 0$

- When $V_{DS} = 0$, the drain current $I_D = 0$, and the voltage between the gate and all points in the channel is also zero. When V_{DS} is increased by small amount the drain current also increases by small amount causing some voltage drop across the channel.
- Due to this the gate-channel junctions are reverse biased by small amount. This causes little depletion region penetration having negligible effect on the channel resistance.
- At first, the drain current I_D increases rapidly with increase in V_{DS} but then becomes constant. The drain-source voltage above which drain current becomes constant is known as *pinch-off voltage* (V_P). The drain current at this point, with $V_{GS} = 0$, is referred as the *drain-source saturation current* (I_{DSS}). The region of the characteristics where I_D is fairly constant is referred to as the *pinch-off region*.
- This region sometimes called as the *channel ohmic region*, because the channel is behaving like a resistance. When V_{DS} is continuously increased a stage will reach when the gate-channel junction breaks down. This is the result of the charge carriers which make up the reverse saturation current at the gate channel junction being accelerated to high velocity and producing avalanche effect. At this point the drain current increases rapidly, and the device may be destroyed.
- The normal operating region for JFET is the characteristics in the pinch-off region.
- The flow of drain current in N-channel JFET is only due to the majority charge carriers i.e. electrons. For this reason, the JFET is called a *unipolar transistor*.
- The operation of P-channel JFET is exactly similar to N-channel JFET except that current carriers are holes and polarities of the battery voltages V_{GG} and V_{DD} are reversed.

5.12 CHARACTERISTICS OF N-CHANNEL JFET

Q. Explain characteristics of FET. [May 11, 4 M]

- Following are the two important characteristics of a JFET :
1. V-I or Drain characteristics
2. Transfer characteristics.

The drain and transfer characteristics of N-channel JFET may be obtained by using an N-channel JFET connected to the common source mode as shown in Fig. 5.24. Here, the potentiometers R_1 and R_2 are used to vary the voltages V_{GS} and V_{DS} respectively.

- The voltages V_{DS} and V_{GS} may be measured by the voltmeters connected across the JFET terminals. The drain current I_D can be measured by the milliameter connected in series with the JFET and the supply voltage V_{DD}.

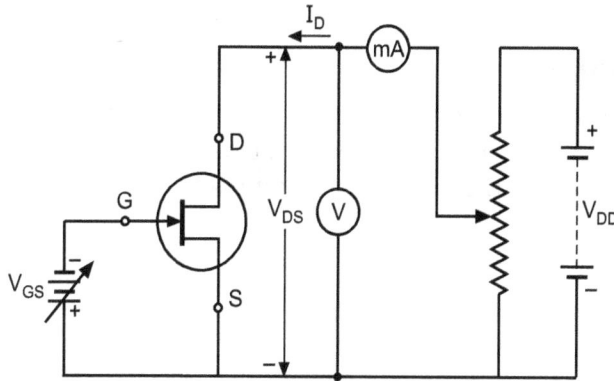

Fig. 5.24 : Circuit arrangement for JFET characteristics

5.12.1 Drain Characteristics

Q. Draw and explain the drain characteristics of FET.	[Dec. 12, 8 M]
Q. Explain drain characteristics of FET.	[Dec. 12, 8 M]
Q. What is the significance of drain characteristics.	[Dec. 10, May 12, 2 M]

- The characteristic curve which gives the relationship between the drain current I_D and drain-to-source voltage V_{DS} for a constant gate-to-source voltage is known as drain characteristics.
- These curves may be obtained by using the circuit arrangement shown in Fig. 5.24. First of all, we adjust the gate-to-source voltage V_{GS} to zero volt. Then increase the drain-to-source voltage V_{DS} in small suitable steps and record the corresponding values of drain current I_D at each step.
- Now, if we plot a graph with the voltage V_{DS} along the horizontal (i.e. X) axis and the current I_D along the vertical (i.e. Y) axis, we shall get a curve marked $V_{GS} = 0$ as shown in Fig. 5.25. A similar procedure may be used to obtain curves for different values of $V_{GS} = -1, -2, -3$ etc.

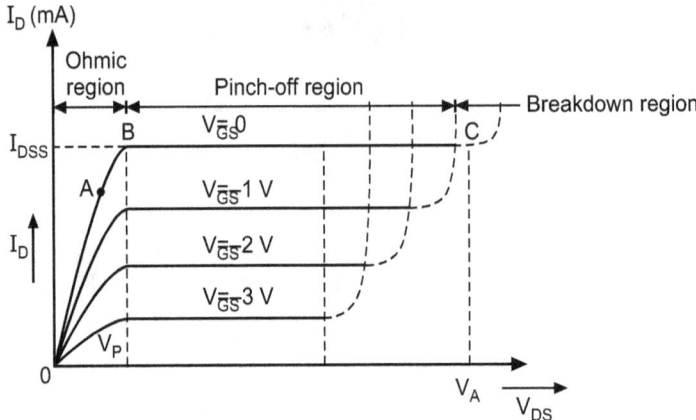

Fig. 5.25 : Drain characteristics of N-channel JFET

The drain characteristic curve may be divided into the following four regions :

(a) **Ohmic region (OA) :**
- This region is shown as a curve OA in the figure. In this region, the drain current increases linearly with the increase in drain-to-source voltage and obeys the Ohm's law. The linear increase in drain current is due to the fact that the N-type semiconductor bar acts as a simple resistor.

(b) **Curve AB :**
- In this region, the drain current increases at the reverse square law rate with the increase in drain-to-source voltage. It means that drain current increases slowly as compared to that in ohmic region. It is because of the fact, that with the increase in drain-to-source voltage, the drain current increases.
- This in turn increases the reverse bias voltage across the gate-to-source junction. As a result of this, the depletion region increases in size, thereby reducing the effective width of the conducting channel.
- At the drain-to-source voltage, corresponding to point B, the channel width is reduced to a minimum value and is known as pinch off. *The drain-to-source voltage at which the channel pinch-off occurs is known as pinch-off voltage (V_p).*

(c) **Pinch-off region (BC) :**
- This region is shown by a curve BC. It is also called *saturation region* or constant current region. In this region, drain current remains constant at its maximum value (i.e. I_{DSS}). The drain current in the pinch-off region depends upon the gate-to-source voltage and is given by

$$I_D = I_{DSS}\left(1 - \frac{V_{GS}}{V_p}\right)^2$$

- This relation is known as *Schockly's equation*. The pinch-off region is the normal operating region of JFET when used as an amplifier.

(d) Breakdown region (CD) :

- This region is shown by the curve CD. In this region, the drain current increases rapidly as the drain-to-source voltage is increased. It happens due to avalanche effect. *The drain-to-source voltage corresponding to point C is called breakdown voltage.*

5.12.2 Transfer Characteristics

> Q. What is the significance of transfer characteristic of FET ? Draw and explain.
> [Dec. 11, May 12, 4 M]

- The characteristic curve which gives the relationship between the drain current I_D and gate-to-source voltage V_{GS} for a constant drain-to-source voltage V_{DS} is known as transfer characteristics.

- These curves may be obtained by using the circuit arrangement shown in Fig. 5.24. First of all, we adjust the drain-to-source voltage V_{DS} to some suitable value. Then increase the gate-to-source V_{GS} in small suitable steps and record the corresponding values of drain current I_D at each step.

- If we plot a graph with the voltage V_{GS} along the horizontal (X) axis and the current I_D along the vertical (Y) axis, we shall get a curve as shown in Fig. 5.26. A similar procedure may be used to obtain curves at different values of voltage V_{GS}.

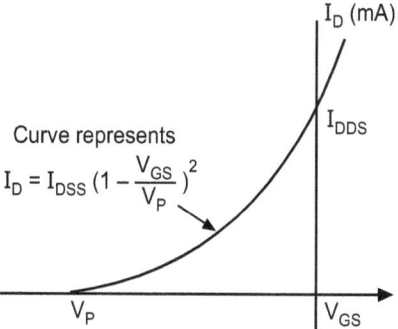

Fig. 5.26 : Transfer characteristics of N-channel JFET

5.13 PARAMETERS OF JFET

> Q. Define transconductance and amplifier factor associated with FET. [Dec. 10, 4 M]

- The electrical properties of JFET may be described in terms of certain parameters called JFET parameters. Such parameters may be obtained from the characteristic curves of JFET. The important parameters are as discussed below :

1. Drain saturation current (I_{DSS}) :

The maximum amount of drain current at zero gate-to-source voltage V_{GS} is known as drain saturation current. It is denoted by I_{DSS} and it is specified by the manufacturer.

2. D.C. drain resistance (R_D) :

It is defined as the ratio of drain-to-source voltage V_{DS} to the resulting drain current (I_D) for a constant gate-to-source voltage V_{GS}. It is also called the *static* or *ohmic resistance* of the channel and mathematically,

$$R_D = \frac{V_{DS}}{I_D}\bigg|_{V_{GS} = \text{constant}}$$

3. A. C. drain resistance (r_d) :

It is defined as the ratio of small change in drain-to-source voltage ΔV_{DS} to the resulting change in drain current (ΔI_D) for constant gate-to-source voltage V_{GS}. It is also called *dynamic drain resistance* and it is the a.c. resistance between the drain and source terminal when the JFET is operating in the pinch-off or saturation region.

$$\Delta r_d = \frac{\Delta V_{DS}}{\Delta I_D}\bigg|_{V_{GS} = \text{constant}}$$

Its value ranges from 10 kΩ to 1 MΩ. Typically, it is about 400 kΩ.

4. Transconductance (g_m) :

It is defined as the ratio of small change in drain current ΔI_D to the corresponding change in gate-to-source voltage ΔV_{GS} for a constant drain-to-source voltage V_{DS}. It is also called *mutual conductance* and mathematically.

$$g_m = \frac{\Delta I_D}{\Delta V_{GS}}\bigg|_{V_{DS} = \text{constant}}$$

The value of transconductance is expressed in siemens S or mhos Ω. Its value ranges upto 5000 μ mhos and typically, its value ranges from 150 μmhos to 250 μmhos.

5. Amplification factor (μ) :

It is defined as the ratio of small change in drain-to-source voltage ΔV_{DS} to the corresponding change in gate-to-source voltage V_{GS} for a constant drain current I_D. Mathematically,

$$\mu = \frac{\Delta V_{DS}}{\Delta V_{GS}}\bigg|_{I_D = \text{constant}}$$

It has no unit. It can be as high as 100.

Amplification factor of a JFET indicates how much more control the gate voltage V_{GS} has over drain current than has the drain voltage V_{DS}.

6. Input resistance (R_i) :

It is the ratio of reverse gate-to-source voltage V_{GS} to a resulting reverse gate current when the drain-to-source voltage is zero.

Mathematically,

$$R_i = \frac{V_{GS}}{I_{GSS}}$$

It is of the order of hundreds of megaohm.

5.14 RELATION AMONG FET PARAMETERS

Q. What is the relation between FET parameters?

The relationship among the FET parameters can be established as under:

We know, $\mu = \dfrac{\Delta V_{DS}}{\Delta V_{GS}}$

Multiplying the numerator and denominator by I_D, we get

$$\mu = \dfrac{\Delta V_{DS}}{\Delta I_D} \times \dfrac{\Delta I_D}{\Delta V_{GS}}$$

$\therefore \quad \mu = r_d \times g_m$

Therefore, the amplification factor (μ) may be expressed as a product of trans-conductance (g_m) and dynamic drain resistance (r_d).

5.15 APPLICATIONS OF JFET

Q. Give some important applications of JFET.

Some of the important applications of JFET are:
1. It is used as a high impedance wideband amplifier.
2. It is used as a buffer amplifier.
3. It is used as an electronic switch.
4. It is used as a phase-shift oscillator.
5. It is used as a constant-current source.
6. It is used as a voltage variable resistor (VVR) or voltage dependent resistor (VDR).

5.15.1 Electronic Switch

- Field-effect transistors control the current between source and drain connections by a voltage applied between the gate and source. In a junction field-effect transistor (JFET), there is a PN junction between the gate and source which is normally reverse-biased for the control of source-drain current.

- The major application of the JFET is analog switching. In this application, the JFET acts as a switch which either transmits or blocks the AC signal. We have two types of switches: (1) Shunt switch and (2) Series switch. To get the switching action, the gate-source voltage V_{GS} has only two values which are either zero or a value that is greater than $V_{GS(off)}$.

(1) Shunt Switch :

Fig. 5.27 (a) shows the circuit diagram of shunt switch using JFET. The JFET will either conduct of cut off, depending on whether V_{GS} is high or low.

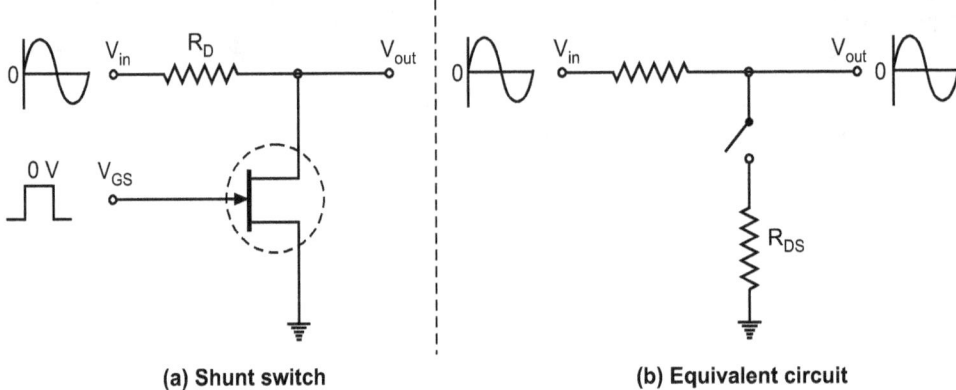

(a) Shunt switch   (b) Equivalent circuit

Fig. 5.27 : Shunt switch

- Remembering that the *controlled* current in a JFET flows between source and drain, we substitute the source and drain connections of a JFET for the two ends of the switch in the above circuit. When V_{GS} is high (0 V), the JFET operates in the ohmic region. When V_{GS} is low, the JFET will be in pinch off, thus forcing it into cutoff. Because of this we can use Fig. 5.27 (b) as an equivalent circuit.

- For normal operation, the a.c. input signal voltage must be small (about 100 mV) so that it ensures that the JFET remains in the ohmic region when the a.c. signal reaches its peak value. Also, the resistance R_D must be very large as compared to drain to source resistance R_{DS} to ensure hard saturation. When V_{GS} is high, the JFET operates in the ohmic region, the JFET conducts and since its resistance R_{DS} is very small, V_{out} is much smaller than V_{in}. In this case, the switch in Fig. 5.27 (b) is closed. When V_{GS} low, the JFET is cut-off and it does not conduct. In this case, the switch in Fig.5.27 (b) is open and V_{out} is equal to V_{in}. Therefore, the JFET shunt switch either transmits the a.c. signal or blocks it.

(2) Series Switch :

Fig. 5.28 (a) shows the circuit diagram of series switch using JFET. Its equivalent circuit is shown in Fig. 5.28 (b). The JFET will either conduct of cut off, depending on whether V_{GS} is high or low.

Remembering that the *controlled* current in a JFET flows between source and drain, we substitute the source and drain connections of a JFET for the two ends of the switch in the above circuit. When V_{GS} is high (0 V), the JFET operates in the ohmic region. When V_{GS} is low, the JFET will be in pinch-off, thus forcing it into cut-off.

- For normal operation, the a.c. input signal voltage must be small (about 100 mV) so that it ensures that the JFET remains in the ohmic region when the a.c. signal reaches its peak value.

- Also, the resistance R_D must be very large as compared to drain to source resistance R_{DS} to ensure hard saturation. When V_{GS} is high, the JFET operates in the ohmic region, the JFET conducts and since its resistance R_{DS} is very small, V_{out} is equal to V_{in}. In this case, the switch in Fig. 5.28 (b) is closed.

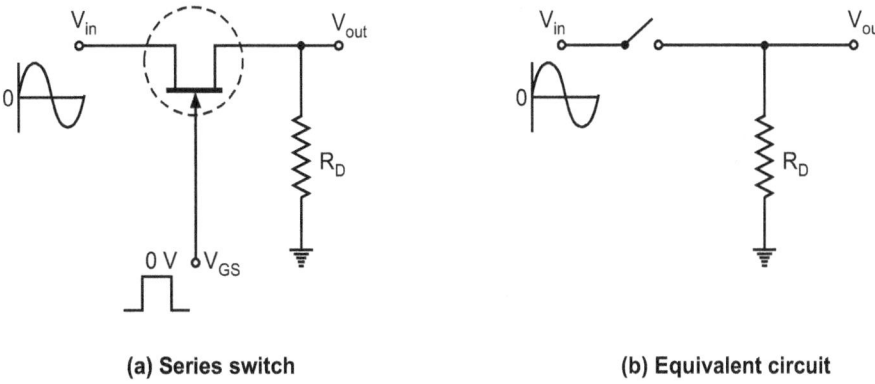

(a) Series switch   (b) Equivalent circuit

Fig. 5.28 : Series switch

- When V_{GS} low, the JFET is cutoff and it does not conduct. In this case, the switch in Fig. 5.28 (b) is open and V_{out} is approximately zero. Therefore, the JFET series switch either transmits the a.c. signal or blocks it.

5.15.2 Analog Multiplexer

- An *analog multiplexer*, a circuit that steers one of the input signals to the output line, is shown in Fig. 5.29. In this circuit, each JFET acts as a single-pole, single-throw switch. When the control signals (V_1, V_2 and V_3) are more negative than $V_{GS(OFF)}$, all input signals are blocked. By making any control voltage equal to zero (i.e. high), one of the inputs can be transmitted to the output. For instance, when V_1 is zero, the signal obtained at the output will be sinusoidal. Similarly when V_2 is zero, the signal obtained at the output will be triangular and when V_3 is zero, the output signal will be square-wave one. Normally, only one of the control signals is zero.

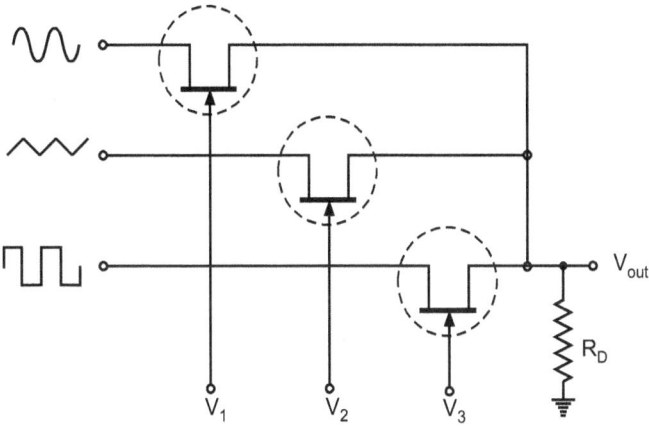

Fig. 5.29 : Analog multiplexer

5.16 ADVANTAGES OF FET OVER BJT

Q. What are the advantages of FET ever BJT ?

Some of the important advantages of FET over BJT are as given below :

- It has extremely high input impedance and low output impedance.
- It has a very high power gain.
- It has a smaller size, longer life and high efficiency.
- It is less noisy.
- It has negative temperature co-efficient of resistance at high current levels and avoids the risk of thermal run-away.
- It is much simpler to fabricate as IC and occupies a less space on IC chip.
- It has better thermal stability.
- The frequency response is high.
- It has high degree of isolation between input and output.
- It is a voltage controlled device. So drain current can be easily controlled by the electric field.

5.17 Disadvantages of JFET

- The main disadvantage of the JFET is the relatively low gain bandwidth product as compared to BJT.

5.18 METAL OXIDE SEMICONDUCTOR FET

Q. What are MOSFETs ?

- The MOSFET is an abbreviation for metal oxide semiconductor field-effect transistor. It is a three terminal semiconductor device. Like JFET, it has a source, gate and drain terminals. Unlike JFET, the gate is a MOSFET, is insulated from the channel and therefore, sometimes it is also known as Insulated Gate Field Effect Transistor (IGFET).

5.18.1 Types of MOSFET

Basically, the MOSFETs are of the following two types :

- Depletion type MOSFET
- Enhancement type MOSFET.

5.19 DEPLETION TYPE N-CHANNEL MOSFET

5.19.1 Construction

- The construction of N-channel depletion type MOSFET is shown in Fig. 5.30 (a) and its basic structure is shown in Fig. 5.31. It consists of a conducting bar of N-type silicon material with an insulated gate on the left and P-region on the right. The free electrons can flow from source to drain through the N-type material. There is only a single P-region and it is called substrate (or body). It physically reduces the conducting path to a narrow channel.

- A thin layer of silicon dioxide is deposited on the left side of the N-type channel. This layer insulates the gate from the channel. It has no P-N junction.

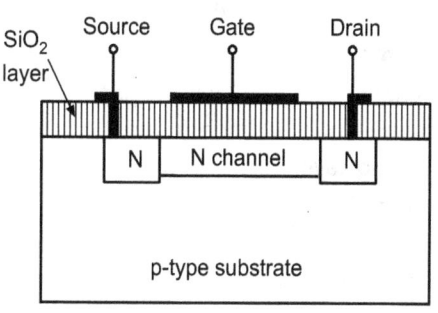
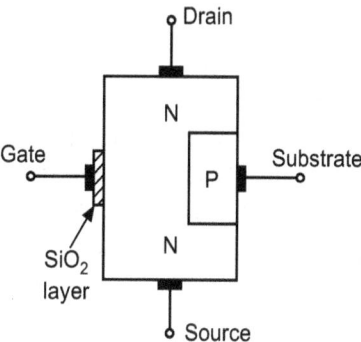

Fig. 5.30 : Depletion type N-channel MOSFET   Fig. 5.31 : Symbol

5.19.2 Working Principle

The depletion-type MOSFET can be operated in the following two different modes :

1. Depletion mode : When the gate voltage is positive with respect to source, the depletion-type MOSFET operates in depletion mode.

2. Enhancement mode : When the gate voltage is negative with respect to source, the depletion-type MOSFET operates with an enhancement mode.

Since the depletion type MOSFET can be operated in either depletion or enhancement mode, the MOSFET is commonly known as depletion - enhancement (DE) type MOSFET.

- The working principle of this MOSFET can be explained easily, if we visualise the entire structure of this MOSFET as a parallel-plate capacitor shown in Fig. 5.32 (b). One of the plates of MOSFET is formed by the gate and the other by the semiconductor channel.

- The plates are separated by a dielectric i.e. SiO_2 layer. We know that if one plate of a capacitor is made negative, it induces a positive charge on the opposite plate and vice-versa.

- The working of depletion-type of 4 MOSFETs on the depletion and enhancement modes are based on the working principle of capacitor.

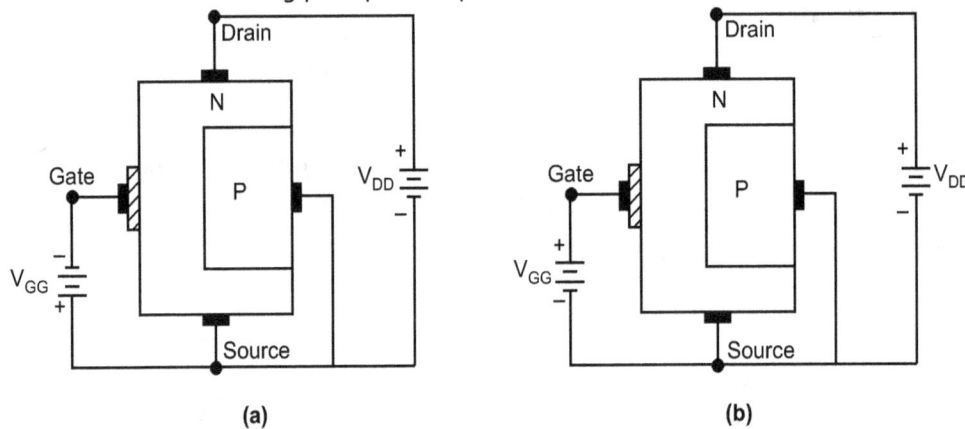

Fig. 5.32 : Working of a depletion-type N-channel MOSFET

1. **Enhancement Mode :** A depletion-type N-channel MOSFET with a positive gate-to-source voltage is shown in Fig. 5.32 (a). The positive gate voltage induces the negative charges in the N-type channel through the insulating layer of SiO_2. Since, conduction of current through the N-type channel is by means of majority carriers (i.e. electrons), the free electrons in the vicinity of negative charges are added together in N-type channel. Thus, the positive gate voltage increases the number of free electrons passing through the N-type channel.

- This increases the drain current passing through the N-type channel. As a result, this enhances the conductivity of the N-type channel. Thus, it increases the drain current flowing through the N-type channel as the gate-to-source voltage is made more positive. Because of this fact, the positive gate operation is called an enhancement mode.

2. **Depletion Mode :** A depletion-type N-channel MOSFET with a negative gate-to-source voltage is shown in Fig. 5.32 (b). The negative gate voltage induces the positive charges in the N-type channel through the insulating layer of SiO_2. Since conduction of current through the N-type channel is by means of majority carriers (i.e. electrons), the free electrons in the vicinity of positive charges are repelled away in the N-type channel. This reduces the number of free electrons passing through the N-type channel. As a result of this, the N-type channel is depleted of free electrons (i.e. majority carriers). Thus, it reduces the drain current flowing through the N-type channel as the gate-to-source voltage is made more negative. At a sufficiently large negative gate-to-source voltage, the N-type channel region near the drain end is totally depleted of free electrons (and hence channel width is almost zero) and therefore, the drain current reduces to zero. This phenomenon is analogous to that of pinch off occurring in the JFET. Thus, the working of a MOSFET with the negative gate voltage is similar to that of a JFET.

- The negative gate voltage depletes the N-type channel of free electrons. Because of this fact, the negative operation is called depletion mode.
- It should be noted that the depletion-type N-channel MOSFET can conduct even if the gate-to-source voltage is zero. Because of this, it is commonly known as Normally-ON MOSFET.

5.19.3 Static Characteristics

Q. Explain static characteristics of MOSFET.
Q. Draw and explain the drain characteristics of MOSFET.

5.19.3.1 Drain characteristics

- The drain characteristics for the N-source configuration is shown in Fig. 5.33 (a). These curves show the relation between drain current and drain-to-source voltage for values of gate-to-source voltages. These curves are plotted for both negative and positive values of gate-to-source voltage.
- The curves shown above the curve for $V_{GS} = 0$ have the positive value, whereas those below have the negative value. When the voltage V_{GS} is zero and negative, the MOSFET operates in the depletion mode. When the voltage is zero and positive, the MOSFET operates in this enhancement mode.

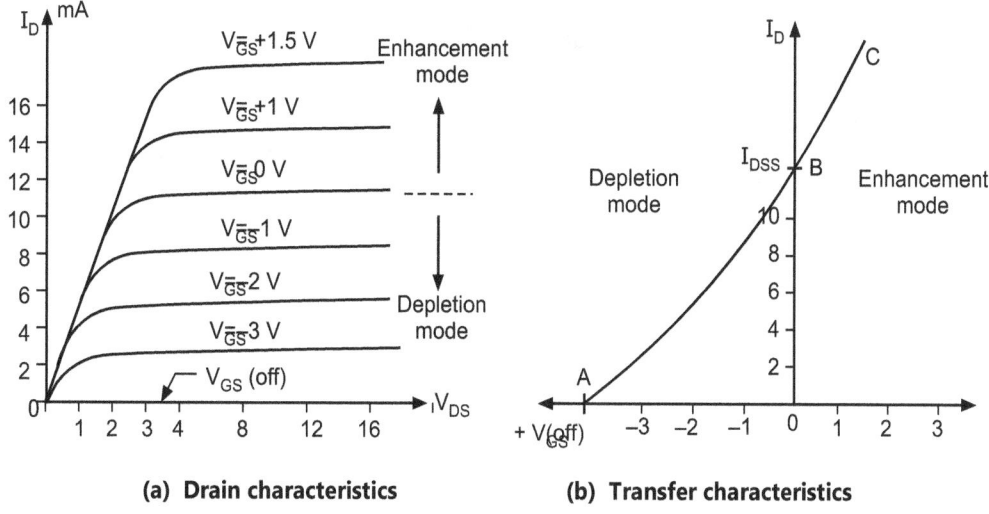

(a) Drain characteristics   (b) Transfer characteristics

Fig. 5.33 : Characteristics of depletion-type N-channel MOSFET

- It may be noted that the drain characteristics of depletion-type MOSFETs are similar to that of JFET. The only difference is that JFET does not operate for positive values of gate-to-source voltage.

5.19.3.2 Transfer characteristics

> Q. Draw and explain the transfer characteristics of a MOSFET.

- The transfer characteristics for the N-channel depletion type MOSFET in common source configuration is shown in Fig. 5.33 (b). These curves show the relation between drain current and gate-to-source voltage for values of drain-to-source voltage. These curves are plotted for both positive and negative values of gate-to-source voltage. This curve is also called transconductance curve.
- It may be noted that the region AB of the characteristic is similar to that of JFET. This curve extends for the positive values of the gate-to-source voltage also. Also, it may be noted that even, if $V_{GS} = 0$, the MOSFET has a drain current end to loss. Because of this fact, it is called Normally-ON MOSFET.

5.20 ENHANCEMENT TYPE N-CHANNEL MOSFET

5.20.1 Construction

- The construction of N-channel enhancement-type MOSFET is shown in Fig. 5.34(a) and its basic structure is shown in Fig. 5.34 (b). On to a lightly doped P-type substrate, two heavily doped N-regions separated by about 25 µm are diffused. These N-regions will act as the source and the drain.
- A thin layer of insulating SiO_2 is then grown over this surface and holes are cut into the oxide layer through which metal (aluminium) contacts for the source and the drain are made. A conducting layer of aluminium which will act as gate is overlaid on SiO_2 over the entire channel region.

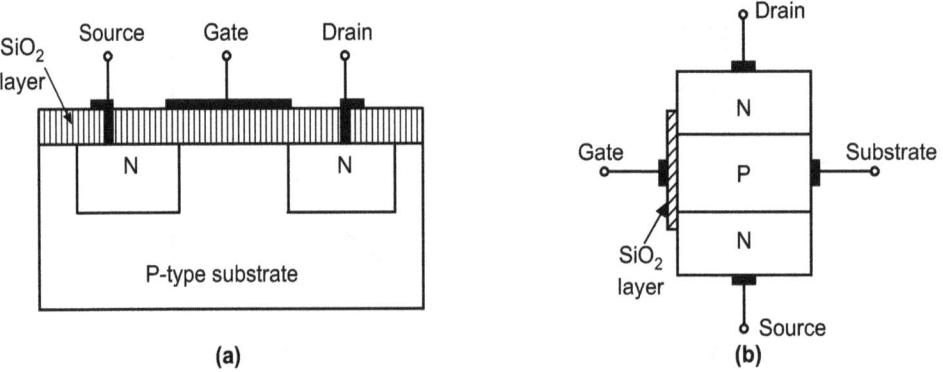

Fig. 5.34 : Enhancement type N-channel MOSFET

- It differs in construction from the depletion-type MOSFET in the sense that it has no physical channel. It may be noted that the P-type substrate extends the SiO_2 layer completely.

5.20.2 Working Principle

- The enhancement-type MOSFET has no depletion mode, but it operates only in enhancement mode.

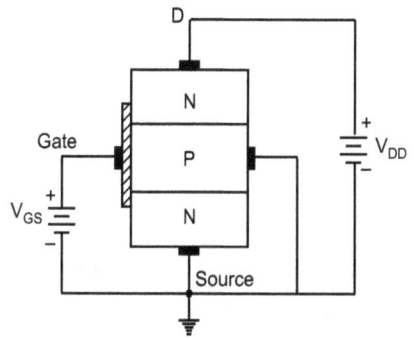

Fig. 5.35 : Normal biasing of enhancement type N-channel MOSFET

- The working of this MOSFET can be explained easily, if we visualise the entire structure of this MOSFET as a parallel-plate capacitance as shown in Fig. 5.35
- The semiconductor channel, the insulating dielectric SiO_2 layer and the metal layer of the gate form a parallel-plate capacitor. We know that if one of the plate of a capacitor is made positive, it induces a negative charge on the opposite plate and vice-versa. The working of enhancement-type MOSFET in the enhancement mode is based on the working principle of a capacitor.

Enhancement mode : Fig. 5.35 shows the enhancement type N-channel MOSFET in common mode configuration with a positive gate-to-source voltage. When the gate-to-source voltage V_{GS} is zero, the supply voltage V_{DD} tries to force the free electrons from source-to-drain. But the presence of P-region does not permit the electrons to pass through it. As a result, there is no flow of drain current for $V_{GS} = 0$. Because of this fact, the enhancement-type MOSFET is also called Normally-OFF MOSFET.

- If a positive voltage is applied at the gate with respect to the substrate, which is usually at grounded, negative charges are induced in the P-type substrates produced by attracting the free electrons from the source. The negative charge thus produced on the P-type substrate consists of free electrons, when the gate is positive enough, it can attract a number of free electrons. This forms a thin layer of electrons which stretches from source to drain. This effect is equivalent to producing a thin layer of N-type channel in the P-type substrate. This layer of free electrons is called N-type inversion layer.

- With the increase in gate-to-source voltage, more of induced negative electrons (minority carrier for the P-type substrate) is formed in the channel and its conductivity increases. Thus, the drain current is enhanced by the positive gate potential.

5.20.3 Static Characteristics

5.20.3.1 Drain characteristics

- The drain characteristics for N-channel enhancement-type MOSFET in the common configuration is shown in Fig. 5.36 (a). These curves show the relation between drain current and drain-to-source voltage for values of gate-to-source voltage. These curves are plotted for positive values of gate-to-source voltage.

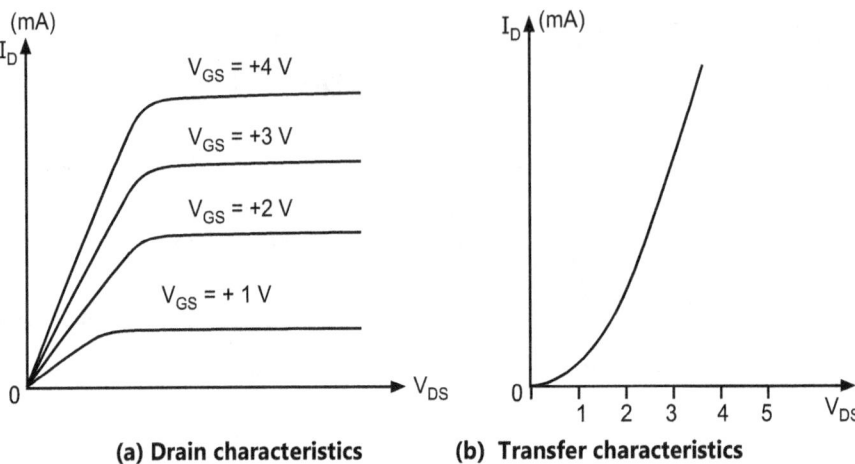

(a) Drain characteristics (b) Transfer characteristics

Fig. 5.36 : Characteristics of enhancement-type N-channel MOSFET

- It may be noted from the drain characteristics that there is negligibly small flow of drain current for the gate-to-source voltage V_{GS} less than threshold voltage $V_{GS(th)}$.

- This flow of current is due to the presence of thermally generated electrons in the P-type substrate. When the voltage V_{GS} is above $V_{GS(th)}$, large drain current flows through the MOSFET.

- The value of drain current increases with the increase in gate-to-source voltage because the width of inversion layer widens for increased value of voltage V_{GS}. Therefore, it allows more number of free electrons to pass through it, the drain current reaches its saturation value.

5.20.3.2 Transfer characteristics

- The transfer characteristics for N-type channel enhancement type MOSFET in the common source configuration is shown in Fig. 5.36 (b).

- These curves show the relation between drain current and gate-to-source voltage for values of drain-to-source voltage.

- The curve is plotted for both positive and negative values of gate-to-source voltage. This curve is also called transconductance curve.

- It may be noted from the transfer characteristics that there is no drain current for the voltage V_{GS} = v. If the voltage V_{GS} is increased above the threshold voltage $V_{GS(th)}$, the drain current increases rapidly.

- It may also be noted that enhancement-type MOSFET does not have loss parameter like JFET and Depletion-type MOSFET.

5.21 SYMBOLS OF MOSFET

5.21.1 Depletion-type MOSFET

Fig. 5.37 shows the circuit symbol of N-channel depletion-type MOSFET. The thin vertical ions represent the channel. The arrow on the P-type substrate points towards the channel. This indicates that the channel is N-type. In some MOSFETs, a connection from the substrate is also taken out. Such MOSFETs have 4 terminals as shown in Fig 5.37. But in most of the MOSFETs the substrate is internally connected to the source. Such MOSEFTs have 3 terminals as shown in Fig. 5.37.

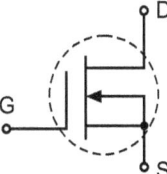
Fig. 5.37 : N-channel

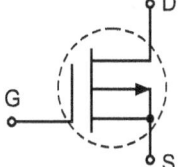
Fig. 5.38 : P-channel

- Fig. 5.38 shows the circuit symbols of P-channel depletion-type MOSFET. The arrow on the N-type substrate points away from the channel.
- This indicates that the channel is P-type. The P-channel MOSFETs having 4-terminals is as shown in Fig. 5.38. But in most of the MOSFETs the substrate is internally connected to the source. Such MOSFETs have 3-terminals as shown in Fig. 5.38.
- It may be noted that the circuit symbol of P-channel depletion type MOSFET is similar to that of N-channel, except the direction of the arrow on the substrate.
- Its direction is away from the channel which indicates that the channel is P-type material.

5.21.2 Enhancement-Type MOSFET

- Fig. 5.39 (a) shows the circuit symbol for N-channel enhancement-type MOSET. The broken line indicates that there is no conducting channel between drain and source. The substrate is internally connected to the source as shown in figure.

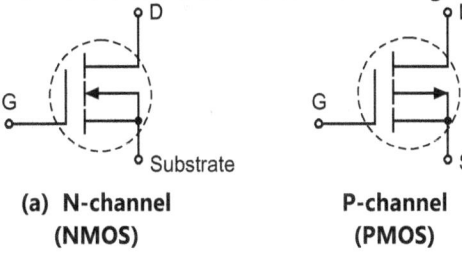

(a) N-channel (NMOS)   P-channel (PMOS)

Fig. 5.39: Symbols of enhancement type MOSFET

Fig. 5.39 (b) shows the circuit symbol for P-channel enhancement-type MOSFET with substrate internally connected to the source.

In actual practice, the N-channel and P-channel enhancement-type MOSFETs are known as NMOS and PMOS FETs respectively.

5.22 APPLICATIONS OF MOSFET

Q. Give some important applications of MOSFET ?

The important applications of MOSFET are
1. It can be used as a passive element e.g. resistor, capacitor and inductor.
2. It can be used as an electronic switch.
3. It can be used as a high frequency amplifier.

5.22.1 Advantages of N-channel MOSFETs over P-channel MOSFETs

Q. What precautions should one take while handling MOSFETs ?

The advantages of N-channel MOSFETs over P-channel MOSFETs are :
1. It has electrons as charge carriers which have very high mobility.
2. It has very high drain current for the same dimension.
3. It has very low ON-resistance.
4. It has very small size.
5. It has higher packing density.

5.22.2 Handling Precautions for MOSFET

If the MOSFETS are not handled properly, it is damaged easily. The damage may occur due to the static electricity. In order to protect a MOSFET from damaging, the following precautionary measures should be taken :
1. It should be kept with its terminals shorted by a ring.
2. The ring shorting the MOSFET should be removed at the time of soldering it in a circuit.
3. It should be kept in a conducting system.
4. It should never be inserted or removed from the circuits with power ON.

5.22.3 Advantages of MOSFET over JFET

Q. What are the advantages of MOSFET over JFET ?

The important advantages of MOSFET over JFET are as given below :
1. It has very high input impedance.
2. It has very low output impedance.
3. It has high gain.
4. It has very small size, longer life and very high efficiency.
5. It avoids the risk of thermal runaway.
6. It has very high frequency runaway.
7. It is very less noisy.

5.22.4 Comparison of JFET and MOSFET

> **Q.** Compare JFET and MOSFET.
> **Q.** What is the difference between a JFET and a MOSFET ?

The difference between JFET and MOSFET are as given below :

JFET	MOSFET
1. It has two P-N junctions.	1. It has only one P-N junction.
2. It has high input impedance.	2. It has very high input impedance.
3. It does not form the capacitance at the channel.	3. It forms the capacitor between the channel and gate.
4. It is operated in depletion mode i.e. gate reverse biased.	4. It is operated in both depletion and enhancement mode i.e. gate is either positive or negative.
5. The gate terminal is directly taken out from the channel.	5. The gate terminal is taken out from the metallic layer deposited over SiO_2 layer which is deposited over the channel.

5.23 CMOS

- Complementary metal oxide semi-conductor devices are chips in which both P-channel and N-channel **enhancement MOSFETs** are connected in push-pull arrangement. The basic connections for CMOS are shown in Fig. 5.40.

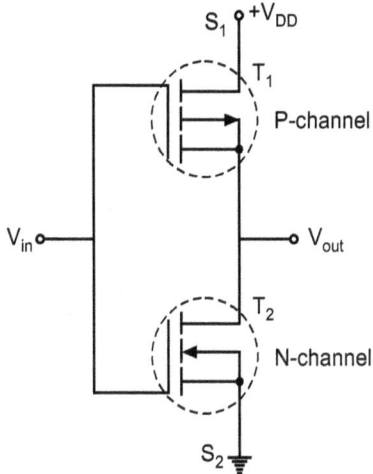

Fig. 5.40 : N-channel and P channel CMOS connections

Fig. 5.40 shows various CMOS connections especially N-channel and P-channel CMOS connections. In Fig. 5.40, T1 is a p-channel MOSFET and T2 is n-channel MOSFET. These two

MOSFETs are connected in series so that source of P-channel device is connected to a positive voltage supply +VDD and the source of N-channel device is connected to the ground. Gates of both the devices are connected as a common input and drain terminals of both the devices are connected together as a common output. These two devices are complementary; that is, they have equal and opposite values of VGS, ID and so on.

5.23.1 Working Principle

- When CMOS circuit like Fig. 5.41 is used in a switching application, the input voltage is either high (+V_{DD}) or low (0 V). When the input is kept low that is at 0 volt, then gate of MOSFET T_1, is at negative potential with respect to the source S_1.
- So MOSFET T_1 will be ON with its resistance R_{ON} = 1 kΩ, while gate of MOSFET T_2, will be at 0 volt relative to its source. So T_2 will be OFF with its resistance R_{OFF} = 10^{10} Ω. Both of these resistances act like a potential divider and the shortened T_1 pulls the output to high and this will be approximately +V_{DD} volts.
- When the input is kept at high level that is +V_{DD} volts then the gate of MOSFET T_1, is at zero potential relative to the source, so T_1 will be OFF with its resistance R_{OFF} = 10^{10} Ω while gate of MOSFET T_2 will be at positive potential relative to its source, so the MOSFET T_2 will be ON with its resistance R_{ON} = 1 kΩ. In this case, the shortened T_2 pulls the output voltage to ground and will be approximately 0 volt. Since the output voltage is inverted, the circuit is called a CMOS *inverter*.

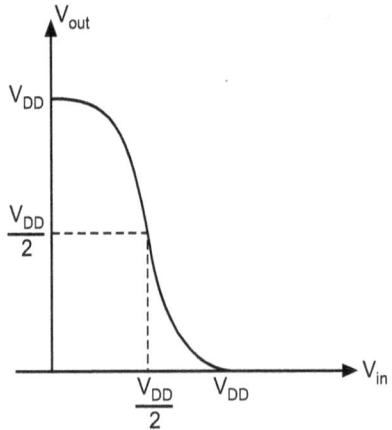

Fig. 5.41 : Input-output graph of CMOS

- Fig. 5.41 shows the CMOS variation of output voltage with input voltage. Except for a short time as the voltage drop from +VDD to zero or rises from zero to +VDD, the series combination of P-channel MOSFET and N-channel MOSFET has one transistor off with no current then drawn from the power supply.
- Thus, the CMOS circuit operates with the input either high or low while drawing no power from the supply except during the brief time while switching between high and low output levels, when both transistors are ON as one is turning ON and the other is turning OFF. In fact, the power consumption of a CMOS circuit is zero at d.c. conditions,

increasing as the applied signal frequency increases since the circuit is switching more often. Between the two extremes, there is crossover point where the input voltage equals VDD/2. At this point both MOSFETs have equal resistance and the output voltage equals VDD/2.

5.23.2 Advantage of CMOS

- The main advantage of CMOS is that the power dissipation is very small typically 50 nW.

5.24 COMPARISON BETWEEN JFET AND BJT

5.24.1 Comparison between JFET and BJT

Q. Compare JFET and BJT.

Sr. No.	Field-Effect Transistor (FET)	Bipolar Junction Transistor (BJT)
1.	It is a voltage controlled device.	It is a current controlled device.
2.	It is a unipolar device, i.e. current conduction is due to either electrons or holes.	It is a bipolar device, i.e. current conduction is due to both electrons and holes.
3.	It is a unijunction device.	It is a bijunction device.
4.	It has very high input resistance.	It has very low input resistance.
5.	It has a negative temperature co-efficient of resistance at high current levels and prevents from thermal breakdown.	It has a positive temperature co-efficient of resistance at high current levels and leads to thermal breakdown.
6.	Thermal stability is very good.	Thermal stability is poor.
7.	It has higher switching speed and cut-off frequency.	It has lower switching speed and cut-off frequency.
8.	It does not suffer from minority carrier storage effects.	It suffers from minority carrier storage effects.
9.	It is less noisy.	It is comparatively more noisy.
10.	It is immune to radiation.	It is sensitive to radiation.
11.	It has less voltage gain.	It has comparatively more voltage gain.
12.	It is much simple to fabricate as an IC and occupies a less space on IC chip.	It is comparatively difficult to fabricate as an IC and occupies more space on IC chip.

5.24.2 Comparison between N-channel and P-channel JFET

Q. Compare N-channel and p-channel JFET.

The comparison between N-channel and P-channel JFET are as given below :

Sr. No.	N-channel JFET	P-channel JFET
1.	The current conduction takes place due to electrons.	The current conduction takes place due to holes.
2.	Its switching speed and cut-off frequency is high.	Its switching speed and cut-off frequency is comparatively low.
3.	Its transconductance is high.	Its transconductance is low.
4.	It is less noisy.	It is comparatively more noisy.
5.	It is superior in circuit applications.	It is comparatively less superior in circuit applications.

Unit - VI

DIODE RECTIFIERS

6.1 INTRODUCTION

- In general, most of the electronic circuits need a source of d.c. power for their operation. Batteries or dry cells are one form of d.c. source which are generally used in laboratories.
- They are easily portable and ripple free (not containing a.c. component), hence they are widely used in pocket transistor, remote circuits and flash of camera. However, they are costly and require frequent replacement after use. Due to decrease in voltage after some use, they are expensive as compared with conventional d.c. power supply.
- Most economical and convenient power supply is the domestic a.c. power usually of 220 V_{rms} and of frequency 50 Hz (in India). Hence, it is advantageous to convert this alternating voltage to d.c. voltage (generally of smaller value).
- This process of conversion of a.c. voltage into d.c. voltage is called rectification and the device is called as rectifier.

6.1.1 Types of Rectifiers

Rectifier is a circuit which converts an alternating voltage into direct voltage. The classification of rectifier is as shown in Fig. 6.1.

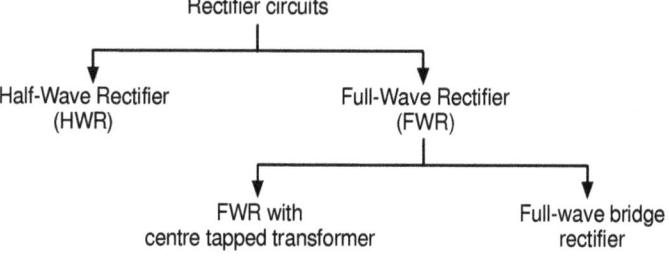

Fig. 6.1 : Classification of rectifiers

6.2 HALF-WAVE RECTIFIER (HWR)

Q. Explain the working of a HWR with waveforms.

- The basic half-wave diode rectifier circuit along with input and output is shown in Fig. 6.2. T is the step-down transformer and R_L is the load resistance.

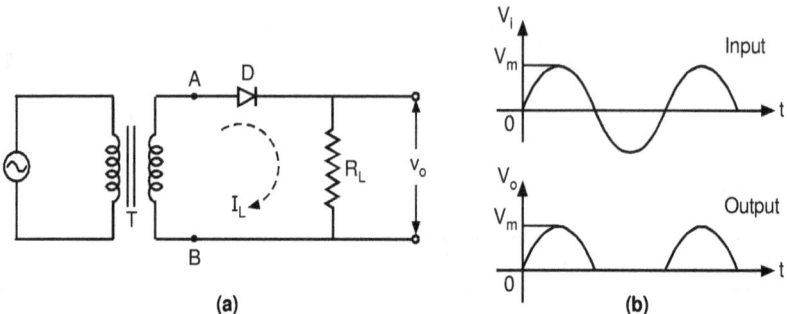

Fig. 6.2 : HWR with R load

Working : During the positive half cycle of the input a.c. voltage, the secondary voltage V_{AB} is positive. The diode D is forward biased and starts conducting. While conducting, the diode acts as short circuit so that circuit current flows and the secondary voltage V_{AB} appears almost as it is across the load resistance (as voltage drop across the diode is very small).

- During negative input half cycle, the secondary voltage across transformer V_{AB} is negative. i.e. A is negative with respect to B. Hence the diode D is reverse bi.ased and offer a high resistance. Hence we can replace it by an open circuited switch. There is no voltage drop across R_L i.e. the load voltage and load current both are zero. The variation of output voltage with input voltage is as shown in Fig. 6.2 (b).

- This circuit is called as half-wave rectifier because it delivers power to the load during only half of the a.c. supply voltage.

6.2.1 Analysis of Half-Wave Rectifier

Q. Explain the rectifier efficiency and ripple factor for a HWR.

1. Average values : We will state the average values of output voltage and current. These are shown in Fig. 6.3.

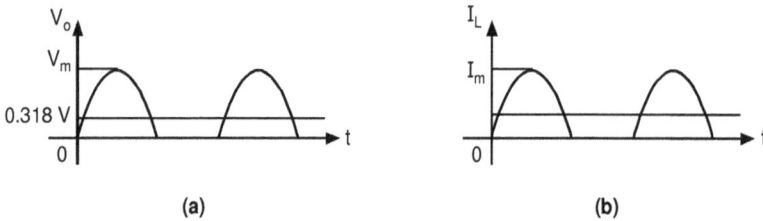

Fig. 6.3

The a.c. input voltage is given by equation

$$V_i = V_m \sin\theta$$

where V_m is the maximum voltage across the transformer secondary.

V_m is given by $\quad V_m = \sqrt{2}\, V$

where V is rms value of supply voltage.

Average load current ($I_{L\,dc}$): The d.c. load current $I_{L\,dc}$ is

$$I_{L\,dc} = \frac{1}{2\pi}\int_0^\pi I_m \sin\omega t\, d\omega t$$

$$= -\frac{I_m}{2\pi}[\cos\omega t]_0^\pi = -\frac{I_m}{2\pi}[\cos\pi - \cos 0]$$

$$= -\frac{I_m}{2\pi}[-1-1]$$

$$I_{L\,dc} = \frac{I_m}{\pi} = 0.318\, I_m$$

The peak current I_m can be calculated as

$$I_m = \frac{V_m}{(R_S + R_F + R_L)}$$

where R_S = Transformer secondary resistance
 R_F = Diode forward resistance
 R_L = Load resistance
 V_m = Maximum or peak secondary voltage

D.C. or Average load voltage ($V_{L\,dc}$):

$$V_{L\,dc} = I_L \cdot R_L$$

$$= \frac{I_m}{\pi} \cdot R_L$$

$$= \frac{V_m}{\pi(R_S + R_F + R_L)} \times R_L$$

R_S and R_F are very small as compared to R_L.

$\therefore\quad R_S + R_F + R_L \approx R_L$

$$V_{L\,dc} = \frac{V_m}{\pi}$$

$$= 0.318\, V_m$$

A.C. or rms load current ($I_{L\,rms}$): Consider one complete cycle of the load current waveform $(0 - 2\pi)$ to write

$$I_{L\,rms} = \left[\frac{1}{2\pi}\int_0^\pi I_m^2 \sin^2\omega t\, d\omega t\right]^{1/2}$$

$$= \left[\frac{I_m^2}{2\pi}\int_0^\pi \left(\frac{1-\cos 2\omega t}{2}\right) d\omega t\right]^{1/2}$$

$$= \frac{I_m}{2}\left[\frac{1}{\pi}\left(\pi - \frac{1}{2}\sin 2\pi\right)\right]^{1/2}$$

$$\therefore \quad I_{L\,rms} = \frac{I_m}{2} = 0.5\, I_m \quad \text{(since } \sin 2\pi = 0\text{)}$$

A.C. or rms value of load voltage ($V_{L\,rms}$) : Since the load is purely resistive, the rms value of load current is

$$V_{L\,rms} = I_{L\,rms} \times R_L$$

$$= \frac{I_m}{2} \cdot R_L$$

$$= \frac{V_m}{2(R_S + R_F + R_L)} \times R_L$$

As $\quad R_S + R_F <<< R_L$

$$V_{L\,rms} \approx \frac{V_m}{2}$$

Ripple factor : Ripple factor is given as

$$r = \frac{\text{RMS value of A.C. component of output}}{\text{D.C. or average value of output}}$$

$$= \frac{\left[V_{L\,rms}^2 - V_{L\,dc}^2\right]^{1/2}}{V_{L\,dc}}$$

$$= \frac{\left[(V_m/2)^2 - (V_m/\pi)^2\right]^{1/2}}{V_m/\pi}$$

$$= \pi\left[\left(\frac{1}{2}\right)^2 - \left(\frac{1}{\pi}\right)^2\right]^{1/2}$$

$$\approx 1.21 \text{ or } 121\%$$

D.C. output power ($P_{L\,dc}$) : D.C. or average output delivered to load is given by

$$P_{L\,dc} = I_{L\,dc}^2 \times R_L$$

$$= \left[\frac{I_m}{\pi}\right]^2 \times R_L = \frac{I_m^2}{\pi^2} \times R_L$$

Substituting value of I_m from Fig. 5.2,

$$P_{L\,dc} = \frac{V_m^2}{\pi^2 (R_S + R_F + R_L)^2} \times R_L$$

If $R_L \gg (R_S + R_F)$ then,

$$P_{L\,dc} = \frac{V_m^2}{\pi^2 R_L}$$

$$= \frac{V_{L\,dc}^2}{R_L} \quad \text{(because } V_m/\pi = V_{L\,dc}\text{)}$$

A.C. input power (P_{ac}): The a.c. input power to a rectifier is the power supplied by the secondary winding of transformer.

$$P_{ac} = I_{S\,(rms)}^2 \times (R_S + R_F + R_L)$$

where $I_{S\,rms}$ = RMS value of secondary current

For a half-wave rectifier, the secondary current is same as the load current.

$$I_{S\,(rms)} = I_{L\,(rms)} = \frac{I_m}{2}$$

$$P_{ac} = \frac{I_m^2}{4}(R_S + R_F + R_L)$$

Rectifier efficiency or Power conversion efficiency: Rectifier efficiency is defined as

$$\eta = \frac{\text{D.C. output power}}{\text{A.C. input power}} = \frac{P_{L\,dc}}{P_{ac}}$$

Using the value of $P_{L\,dc}$ and P_{ac} from equations (5.8) and (5.9),

$$\eta = \frac{I_{L\,dc}^2 \cdot R_L}{I_{S\,(rms)}^2 (R_S + R_F + R_L)}$$

$$\eta = \frac{(I_m/\pi)^2 R_L}{\left(\frac{I_m}{2}\right)^2 (R_S + R_F + R_L)}$$

$$= \frac{4}{\pi^2} \cdot \frac{R_L}{(R_S + R_F + R_L)}$$

If $R_L \gg R_S + R_F$ then,

$$\eta_{max} = \frac{4}{\pi^2}$$

$$= 0.406 \text{ or } 40.6\%$$

Rectification efficiency of a rectifier indicates the percentage of a.c. input power, actually converted into average load power. Hence it should be as high as possible.

Peak Inverse Voltage (PIV) : Peak inverse voltage is the maximum negative voltage which appears across a non-conducting reverse biased diode.

$$\therefore \quad PIV = V_m \text{ volts}$$

6.2.2 Disadvantages of Half-Wave Rectifier

> Q. What are the disadvantages of HWR ?

1. The current passing through the transformer is unidirectional, hence there is possibility of core saturation. To avoid this we have to increase size of a transformer.
2. Ripple factor is high (121%).
3. Rectification efficiency is low (~ 40%).
4. Output D.C. voltage and current is low.
5. Larger filter components are required while using half-wave rectifier in power supply.

6.3 SINGLE PHASE HALF WAVE RECTIFIER WITH RL LOAD

> Q. Explain the working of a single phase HWR with RL load.

- Fig. 6.4 shows the circuit diagram of single half wave rectifier with inductive (RL) load. The waveforms and operations change in this case because of the property of the the inductance to store the energy.
- The diode turns ON when its anode is positive w.r.t its cathode. It will conduct if the forward voltage is greater than the threshold voltage.
- During the interval 0 to $\pi/2$, the applied source voltage increases from zero to maximum. Due to the property of inductance, the voltage across the inductor opposes the change in the current, through the load. So, the current gradually increases till it reaches its maximum value.
- We know that the current lags the applied voltage in an inductive circuit. So, the current does not reach its peak when the voltage is at its maximum. During this time, energy is transferred and is stored in the magnetic field of the inductor.
- For the decreasing source voltage, the induced voltage in the inductor reverses polarity. It again opposes the decrease in current. The net voltage across the diode forward biases the diode and keeps it conducting. Hence, the current starts decreasing gradually and becomes zero when all the energy stored by the inductor is released to the circuit.
- At $\omega t = \pi$, the load current across diode D still exists even after the source voltage has dropped below zero.
- Fig. 6.5 shows the load voltage waveform.
- Note that the shaded region shows negative load voltage from π to σ. This negative load voltage appears due to energy stored in load inductance.

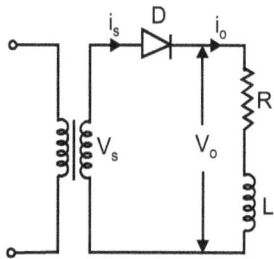

Fig. 6.4 : Half wave rectifier with RL load.

- When output current becomes zero, the diode D stops conducting. The negative supply voltage appears across the diode. At 2π, the diode starts conducting again.

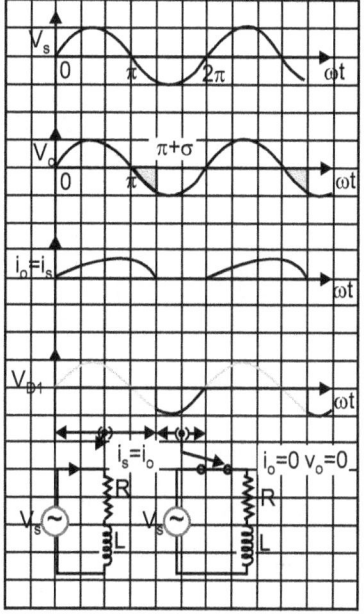

Fig. 6.5 : Waveform

Mathematical analysis

Output average voltage

$$V_o = \frac{1}{T}\int_0^T v_o(\omega t)\, d\omega t$$

From the waveforms of Fig. 6.2.4

$$V_{o(av)} = \frac{1}{2\pi}\int_0^{\pi+\sigma} V_m \sin\omega t\, d\omega t = \frac{V_m}{2\pi}[-\cos\omega t]_0^{\pi+\sigma}$$

$$\therefore \boxed{V_o = \frac{V_m}{2\pi}[1 - \cos(\pi+\sigma)]}$$

6.3.1 Single Phase Half Wave Rectifier with RC Load

Q. Explain the working of a single phase HWR with RC load.

- A capacitive load is generally a battery or a cell load.
- Fig. 6.6 shows the battery charger circuit. Fig. 6.2.7 shows the waveforms of this circuit.
- The Diode D conducts only when $V_s > E$, i.e. supply voltage is greater than the voltage across the battery and the diode starts conducting at $\omega t = \alpha$.

Now, $V_m \sin \omega t = E$ at $\omega t = \alpha$.

$\therefore \quad V_m \sin \alpha = E$

or $\quad \alpha = \sin^{-1} \dfrac{E}{V_m}$

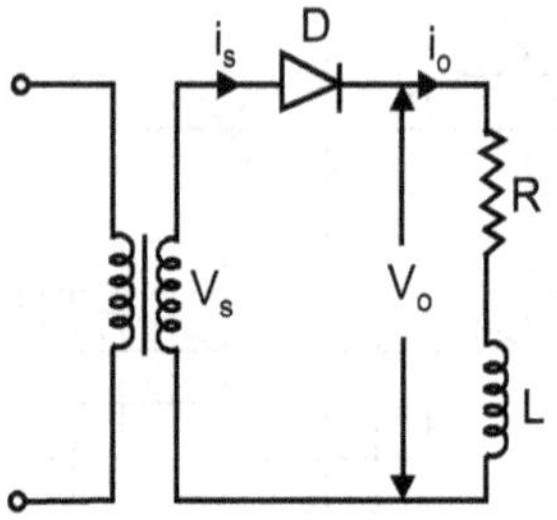

Fig. 6.6

- The diode stops conducting at $\omega t = \beta$ where $\beta = \pi - \alpha$
- The charging current of the battery is given by the formula,

$$i_o(t) = \dfrac{V_m \sin \omega t - E}{R}$$

6.3.2 Single Phase Half Wave Rectifier with Freewheeling Diode

- The circuit diagram shows a single phase HWR with freewheeling diode. A diode is connected parallel to the RL load. This is known as the freewheeling diode.
- The waveforms of single phase HWR are shown in Fig.
- Observe that the output current flows from 0 to $\pi + \sigma$ just like in resistive – inductive RL load circuit.
- The load inductance generates the voltage at $\omega t = \pi$, with polarities as shown in Fig. which forward biases both D and D_{FW}. But the freewheeling diode D_{FW} is more forward biased compared to D. Due to negative v_s, the diode D has reduced forward bias.
- Therefore, the freewheeling diode D_{FW} conducts from π to $\pi + \sigma$ and the output voltage becomes zero during freewheeling, neglecting the drop across the freewheeling diode.

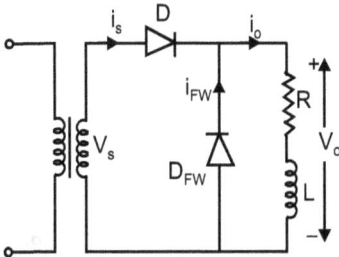

Fig. 6.7 : HWR with freewheeling diode

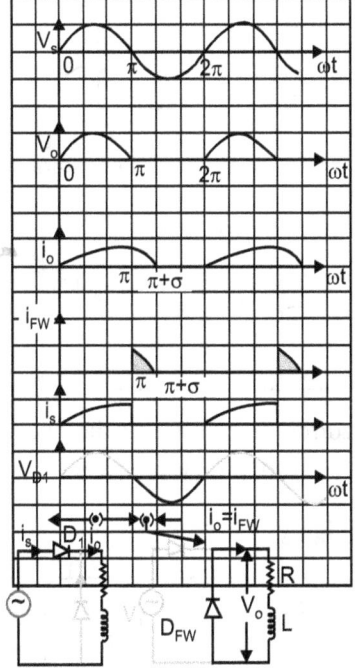

Fig 6.8 : Waveforms of HWR with freewheeling diode.

6.3.3 Diode Circuit with RL Load

- Let us analyze a diode circuit with RL load having a fixed voltage dc supply.
- Fig. 6.9 shows the diode circuit with RL load.

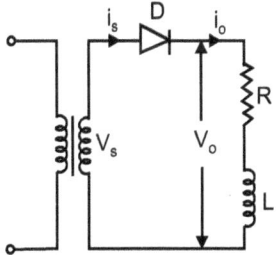

Fig. 6.9 : Diode circuit with RL load

- When the switch S1 is closed, the current 'i' starts flowing through the circuit. Applying KVL to the RL circuit we get,

$$V_s = V_R + V_L$$

$$\therefore V_s = iR + L\frac{di}{dt}$$

Initially, at t = 0, current i = 0. So, solving the differential equations we get,

$$i(t) = \frac{V_s}{R}(1 - e^{-tR/L})$$

or

$$\boxed{i(t) = \frac{V_s}{R}(1 - e^{-t/\tau}), \tau = \frac{L}{R}}$$

where $\tau = \frac{L}{R}$ is called time constant of the RL circuit.

- The voltage across inductor can be expressed as,

$$V_L = L\frac{di}{dt} = L\frac{d}{dt}\frac{V_s}{R}(1 - e^{-tR/L})$$

$$\boxed{V_L = V_s e^{-tR/L} = V_s e^{-t/\tau}}$$

- The inductor voltage and current according to the above equations can be graphically expressed as shown in the Fig. 6.10. It is clear that the current reaches to maximum value of $\frac{V_s}{R}$ as inductance fully saturates.

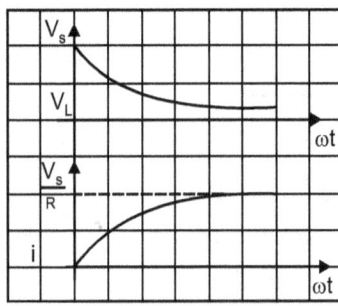

Fig. 6.10

6.3.4 Diode circuit with RC Load

- A diode circuit with fixed supply voltage or a dc source voltage with RC load is shown in Fig. 6.11.
- At time t=0, when the switch S is closed, current starts flowing through the RC circuit and capacitor starts charging. Applying KVL to RC circuit,

$$V_S = V_R + V_C$$
$$= iR + \frac{1}{C}\int i\, dt + V_C(t=0)$$

- Initial voltage across the capacitor is zero. Hence $V_C(t=0) = 0$. Solving the above equation, we get,

$$i(t) = \frac{V_S}{R} e^{-t/RC}$$

or

$$\boxed{i(t) = \frac{V_S}{R} e^{-t/\tau}, \tau = RC}$$

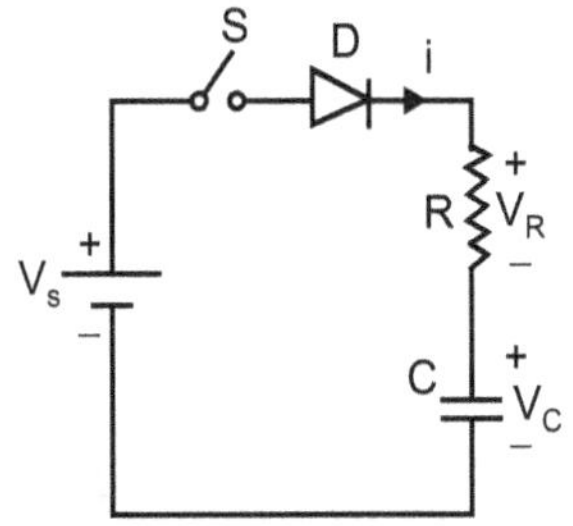

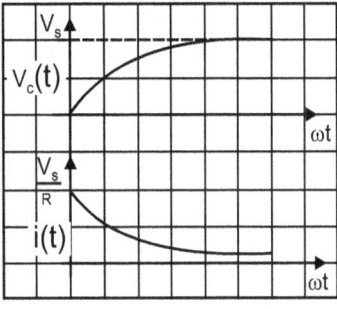

Fig. 6.11 : Diode circuit with RC load

where $\tau = RC$ is called time constant of the RC load.

The voltage across the capacitor is,

$$V_C(t) = \frac{1}{C}\int_0^t i(t)\, dt$$

$$\boxed{V_C(t) = V_S(1 - e^{-t/RC}) = V_S(1 - e^{-t/\tau})}$$

- The sketches of current and voltage are shown in Fig 6.12. Observe that initial capacitor current is $\frac{V_S}{R}$ and it reduces gradually as capacitor charges.

Fig. 6.12 : Waveform

6.4 FULL-WAVE RECTIFIER WITH CENTRE TAPPED TRANSFORMER (FWR)

Q. Explain the working of a FWR with centre tapped transformer.

- In full-wave rectifier, both half cycles of the input are utilized with the help of two diodes working alternately. The full-wave rectifier consists of two diodes and a centre tapped transformer. [Fig. 6.13 (a)]

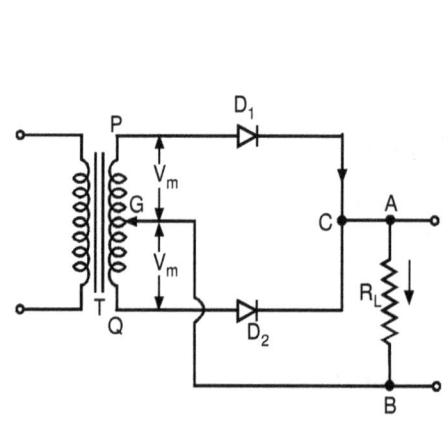
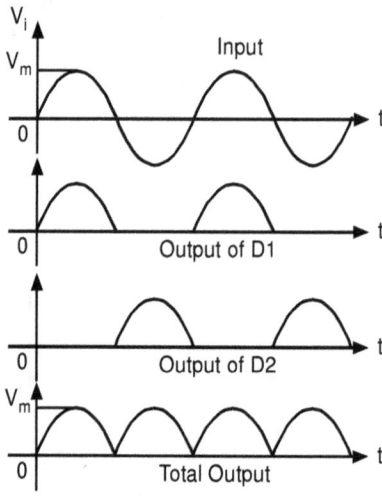

(a) Centre tapped full-wave rectifier   (b) Input and output waveforms

Fig. 6.13

Working :
- When input a.c. power supply is switched ON, two ends P and Q of the transformer secondary become +ve and −ve alternately. During positive half cycle of a.c. input, terminal P is positive, terminal G is at zero potential and terminal Q is negative.
- During this diode D_1 is forward biased and conducts (but D_2 is reverse biased). Current flows along PD_1CABG. As a result, voltage appears across R_L.
- During negative half cycle, the terminal Q becomes positive and diode D_2 conducts (but not D_1). The current flows across QD_2CABG. Thus, we find that current keeps on flowing through R_L in the same direction from A to B in both half cycles of ac input.
- It means that both the half cycles of a.c. input are utilized as shown in Fig. 5.4. Frequency of rectifier output is twice the frequency of supply. The input and output waveforms of centre tapped transformer are as shown in Fig. 6.13 (b).

6.4.1 Analysis of Full-Wave Rectifier Circuit

Let us obtain expression for various performance parameters. Expression for the peak load current I_m is given as

Peak load current, $\quad I_m = \dfrac{V_m}{(R_S + R_F + R_L)}$

ANALOG AND DIGITAL ELECTRONICS (S.E.ELECTRICAL) — DIODE RECTIFIER

Average load current ($I_{L\,dc}$):

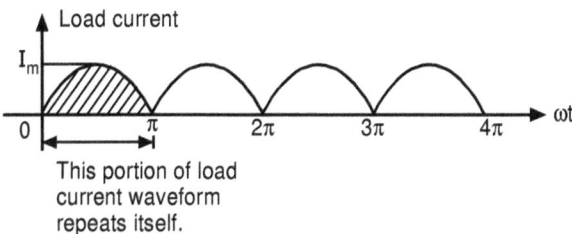

Fig. 6.14 : Load current for FWR

- Here we are going to consider load current waveform extending from 0 to π because shaded portion in Fig. 6.14 repeats again and again.

$$I_{L\,dc} = \frac{1}{\pi}\int_0^\pi I_m \sin\omega t\, d\omega t$$

$$= -\frac{I_m}{\pi}[\cos\omega t]_0^\pi = -\frac{I_m}{\pi}[\cos\pi - \cos 0]$$

$$I_{L\,dc} = \frac{2I_m}{\pi} = 0.637\, I_m$$

- For full-wave rectifier, the average load current value is twice that of half-wave rectifier.

Average load voltage ($V_{L\,dc}$): As load is purely resistive, the average load voltage of a full-wave rectifier is

$$V_{L\,dc} = I_{L\,dc} \times R_L$$

Substituting the value of $I_{L\,dc}$, we get

$$V_{L\,dc} = \frac{2I_m}{\pi} R_L = \frac{2V_m}{\pi (R_S + R_F + R_L)} R_L$$

Assuming $(R_S + R_F) \ll R_L$

$$V_{L\,dc} = \frac{2V_m}{\pi} \text{ (approximate)}$$

∴ Average value of load current voltage for FWR is twice the average load voltage for HWR.

RMS load current ($I_{L\,rms}$): Referring to load current waveform of Fig. 6.14, we consider waveform extending from 0 to π, the rms value of load current is given by

$$I_{L\,rms} = \left[\frac{1}{\pi}\int_0^\pi I_m^2 \sin^2\omega t\, d\omega t\right]^{1/2}$$

$$= \left[\frac{I_m^2}{\pi} \int_0^\pi \left(\frac{1-\cos 2\omega t}{2}\right) d\omega t\right]^{1/2}$$

$$= \frac{I_m}{\sqrt{2}} \left[\frac{1}{\pi}\left(\pi - \frac{1}{2}\sin 2\pi\right)\right]^{1/2}$$

$$\therefore \quad I_{L\,rms} = \frac{I_m}{\sqrt{2}} \quad (\because \sin 2\pi = 0)$$

$$I_{L\,rms} = 0.707\, I_m$$

As compared to HWR, the value of $I_{L\,rms}$ for FWR is higher by 20.7%.

RMS load voltage ($V_{L\,rms}$):

$$V_{L\,rms} = I_{L\,rms} \times R_L$$

$$= \frac{I_m}{\sqrt{2}} R_L$$

Substituting the value of I_m

$$V_{L\,rms} = \frac{V_m}{\sqrt{2}\,(R_S + R_F + R_L)} \times R_L$$

$$= \frac{V_m}{\sqrt{2}\left[1 + \frac{(R_S + R_F)}{R_L}\right]} \quad \text{(exact)}$$

Assuming $\quad R_S + R_F \ll R_L$

$$V_{L\,rms} = \frac{V_m}{\sqrt{2}} \quad \text{(approximately)}$$

Thus, the rms load voltage for FWR is higher than that of HWR.

Ripple factor:

$$\text{Ripple factor (RF)} = \gamma = \frac{\left[V_{L\,rms}^2 - V_{L\,dc}^2\right]^{1/2}}{V_{L\,dc}}$$

Substituting the values, we get

$$\gamma = \frac{\left[(V_m/\sqrt{2})^2 - (2V_m/\pi)^2\right]^{1/2}}{2V_m/\pi}$$

$$= \left[\frac{\pi^2}{8} - 1\right]^{1/2} = 0.48$$

$$\therefore \quad \gamma = 0.48 \text{ or } 48\%$$

The value of ripple factor for a FWR is much lower than ripple factor of a HWR (which is 1.21 or 121%). Therefore, the quality of the dc voltage at full-wave rectifier is much better than a HWR.

D.C. output power :
$$P_{L\,dc} = I_{L\,dc}^2 \times R_L = \left(\frac{2I_m}{\pi}\right)^2 \times R_L = \frac{4I_m^2}{\pi^2} \times R_L$$

$$= \frac{4}{\pi^2} \cdot \frac{V_m^2}{(R_S + R_F + R_L)^2} \times R_L$$

A.C. output power :
$$P_{ac} = I_{S\,rms}^2 \times (R_S + R_F + R_L)$$

$$= \left(\frac{I_m}{\sqrt{2}}\right)^2 \times (R_S + R_F + R_L)$$

Substituting the value of I_m, we get

$$P_{ac} = \frac{V_m^2\,(R_S + R_F + R_L)}{2\,(R_S + R_F + R_L)^2}$$

$$P_{ac} = \frac{V_m^2}{2\,(R_S + R_F + R_L)}$$

Rectifier efficiency :
$$\eta = \frac{P_{L\,dc}}{P_{ac}} = \frac{I_{L\,dc}^2 \times R_L}{(I_{S\,rms})^2\,(R_S + R_F + R_L)}$$

Substituting the values of $I_{L\,dc}$ and $I_{S\,rms}$ as

$$I_{L\,dc} = \frac{2I_m}{\pi} \text{ and } I_{S\,rms} = \frac{I_m}{\sqrt{2}}$$

$$\eta = \frac{(2I_m/\pi)^2\,R_L}{(I_m/\sqrt{2})^2\,(R_S + R_F + R_L)}$$

$$\eta = \frac{8R_L}{\pi^2\,(R_S + R_F + R_L)}$$

Assuming $(R_S + R_F) << R_L$

$$\eta = \frac{8}{\pi^2} = 0.812 \text{ or } 81.2\%$$

Note that the rectifier efficiency of FWR is almost twice the rectifier efficiency of HWR.

Peak Inverse Voltage (PIV) : In FWR, when D_1 conducts, it is assumed to be equivalent to closed switch and D_2 acts as open since it is reverse biased. A voltage v_m is developed across R_L.

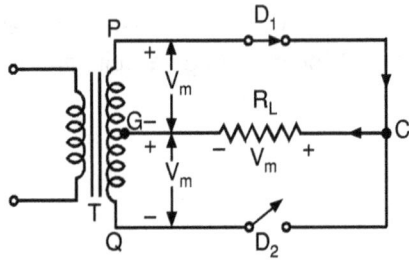

Fig. 6.15

As shown in Fig. 6.15, the voltage across D_2 is equal to the sum of voltage across the lower half of GQ of transformer secondary and the load resistor. Hence PIV of D_2 = $2V_m$. Same is the value of D_1.

Advantages of FWR :
1. Low ripple factor as compared with HWR.
2. Better rectification efficiency.
3. No possibility of transformer core saturation.

Disadvantages of FWR :
1. Since PIV = $2V_m$, size of diodes is larger and they are more expensive.
2. Cost of centre-tapped transformer is high.

6.4.2 Single Phase Full Wave Rectifier with RL Load

- Fig. 6.16 shows a single phase full wave rectifier with RL load with center tap connection.
- The current waveform will be sinusoidal as the load is inductive.
- Supply current waveform of both the phases i_{s1} and i_{s2} si just closed to square wave.

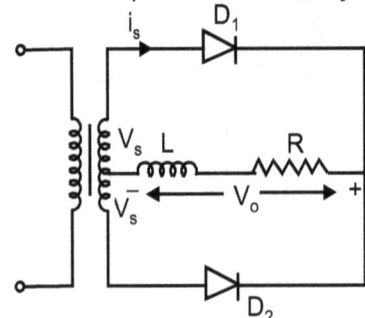

Fig. 6.16 : FWR with RL load

Mathematical analysis

Since load voltage is similar for R and RL loads,

$$\therefore \quad V_{0(av)} = \frac{2V_m}{\pi} = 0.637\ V_m$$

and

$$V_{0(rms)} = \frac{V_m}{\sqrt{2}} = 0.707\ V_m = V_{s(rms)}$$

FF = 1.11 or 111%
RF = 0.4817 or 48.17%
η = 0.812 or 81.2%
PIV = 2 V_m

6.5 BRIDGE RECTIFIER

- The disadvantages of the full-wave rectifier such as high PIV and use of centre-tapped transformer are overcome in bridge rectifier circuit.
- It requires four diodes, but the transformer used is not centre tapped and has a maximum voltage of V_m.

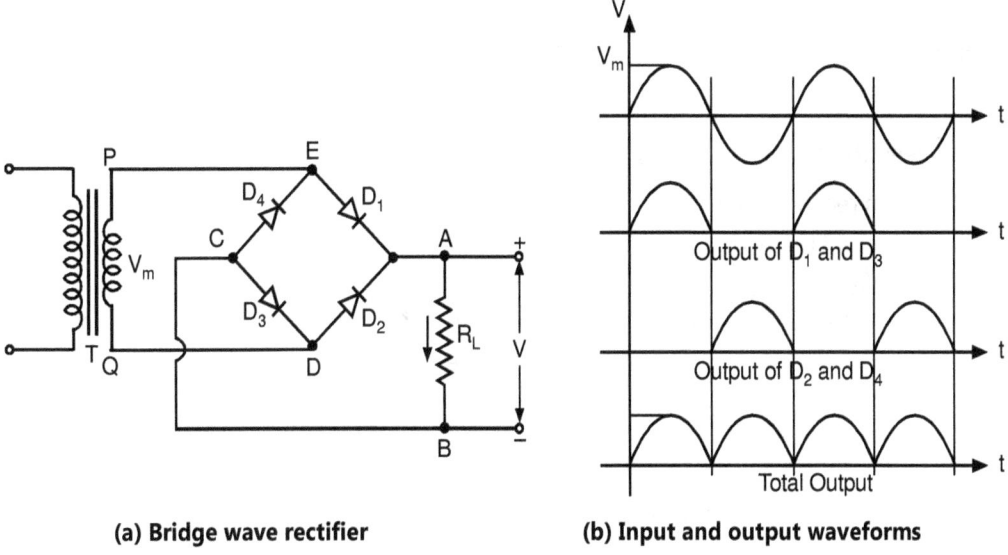

(a) Bridge wave rectifier   (b) Input and output waveforms

Fig. 6.17

Working : During the positive half cycle of input, terminal P of secondary is positive and terminal Q is negative. During this cycle, diodes D_1 and D_3 become forward biased (ON), whereas D_2 and D_4 are reverse biased (OFF). Hence current flows along PED_1ABD_3DQ producing a drop across R_L.

- During the negative half cycle of input, secondary terminal Q becomes positive and P negative. Now D_2 and D_4 are forward biased and D_1 and D_3 reverse biased. Circuit current flows along QDD_2ABD_4EP as shown in Fig. 6.17 (a). We find that current keeps flowing through R_L in same direction AB during both cycles of the input. Point A of bridge rectifier always acts as anode and point C as cathode.
- The output voltage across R_L is as shown in Fig. 6.17 (b).
- Its frequency is twice that of supply frequency.

6.5.1 Performance Parameters of a Bridge Rectifier

- Bridge rectifier is basically a full-wave rectifier. Hence all the parameters such as $V_{L\,dc}$, $V_{L\,rms}$, $I_{L\,dc}$, $I_{L\,rms}$, etc. will have the same expressions as those derived for centre-tapped FWR circuit earlier.
- These parameters are as listed below :

(1) D.C. or average load current = $I_{L\,dc}$ = $\dfrac{2I_m}{\pi}$.

(2) Maximum average load voltage = $V_{L\,dc}$ = $\dfrac{2V_m}{\pi}$.

(3) R.M.S. load current = $I_{L\,rms}$ = $\dfrac{I_m}{\sqrt{2}}$.

(4) R.M.S. load voltage = $V_{L\,rms}$ = $\dfrac{V_m}{\sqrt{2}}$.

(5) D.C. load power = P_{dc} = $\dfrac{4I_m^2}{\pi^2\,R_L}$.

(6) Maximum rectification efficiency = η = 81.2%.

(7) Ripple factor, r = 48%.

(8) PIV = V_m.

- However, the expression for peak load current I_m gets modified slightly. In bridge rectifier, as two diodes conduct simultaneously, the maximum value of load current is given by

$$I_m = \dfrac{V_m}{(R_S + 2R_F + R_L)}$$

The peak inverse voltage (PIV) of diode connected in bridge rectifier is V_m volt and not $2V_m$ like FWR.

Advantages of Bridge Rectifiers :
1. Bridge rectifier requires small transformer instead of centre tapped used on full-wave rectifier. This reduces cost of the bridge rectifier.
2. This circuit is most suitable for high voltage application. This is because the maximum negative voltage that appears across each diode is $-V_m$. Hence diodes with PIV rating of + V_m are needed. (But PIV of FWR is + $2V_m$.)
3. Core saturation does not take place. Therefore, transformer losses are reduced. Core losses are avoided because equal and opposite currents flow through the transformer in each cycle.
4. It has less PIV rating for diode.

Disadvantages of Bridge Rectifiers :
The number of diodes used are four instead of two for FWR. As two diodes conduct simultaneously, the voltage drop increases and output voltage reduces.

6.5.2 Single Phase Bridge Rectifier with RL Load

- Fig. 6.18 shows the circuit diagram of 1φ bridge rectifier with RL load. Diodes D_1 and D_2 conduct in positive half cycle and diodes D_3 and D_4 conduct in negative half cycle.
- Fig. 6.18 shows the waveforms of bridge rectifier with RL load.

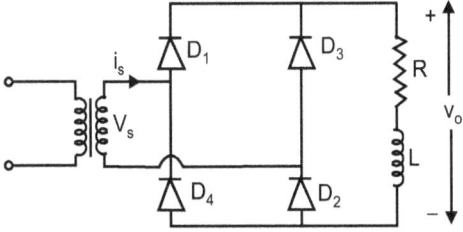

Fig. 6.18 : Bridge Rectifier with RL load

Mathematical analysis

- Note that the waveforms of bridge rectifier for RL load are same as that for center tap transformer based full wave rectifier. Hence we can write,

$$\therefore \quad V_{0(av)} = \frac{2V_m}{\pi} = 0.637 \, V_m$$

and

$$V_{0(rms)} = \frac{V_m}{\sqrt{2}} = 0.707 \, V_m = V_{s(rms)}$$

$$FF = 1.11$$
$$RF = 0.4817 \text{ or } 48.17$$
Rectifier efficiency $\eta = 0.812$ or 81.2%
$$PIV = V_m$$

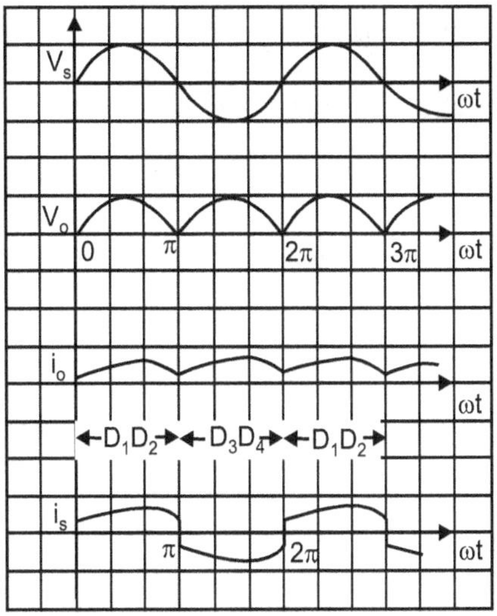

Fig. 6.19 : Voltage and current waveforms

6.6 THREE PHASE RECTIFIERS

6.6.1 Three Phase Bridge Rectifier with R Load

- The circuit diagram of a three-phase bridge rectifier with R load. The six diodes D_1 to D_6 form the bridge.

- At any point of time, only two diodes conduct.

- Fig. 6.20 shows the phasor diagram of V_R, V_Y and V_B. The three phasors are $120°$ out of phase.

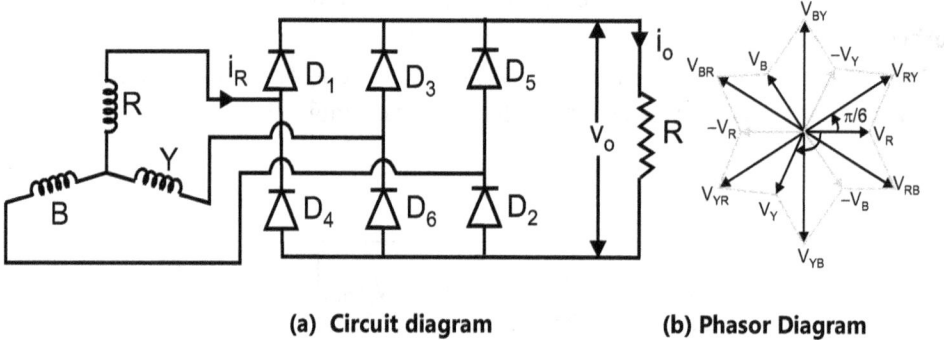

(a) Circuit diagram   (b) Phasor Diagram

Fig. 6.20 : Bridge Rectifier with R load

- The V_R and $-V_Y$ form line voltage V_{RY}. The line voltages are $60°$ phase shifted.

- When any two diodes conduct, highest of the line voltage appears across the load.

- From the waveforms observe that D_6 and D_1 counduct when V_{RY} is highest of all other line voltages. Similarly when V_{RB} is highest, D_1 and D_2 conduct.

- The waveforms of output voltage and current are same because for a resistive load,

$$i_0 = \frac{V_0}{R}$$

- Phase current through R is positive when diode D_1 is conducting and it is negative when diode D_4 is conducting.

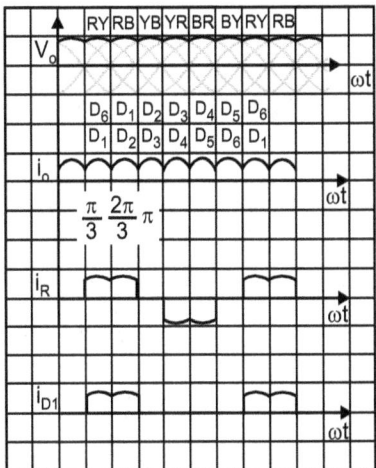

Fig. 6.21 : Waveforms

Mathematical analysis

The output voltage waveform is redrawn for convenience and shown in Fig. 6.22. Since output voltage is line voltage, it will be $\sqrt{3}\, V_m \cos \omega t$.

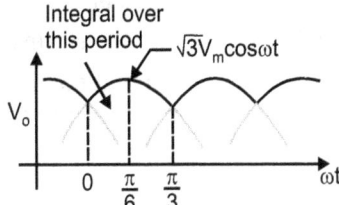

Fig. 6.22 : Output waveform

1. $$V_{0(av)} = \frac{2}{2\pi/6} \int_{0}^{\pi/6} \sqrt{3}\, \cos\omega t \, d\omega t$$

$$= \frac{3\sqrt{3}\, V_m}{\pi} = 1.654\, V_m$$

2. $$V_{0(rms)} = \left[\frac{2}{2\pi/6} \int_{0}^{\pi/6} \sqrt{3}\, V_m \cos\omega t \, d\omega t \right]^{\frac{1}{2}}$$

$$= V_m \sqrt{\frac{3}{2} + \frac{9\sqrt{3}}{4\pi}} = 1.66\, V_m$$

3. $$FF = \frac{V_{0(rms)}}{V_{0(av)}} = \frac{1.66\, V_m}{1.654\, V_m} = 1.003 \text{ or } 100.3\%$$

4. $$RF = \sqrt{FF^2 - 1} = 0.085 \text{ or } 8.5\%$$

5. $$TUF = I_{s(rms)} = 0.78\, \sqrt{3}\, V_m / R$$

Transformer secondary VA $= 3\, V_{s(rms)}\, I_{s(rms)}$

$$= 3 \times \frac{V_m}{\sqrt{2}} \times 0.78 \times \sqrt{3}\, V_m / R$$

$\therefore\quad$ TUF $= \dfrac{P_o(av)}{\text{Transformer secondary VA}}$

$$= \frac{V_{o(rms)}^2 / R}{3 \times \dfrac{V_m}{\sqrt{2}} \times 0.78 \times \sqrt{3}\, V_m / R}$$

$$= \frac{(1.66 V_m)^2 / R}{3 \times \dfrac{V_m}{\sqrt{2}} \times 0.78 \times \sqrt{3}\, V_m / R} = 0.9615 \text{ or } 96.5\%$$

6. PIV = $\sqrt{3}\, V_m$, since peak value of supply line voltage appears across any diode.

6.6.2 Three Phase Bridge Rectifier with RL Load

- Fig. 6.23 shows the circuit diagram of a 3-phase bridge rectifier with RL load.
- Compared to circuit with only R load, here the waveforms of only current change.
- Fig. 6.24 shows the waveforms. It can be seen that the ripple in output current is reduced.

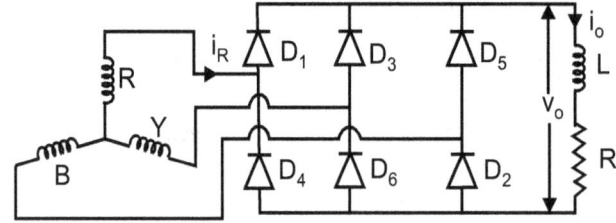

Fig. 6.23 : 3-phase bridge rectifier with RL load

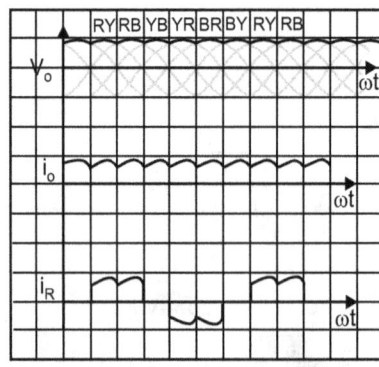

Fig. 6.24 : Waveforms

Mathematical analysis

Since the output voltage waveform of R load and RL load for three phase bridge rectifier is same we have following,

$$PIV = \sqrt{3}\, V_m$$
$$V_{0(av)} = 1.654\, V_m$$
$$V_{0(rms)} = 1.66\, V_m$$
$$RF = 0.085 \text{ or } 8.5\,\%$$
$$FF = 1.003 \text{ or } 100.3\,\%$$
$$TUF = 0.9615 \text{ or } 96.15\,\%$$

6.7 COMPARISON OF DIODE RECTIFIERS

6.7.1 Comparison of Single Phase Half Wave and Full Wave Rectifiers

Q. compare single phase HWR and FWR.

Table 6.1

Sr. No.	Parameter	Half wave rectifier	Full wave rectifier
1.	PIV	$\dfrac{V_m}{\pi}$	$\dfrac{2V_m}{\pi}$
2.	Output rms voltage	$\dfrac{V_m}{2}$	$\dfrac{V_m}{\sqrt{2}}$
	RF	1.21	0.4817
4.	Output average voltage	V_m	V_m for bridge $2V_m$ for center tapped
5.	Cycles rectified	Half cycle	Complete cycle
6.	FF	1.57	1.11
8.	Applications	Simple low power supplies	DC electronic circuits

6.7.2 Comparison of Single Phase and Three Phase Bridge Rectifiers

Q. Compare single phase and three phase bridge rectifiers.

Table 6.2

Sr. No.	Parameter	Single phase full wave bridge	Three phase full wave bridge
1.	PIV	V_m	$\sqrt{3}\,V_m$
2.	Output rms voltage	$\dfrac{V_m}{\sqrt{2}}$	$1.66\,V_m$
3.	RF	0.4817	0.085
4.	Output average voltage	$\dfrac{2V_m}{\pi}$	$\dfrac{3\sqrt{3}V_m}{\pi}$
5.	FF	1.11	1.003
7.	Ripple content	More	Less
8.	Filter requirement	Heavy filters are required	Small filters are enough
9.	Applications	Low power DC electronic circuits	High power supplies, UPS

❖ ❖ ❖